NASCAR Legends

NASCAR

Legends

Memorable Men, Moments, and Machines in Racing History

Robert Edelstein

THE OVERLOOK PRESS
New York, NY

This edition first published in paperback in the United States in 2012 by
The Overlook Press, Peter Mayer Publishers, Inc.
141 Wooster Street
New York, NY 10012
www.overlookpress.com
For bulk and special sales, please contact sales@overlookny.com

Library of Congress Cataloging-in-Publication Data

Edelstein, Robert
NASCAR legends : memorable men, moments, and
machines in racing history / Robert Edelstein.
p. cm.
I 1. NASCAR (Association)—History. 2. Stock car racing—History.
3. Stock car drivers—History. I. Title.
GV1029.9.S74E34 2011   796.72092'2—dc22 [B]   2010052007

Book design and typeformatting by Bernard Schleifer
Printed in the United States of America
1 3 5 7 9 10 8 6 4 2
ISBN 978 1 59020 731 4

For Loren, Dave, and my mom,
and in memory of my dad

Contents

By 1969, Bobby Allison was already a popular NASCAR star on the rise.

Introduction:
Bobby

November 1993

"I have shied away from proclaiming that I am retired with the idea that maybe I will do a race somewhere, someday, rather than to be injured and put out of a career. Then I could take that checkered flag and step out of the car and say, okay, now I quit. It's a thought that makes me smile."

—BOBBY ALLISON, Waldorf-Astoria Hotel, November 1993

T HEY HAD SET UP A MAKESHIFT STAGE, A WIDE PLATFORM ON RISERS, in a spacious hallway outside several ballrooms in the Waldorf-Astoria. It seemed an informal setting in such a space of old New York grandeur but it appeared to fit the occasion: a NASCAR press conference introducing the top drivers of the 1993 season. Two days later, the sport's big post-season event—the NASCAR Winston Cup championship banquet—would be held in the Waldorf's Grand Ballroom, honoring champ Dale Earnhardt. The tuxedos would be out for that one.

I was there to do my first-ever in-person interview with a stock car racer. I had done two other interviews with NASCAR drivers the previous year. The first one, with Richard Petty, had been conducted through the mail; with word that the King had hearing difficulties, his PR rep, Chuck Spicer, read me Petty's answers to questions I'd sent to him. And then I did a brief phone interview with Richard's son, Kyle. I found Richard Petty's answers especially intriguing. His father had knocked him out of the way in his first-ever race, and he'd broken just about every bone in his body at one time or another. The quote I remember most was, "I never should have driven with a broken neck."

At the Waldorf, I was going to be talking to Bobby Allison for a short 150-word item about his induction into the International Motorsports Hall of Fame. The incoming class would also include Henry Ford and Cale Yarborough—with whom, I'd later learn, Allison had fought at the end of NASCAR's most famous race, the 1979 Daytona 500.

I felt completely outside my element as I stood in the hallway, watching the area fill with unfamiliar faces. It was odd to be standing around, listening in on conversations, as guys made in-jokes about other members of the press and traded anecdotes; it was all over my head.

Two guys in front of me began talking about Earnhardt, who'd soon be ushered in to make some comments. The impression I got from these writers was that Earnhardt loved talking about Earnhardt, and the joys of a run of success that showed no signs of abating. Their gentle complaints were not so much about Earnhardt's ego as they were about the fact that the guy had won yet again. What the hell do you write about a guy who's just won his sixth title, and his third in four years?

The Nashville Network publicist appeared suddenly; his familiar face immensely welcome. He ushered me to a corner near the back and quickly introduced me to Bobby Allison, a gray-haired man with a slightly doughy face, a shy and uncomfortable look in his eyes, and a prominent limp. He nodded and absently took my hand as I said hello. Recalling now, I might have guessed he was close to seventy. In fact, he was one day shy of his fifty-sixth birthday.

I knew his story in a sketchy way. He had lost his sons Davey and Clifford within that past year; Clifford in an on-track crash in 1992, and Davey in a helicopter accident four months before, in mid-July. He'd also had a terrible wreck five years earlier that had nearly killed him and left him physically impaired. I also knew that Bobby had won the 1983 NASCAR Winston Cup title, and a few Daytona 500s; beyond that, I hadn't researched too much—the story was only going to be 150 words.

I was no NASCAR fan. I'd vaguely heard of the new kid, Jeff Gordon. To me, motorsports was Indy Racing, with Andretti, Foyt,

Gordon Johncock, and the Unsers screaming around the track in those sleek mantis-like cars.

I was thirty-three years old, a newlywed, a Jewish kid from New York; I'd been talking to my wife about starting a family.

I had no idea my life was about to change, that NASCAR was soon going to become an interest, at times an obsession, and an endless fascination, and my form of fraternity with millions of strangers across the nation. Or that I'd one day pride myself on knowing tiny facts about races that had been run years before I was born on gleaming dirt tracks. And that one day I'd strongly consider naming my third child after Kyle Petty's oldest son.

But meeting Bobby Allison will change a person like that.

Someone came up onto that makeshift Waldorf stage and introduced Earnhardt, who climbed up the steps in boots and some kind of dark sponsor's jacket, to polite applause and some smiling shouts. He grinned a lot under that mustache. He told a few jokes about the season, about winning again, and the spoils of victory, and everybody laughed their knowing laugh. I looked at Bobby once with a polite smile. He was looking down, not paying much attention.

Earnhardt called Rusty Wallace to the stage. Wallace had finished second in the points standings and it had apparently been close. They joked in that poking, friendly, competitive way; if memory serves, Rusty mentioned a race or two that spelled the difference. Again, everybody laughed knowingly.

And then Earnhardt got quiet and shushed the crowd; and he said something about how, "It was a good year, but a hard year, too. We lost two good friends. So I'd like to ask you all to bow your heads, and take a moment to remember Davey Allison and Alan Kulwicki."

We all bowed our heads; everyone closed their eyes and I closed mine. And I waited a good few seconds.

I know now as I knew then that it was wrong, but I felt compelled. I opened my eyes, and I turned to look at Bobby Allison.

His head was bowed slightly, his eyes were closed. And then his eyelids grew tight, and then relaxed, tight again, relaxed again. It was the look of a man trying to fend off darts of anguish. Terribly embarrassed, I quickly closed my eyes; and then I waited for Dale Earnhardt to tell me I could open them again.

* * *

I had said yes to this assignment because of Dave Glatter, my best friend when I was growing up. When we were about fourteen, we talked all the time about our crushes; I had this terrible thing for a dark-haired girl named Bobbi, and Dave liked a blonde girl named Allison. As a way to honor this secret, Dave, who was a talented artist as a kid, drew a perfect rendition of Bobby Allison's No. 12 Coca-Cola Chevy and hung it on the wall between his desk and his bed. There it remained, like some brilliant siren image, part of a life's code that had become the great subtext language of best friends. I never forgot the clean, vibrant colors of that car. Plus, Bobby Allison shared my name, and had that cool nickname, just like one of my first heroes, Bobby Kennedy. It all seemed quite right.

So, as managing editor of *The Cable Guide*, when the opportunity arose to interview Bobby Allison in conjunction with the televised Hall of Fame ceremony, I thought, Sure, I'll do that.

Bobby, his wife, Judy, and I shared an elevator to their suite at the Waldorf, and we settled down to talk.

As it turned out, asking basic biographical questions worked just fine. For Bobby, it provided a perfect structure to go through points he'd been asked many times before. Plus, talking about Clifford and Davey appeared to be therapeutic.

It was an honor, he said, to be inducted into the Hall of Fame with such a stellar class; he'd twice been selected as NASCAR's Most Popular Driver, and relished that; it celebrated the communication he had with fans who "felt they could walk up to me anytime and say hello."

For all the difficulty of making small talk that we'd just experienced, I found Allison to be especially warm and forthcoming. I'd worked at a music magazine called *RockBill* in the 1980s, interviewing rock stars and star wannabes, and found that many of them were so caught up in either themselves or their fame, that it was difficult to discuss the subtlety of their music—or lack thereof. I kept finding myself pressed up against the rampant egos, and at times, the inanity of the exercise. I interviewed at least three musicians who considered themselves the best songwriters of their era. Later, I often interviewed TV and movie stars. They were better than the musicians, by and large, but you were still getting people promoting a project, usually without much of a backstory.

Bobby Allison, on the other hand, was instantly disarming, incredibly humble, seemingly grateful. Judy sat stoically at his side, sometimes with a little smile. I had no idea that their marriage would, in the months to come, slowly crumble, undone by overpowering grief; or that, years later, the Petty family's terrible grief would bring them back together. I remember them that day in 1993 looking and acting like simple folks, without trappings. Speaking to Bobby was refreshing and powerful.

The conversation grew more profound. Knowing the losses he'd suffered, it seemed appropriate to bring up the good memories, like the 1988 Daytona 500, when he'd finished first, with Davey coming in second. But I had no idea how wistful this event now made him.

"I'm in a real bind on that one," Bobby said, "because that one race, the one I know has to mean the most to me, is the one that I can't remember. It continues to be covered up with the dust back there."

His injuries at Pocono months after Daytona had wiped away the recollections of that triumph. It seemed a terrible injustice: Four months earlier, he'd lost Davey, and yet he had no recollection of their proudest moment as father and son.

We talked about how he got into racing, how his parents first disapproved but eventually became his biggest fans. "They pulled for Donnie, too," he said, talking about his younger brother, "but he didn't pursue it like I did."

And long into Bobby's great career, Davey said he wanted to get into racing. When Bobby and Judy insisted he get his high school diploma first, he took summer classes after his junior year so he could graduate early. Bobby, I would later learn, didn't give Davey much in the way of help, wanting the kid to earn it all on his own. Eventually, Davey became one of the greatest drivers on the NASCAR Winston Cup circuit.

He talked of his boys and the "fine Christian young men" they'd become.

"I still cry a lot," Bobby said. "You know, when we lost Clifford it was really, really a tough situation. But a lot of people helped, and Davey helped me. Davey had been a special son from real early on anyway. He and Clifford were quite different young men. Clifford was the one who looked for the fun things, the things to play with. Before he got killed, he'd gotten serious and was really applying himself, but his basic lifestyle was looking for the fun in life, and Clifford got killed working. Davey worked. Davey absolutely from very early on planned what he wanted to do, he was very well focused and he worked. And Davey got killed playing. And that's kind of the irony of life."

He told an incredible story of a time when Clifford started driving around one day in an old junk car the family had, banging it into trees for fun. Bobby heard a crash and ran outside and warned Clifford to stop. But he kept at it, and the next time Bobby heard a crash, he looked and saw the car was turning over down a hillside, and Bobby rushed back outside.

"And Clifford gets out of the car and he's got a grin across his face and these three or four teenage girls from the neighborhood start crawling out of the car. And they said, 'Oh, Mr. Allison, that was so much fun; Clifford told us he'd turn us over and he did and it was so much fun.' Now anyone of those little girls could have gotten hurt so easy, but he had told them that he would turn the car over. It disarmed me so completely that I couldn't choke him like I wanted to do."

I laughed at the story. Given my upbringing, this was perhaps the last thing on earth I would have ever done, and I can't imagine how my own parents would have punished me. But it wasn't the point. Clifford was the playful son of a racecar driver, hanging around in the backyard with a bunch of kids, testing his limits.

Judy smiled at the story. She got up silently a few moments later and walked into the adjoining bedroom. Bobby and I were alone.

He looked at me with a strange level of depth in his eyes, and I felt myself suddenly anxious.

"With all due respect to her," he said, pointing at the door with Judy on the other side of it, "sometimes I think, boy, I wish I hadn't have lived. I wish I wouldn't have made it. But I did, and maybe I can do something constructive. You know, something where I can sit down and say, it's been a good day.'"

We heard the doorknob and Judy returned, and our conversation continued. We talked of all the supportive fan mail he got, with many letters coming from people worse off than himself. And we talked about new safety measures that NASCAR would be well served to add. Perhaps putting heavy foam in the side panels of cars.

Our time soon ended. I shook Bobby's hand and his grip was firmer than when we'd first met, and Judy couldn't have been more gracious. I walked back to the office in a daze. Lisa Bernhard, the editor who'd assigned me the piece, asked, "How did it go?" So I told her the story of Bobby Allison. And when she was done crying, we marched into the editor in chief's office, and the 150-word item became an 800-word two-page story.

In the years since, I've written two other books about NASCAR, one on families in the sport, the other a biography of Curtis Turner, perhaps the first superstar of the sport, who also co-built Charlotte Motor Speedway. While writing, or doing anything else in my life, I've sometimes felt particularly lazy or uninvolved. Whenever that happens, I remind myself that it's important to do something constructive with my life. After that, I'm just fine.

* * *

I began working on this project after Peter Mayer, publisher of The Overlook Press, handed me a copy of *Legends of the Samurai* by Hiroaki Sato one evening and said, "I want you to try to do for NASCAR what this book does for Samurai."

That would be no small task. I decided to write a history of this fascinating sport through stories that encompass some of its most compelling figures and moments. There are tales of amazing races, incredible series, even a number that carries extraordinary meaning.

There is the sport's founder, Big Bill France, showing incredible resolve in staging the first-ever "strictly stock" NASCAR race that gave birth to the sport. And there is the wild and remarkable ending to the 1999 Night Race at Bristol, which stands as a towering monument to two of the sport's most beloved presences: Dale Earnhardt Sr. and Bristol Motor Speedway. There was the generation of racers who thrilled fans by sliding their cars sideways into turns on dusty dirt tracks. And there is Tony Stewart, calmly conquering demons by winning at his hometown Indianapolis Motor Speedway. And it would be hard to come up with a more gripping figure in the sport today than Dale Earnhardt Jr., the sport's most popular driver, whose path in NASCAR was forever altered by the death of his father.

NASCAR has an amazing ability to thrill with triumphs, and too heavy a share of tragedy. I've thought of both on the several occasions I've seen Bobby Allison in the years since our first meeting. Like him, I've watched the stirring closing laps of the 1988 Daytona 500 several times. It was like so many great finishes at Daytona: The man in second waits until the last minute and attempts the final slingshot pass to victory. On that day, Davey Allison didn't have enough horsepower to win. But he had more than enough energy, pride, respect, and love to pour the bubbly over his father's head in victory lane.

Sadly, Bobby and I greet the race the same way: as observers. It would be a fine thing if he were to regain his memories of that day, and relive it from his place in the driver's seat.

Some things cannot be changed. Some losses cannot be reversed. All we can do, whatever we do, is learn from it all, and bring something constructive to the process, as the drivers and innovators in this sport, from one generation to the next, have long done.

That has always been one of the great appeals of stock car racing. You know the consequences of what may happen when you turn on the engine and career around the track at close to two hundred miles per hour, but you approach what you do with joy, purpose, and determination. You hope, at the end of the day, that you find success. And if you don't, that you at least do your best, and, like the great Bobby Allison, that you practice your craft the same way you live your life—with great courage. And your foot pressed firmly to the floorboard.

Lee Petty's NASCAR debut in the first "strictly stock" race was inauspicious, but it led to a Hall of Fame career for himself and his son Richard.

Chapter One
The First of
Its Kind

"Somebody could find a place, take a bulldozer and make a circle and that's the way it was, to begin with. They got better. But you still had all that dust and sand flying. . . . You bang fenders, you get out, you fight, you carry on. That was the life."

—PAUL CAWLEY, stock car racer from the 1940s,
talking about the early days of racing

B Y TEN O'CLOCK IN THE MORNING, WITH THE TEMPERATURE ALREADY pushing 80 degrees, Bill France knew—as he'd feared—that it was going to be a scorcher, a day made for white T-shirts, and ice water-soaked handkerchiefs to cool the sweat on the back of your neck. The people would be hot; the racecars, perhaps grinding to a halt in the baking sun, would be hotter.

France distractedly paced the gravel, and began climbing up the long wood grandstands: theater seating for the front stretch of Charlotte Speedway. Located five miles west of the center of Charlotte, North Carolina, the track was only about a year old, a three-quarter-mile dirt oval with fresh dust clinging to it from the previous day's action.

The wood below France's feet gave a little and it shook him, though he was a little shaky to begin with. He hadn't gotten much sleep the night before, and he woke up on this mid-June morning worrying about the size of the crowd and the importance of the event. That afternoon the speedway would host the first-ever official "strictly-stock" race for

NASCAR, France's two-year-old racing organization. The race was open only to drivers of newly built American factory cars produced in the years since the end of World War II, four years before. France was gambling plenty on the success of this event, hoping it would cement NASCAR's standing ahead of the glut of stock car sanctioning groups. This had become a "push all your chips in" kind of day.

Now standing at the top of the bleachers, France cupped his eyes with his hands, staring out toward Wilkinson Boulevard. The cars of race fans were lining up, groups of them spreading out, inching in from everywhere, hundreds of them, with hundreds more beyond, funneling in. The black hard tops in the distance were like a swarm of ants. The crowd was much greater than France had expected, and he permitted himself a smile. It was still hours before race time.

The planning for this event, the endless promoting, had taken a real toll, even on France, who was normally an indefatigable, determined man. He could be leaning easily against a car with his arms folded, wearing a squint and a smile and he'd still look somewhat imposing. In a room full of powerful men, you'd be hard pressed not to single him out. It wasn't only for his six-foot-five-inch frame that he'd long been called Big Bill. He had a talent, irritating though it could sometimes be, for making anybody realize the advantage, the necessity, and finally the inevitability of being on his side. That he frequently did his convincing with a characteristic grin only added to the power of his charm and reputation.

"He had an iron fist and a velvet glove that was needed at times," said longtime racing historian Greg Fielden. "And Bill France aligned himself with good-quality people, which was one of his finer points. He had a far vision."

"Bill France was a very likeable person," recalled renowned car owner Ray Fox, "but he could talk anybody out of their breakfast."

* * *

For all of France's persuasive talents, there had been too many uncontrollable moments of huge import in his life of late, and keeping his focus had become an extreme challenge. He'd promoted Charlotte Speedway's first race of the season two months earlier, at the beginning of April. Within days of the event, he was heading back to his hometown of Washington, DC, to attend the funeral of his father, William Henry France, who'd passed away after a lengthy illness. France Sr. had been a clerk at the Park Savings Bank in Washington. It was by sneaking off in his dad's Model T Ford that Bill France first came to fulfill his own dreams of speed. Standing on the bleachers now, his hands still up at his eyes, France could recall the memory of trying to steady the casket's weight on his shoulder when he and his fellow pallbearers carried his father's body to its rest.

And then yesterday, taking a break from prerace preparations, France and Bill Tuthill, a fellow racing promoter and one of his right hands in NASCAR, and two other men were in the air, demonstrating a new model of a small private plane. France, an avid flyer, could sense trouble as it developed, and he sat helplessly as the plane began to descend maniacally. Jerking downward, with everyone aboard bracing inside, the small plane overran the runway, pounded to the ground, bounced a moment, and kept rolling across the adjoining highway, slamming finally to a rest in a ditch. Cars had barely managed to swerve away and miss it.

Later on, achy but intact, he returned to the speedway and watched as practice sessions for the next day's race began in earnest. The track had been well watered to keep it moist enough for the action, but the heat of the day—the temperature was topping out at 90 degrees—was unrelenting, and as cars continued to dig into the turns, red clay dust rose up past the fence and out toward Wilkinson Boulevard. You couldn't hear the accidents being caused on the road over the din of the racing engines, but soon enough the county police arrived and delivered a threat: They would shut down the track twenty-four hours before the race began if France couldn't fix the dust problem.

The cure was to grade calcium chloride into the dirt. A local Charlotte racer recalled that a large stash of the stuff remained stored under the scoring stand. There was not enough of it to fully work in, but France had officials bring out the grading machine. They made a sporting show of it while France talked to the police about what a fine event it was going to be, for racing and for the town. France had dealt with enough policemen in his time. Given that stock car racing's roots were intertwined with the illegal running of moonshine, he well understood the need to establish that everything was under rigid control, with rules and propriety well in place.

Imagine if they had shut it down, France thought now. The idea that he might be a little nuts for insisting on this strictly stock thing had struck some as an extremely valid point. Would seeing gleaming new cars getting smacked up in dirt track battles really be good for the car business? Besides, fans already accepted stock car racing as a thing of brutal beauty, dominated by old cars that could be modified to make them swifter. Winning frequently required getting an edge under the hood, in the springs or anywhere else that allowed for hidden tweaks. This wasn't Indianapolis, after all. This was proud Southern racing.

France took one last look at the approaching crowd and scratched the back of his neck. By 2:00 p.m. on June 19, 1949—race time—it would be 91 degrees in Charlotte. And yet they came, many in the crowd showing up as much as four hours early. The orderly traffic looked a lot like what some fans loved best about auto racing: the sense that you were getting a grand view of controlled chaos.

* * *

"The credit for the popularity of Stock Car Racing belongs to the South, the 'Rebels' as the boys like to call themselves," wrote *National Speed Sport News* technical editor Carl Green in an editorial six weeks before the Charlotte race.

The "Rebels" had for years gotten together for races on local dirt tracks on Saturday nights and Sundays, and in midweek features, wherever the money took them if the money was good enough. Farmers, moonshiners, truck drivers, family men, a great deal of them were kind, generous, civilized people who became pit bulls once they strapped themselves into cars and the races began. And beating and banging often led to frustration and anger.

"You used to drive thirty minutes and fight thirty minutes," said Buck Baker, a thick-browed, short-tempered truck driver turned racer from Charlotte.

"You had to be insane to mess with any of those people," added his son Buddy, himself a talented race winner who grew up watching his father battle on and off the track. "They made their living with their wit. You knock somebody in the fence, you better be able to either outrun him or whip his fanny 'cause those guys went to it. There weren't any regulations and there weren't any penalties. You had to be able to survive till the next week and those guys made sure that it wasn't pleasant if you [hit] them."

Many of the racers, track owners, and promoters had long done well for themselves in the moonshine business. Stock car racing grew in the South at least in part from dares and brags among those who carried loads of white lightning in their trunks and eluded the state troopers. Whose 'shine-running car was fastest? Answering the question required taking those cars to a makeshift track in an anonymous field to find out.

"Somebody could find a place, take a bulldozer, and make a circle and that's the way it was, to begin with," said Paul Cawley, who ran a popular filling station on Grandon Street in Roanoke, Virginia, where a large group of stock car racers congregated in the 1940s and '50s. "Everybody tried it. Finally it ended up getting like [better tracks in] Martinsville, Starkey, Lynchburg, and different places in West Virginia. A lot of quarter-milers. Start with a guy with a bulldozer, but they got better. But you still had all that dust and sand flying.

"You bang fenders, you get out, you fight, you carry on," he added with a smile. "That was the life."

If there was a sense of lawlessness—and several drivers and owners kept their guns with them at the track—it extended to promoters, a number of whom would skip town with the profits in the middle of the race, leaving many competitors in need of gas money to get home. In other cases, a prize would hardly match the effort and expense.

"I won a damn race once and I got a fifth of wine and a damn ham meat," Buck Baker said.

Bill France had come to know this truth well, having begun racing in the late 1920s on local tracks near home. He'd run in 1930 at a well-promoted race promising a $500 winner's share, and after collecting only $10 for finishing third, he was told the promise had been made simply to bring in drivers and fans.

As good a racer as France was—"And he was a much better racer than he ever got credit for," according to Fielden—mentioning his driving skills is like remembering Babe Ruth solely as a fine pitcher. France's acumen suited him better off the track. He'd been named William Henry Getty France by his parents—the additional middle name recalling the business vision of the Getty name—and he took the mantle seriously.

France had moved to Daytona Beach, Florida, in 1934, at twenty-five, with his wife, Anne, and young son Billy. Daytona was then among the land speed capitals of the world, and for France, setting up a car repair shop in an auto-happy town seemed a savvy move to combat the sting of the Great Depression.

Months after his arrival, he watched Sir Malcolm Campbell run his long and sleek Rolls Royce–powered Blue Bird Streamliner over the hard packed Daytona sand at 276.82 miles per hour—short of the record but swift nonetheless. When the land speed demons packed up and left the next year, preferring the surface at Utah's Bonneville Salt Flats, nervous Daytona town officials, by then used to big local-event revenue, sanctioned a 1936 stock car race. The course wound along a stretch of beach and its parallel road, with the two straightaways joined by north and south dirt turns that, once the cars began grinding their way over them, became terribly rutted, turning quickly into surfaces more inclined for demolition than speed.

Economically, the race proved disastrous, as fans had an easy time sneaking in without paying. France finished fifth, but more important, he saw the greater potential for a Daytona event if done right. Within two years, the races on the 4.1-mile beach-and-road course were run by France, who partnered with Charlie Reese, a popular Daytona restaurateur. Through heavy promotion and crowd control (France and his wife had staffers put up signs warning of rattlesnakes to keep nonpaying customers from sneaking in through the rock and brush), he began to operate races on the beach successfully. He didn't do too badly behind the wheel either.

* * *

After the war (France had spent those years at the Daytona Boat Works), servicemen returned in victory, and a feeling of normalcy and expectant prosperity filled the country. Few symbols could match the new mindset better than a new factory car stamped out of Detroit.

When Detroit began auto production once again, France became enamored with the idea of Everyman racing those brand-new cars to victory. Why couldn't stock car racing be a bit more like Indianapolis, the motorsports mecca where, thanks to postwar renovations, Continental and European champions once again vied for racing glory on the dazzling asphalt and brick surface? In order to be that, Southern racing needed rules, and safety measures, and guarantees.

And the moonshining sport would also need an image adjustment.

France fit in with the drivers, promoters, and owners. Wearing, at various times, most of those hats earned him trust across the board in a sport where each group was often wary of the others.

And he could easily slip into the role of the slightly older, more responsible, regular guy. "Big Bill, he loved to party," said Paul Sawyer, longtime owner of Richmond International Raceway. "He'd come to the parties in Daytona, or anywhere, Atlanta, didn't make no difference to him. But in those days, the fraternization was closer."

For all his camaraderie, France remained adamant about his ideas for growing the sport. On December 14, 1947, he invited thirty-five of the nation's chief representatives of the sport to join him in the Ebony Room at the top of Daytona's Streamline Hotel. During a series of meetings over several days, France laid out his vision for a necessary organization. "I believe stock car racing can become a nationally recognized sport by having a national point standing, which embraces the majority of large stock car events," he offered.

But image, he told those assembled, was key, and the cars on the tracks—along with the conditions of the facilities—would spell the difference. A racer might be driving what was once a spanking-new Cadillac, but after letting the thing get dirty and overused—he didn't bring up the idea of mechanics reworking the shocks and springs to make them moonshine-ready—it would look like, as he put it, a "jalopy."

Many of the participants came to the meeting out of curiosity more than anything else. Given the disorganized state of racing at the time, from the arguing factions to the lack of a presence beyond the South, the notion that France might somehow rise up and corral everybody inside one circus-like big top struck a percentage of those in the Ebony Room as pretty comical.

But whatever France may have lacked in traditional book smarts—he'd dropped out of high school after two years—he more than made up for in his understanding of human nature, and the independent streak that drove competitors to get behind the wheel.

He was more than happy to lose the National Champion Stock Car Circuit designation that he'd been promoting races under. At the meetings, well-known mechanic Red Vogt suggested the title National Association for Stock Car Auto Racing, or NASCAR. The new association's slogan was, "Racing that is open to everyone."

The meetings produced a charter, guaranteed purses, basic benefits, the beginning of a plan to deal with "after-race arguments," and general guidelines for conduct and misconduct.

There would be three divisions, and while the Modifieds were the bread and butter of stock car racing, France was banking on strictly stock as his wild card.

The Modifieds had always been the sport's reliable, comfortable, profitable option. It was also the perfect symbol for a sport whose players were long used to doing things entirely on their own terms. You could fashion something fast out of the extra parts in the junk heap. And pushing the modification envelope was the normal practice, the secrets of speed and better grip on the track being jealously guarded by mechanics. The only people who cheated to get further ahead, as the saying went, were those who got caught.

* * *

Strictly stock became more viable by 1949. New car manufacturing was way up. While auto factories sold 2.1 million units in 1946—the first full year of postwar production—the number nearly doubled by 1948.

In January 1949, France flew his plane to Detroit to keep up discussions with automakers and spread the word about strictly stock. A brand-new racecar that wins on a Sunday, he told all who would listen, would be a boon for sales come Monday. What better way to sell new cars than to promote them as winners on racetracks?

Detroit remained skeptical. There could be only one winner, and the losers might find themselves driving brand-new wrecks.

Detroit wasn't alone in its doubt. NASCAR not only faced competition from rival governing bodies, but it continued to suffer from a general lower-class whiff it gave off.

"These cars are not second-hands for sale—it's what we will see a lot of on our Speedways during '49," began a January cover-photo caption in *National Speed Sport News*, featuring shots of proudly down-and-dirty Modifieds. "Just how popular stock car races will be throughout the country will be determined this summer," it continued, more than implying the dominance of the retooled set.

Moonshine's association with stock car racing, France knew, represented the sport's biggest hurdle. The fans who showed up at the track didn't care that a guy like Curtis Turner, a tall, tousle-haired timberman and arguably Virginia's most popular racer, had also spent years performing weekly, startling 'shine runs. But the good townsfolk throughout the South, the ones who spoke up for decency at community meetings, did not take kindly to the practice.

France needed a way to combat racing's reputation. Since there would be no way to eradicate moonshining, he'd have to use strictly stock to help establish an appearance of decorum. The series was poised to be a symbol for all that was clean, new, right, and American about the sport.

France's understanding of what drivers wanted and—in his opinion—needed informed what would become his most important decision in the formation of NASCAR. Though the ruling body was listed as an "Association," NASCAR was in fact a corporation, with France as president. There were other officers at the top of the board, but France quickly established himself as the ultimate decision maker. Without checks and balances, he instituted stringent rules. There would be consistent prize money, safety, and protection. But the drivers—and everyone else involved—would have to play along if they wanted to play at all.

Incorporating NASCAR meant that drivers were free to join if they so wished, and just as free not to. They'd be accepted and welcome if they followed the rules, and disciplined and suspended if they did not. NASCAR was not there to organize anybody; France understood intrinsically that attempting to organize drivers went against their grain.

France continued to hold the reins, lightly when possible, tightly when it felt necessary. And he'd bank on the drivers, owners, and promoters resembling a phrase philosopher Harold Rosenberg had famously written one year earlier in *Commentary* magazine: "a herd of independent minds." NASCAR members might chafe at times but it would be up to France to make the corporation the first name in stock car racing.

"I guess back then he had to be hardheaded and everything else," said Cawley, who was once suspended by France after someone was caught using stolen pit passes that had been in his name. "But it was like you were behind locked gates in prison because of all the rules."

* * *

The National Stock Car Racing Association, a rival racing body, was then under the control of twenty-two-year-old Charlotte promoter Bruton Smith, a spark plug of a man who, like France, had begun his career as a racer before turning his energy toward promoting. Smith understood that marquee events and drivers would be the requisite raw materials to create the ruling racing body, and he went about trying to lure Red Byron, NASCAR's top champion, to race under his NSCRA tent.

France bristled at the cherry-picking and the possibilities it could lead to. It would require a response in kind, and he announced the running of the first-ever strictly stock race in NASCAR history, to be held at Charlotte Speedway's three-quarter-mile dirt oval in mid-June. That the race would run in Smith's hometown seemed most appropriate. France planned the event for 150 miles, calling it a marathon, and offering, as bait, a generous $2,000 to the winner, part of a $5,000 total purse. Only eligible drivers—those who weren't racing for Smith, for instance—could compete for the big money.

Like many businesses in racing at the time, Charlotte Speedway boasted a split heritage, its planks and pegs a part of racing's sordid past and—France hoped—its bright future. It had been built on land owned by Carl and Catherine Allison. Carl, a forty-two-year-old North Carolina farmer, and Catherine had agreed to lease some of their land to a couple of local brothers, Harvey and Pat Charles. The brothers bulldozed and carved and shaped the place, lending the oval its character and style. And soon they were off to federal prison, convicted of bootlegging, even missing the track's grand opening event on June 6, 1948.

As soon as France made the announcement, he went on the stump, working the phones and taking out ads, campaigning to drivers, car owners, fans, and the media that this event would stand out. And then there was the power of Zack Mosley, a popular syndicated cartoonist whose aviation strip *Smilin' Jack* was a popular read for anyone from veterans to kids in the years after the war. While detailing the daredevil lives of Jack and his sidekick Downwind, Mosley would also alert readers to upcoming races and air shows by hiding announcements in the panels, perhaps on the roof or hood of a car, or a door sign. And in early June, as popular bad boy Hot-Rod Happy was getting himself into trouble again, Mosley, as a favor to his friend France, alerted readers to the first Strictly Stock race in Charlotte on June 19.

France planned to narrow his field of drivers for the race down to thirty-three, matching the starting grid running every Memorial Day weekend in the Indianapolis 500. The great race in Indianapolis had just been run, won by Bill Holland, with rookie Johnnie Parsons finishing second. Holland collected about $51,000, the winner's share of the whopping $179,000 prize pool.

* * *

Nearly four inches of rain had fallen in Charlotte on Monday, June 13, a thunderstorm that washed out any practice. Some local racers were showing up in the days leading up to the event, trying to find rides either from car owners or curious onlookers. Those lucky enough to already have shiny new cars were testing the track surface, while some curious onlookers drove up to see what all the fuss was about.

The regular drivers hoping to make a run at Charlotte were as different and talented as, say, the three Flock brothers: Bob, Fonty, and Tim. Bob, the oldest and perhaps the greatest natural racer of the three, had piercing blue eyes in his drawn face and a lanky man's gait. Bob Flock didn't like to be touched; rumor had it that laying a hand on his shoulder, even as a fraternal gesture, could earn you a beating. He was one of the more prominent, elusive moonshine runners at Atlanta. Hank Schoolfield, a longtime promoter and motorsports journalist, recalled the time the famed Lakewood Speedway was owned by the city of Atlanta, and Bob was banned from racing by the city's mayor. "He said Bob Flock would not be allowed to race. And there was an interesting story of him sneaking in and racing under another name. And when they'd line up for the start of a race, he'd park on the back stretch so he wouldn't be seen and then come around and join the field after the start."

Fonty was the first of the sport's true showmen, with a bright smile under a pencil mustache and Clark Gable looks. He frequently raced, as he put it, in "bamooda shorts," and though he might lead a crowd in song while standing in victory atop of the hood of his coupe, he also wasn't immune to the lure of a fight. Cawley remembered a time when Fonty tangled with Curtis Turner at Virginia's Martinsville Speedway after a wreck.

"They got out of the car, Curtis is standing there with his helmet on and Fonty comes down there with a tire iron. And he hit Curtis over the head and busted up his helmet. And Curtis just shook his head, and that Fonty could run. Curtis lit up after Fonty but Fonty got a running start."

Tim, the youngest, would soon begin outrunning his brothers on the way to becoming one of the winningest drivers of his day, frequently emerging from his car with a handsome dirt-caked face dominated by a large mouth and a brilliant smile. And yet Tim suffered from ulcers that flared up even during his most successful seasons.

"Tim was just a super, super smooth race car driver," recalled racing great Richard Petty. "He was a class act, a real class act."

But on the Wednesday before the Charlotte race, Tim was still without a ride, when Bob pointed to a new Oldsmobile 88 sitting beside the track.

"Why don't you go over there and see if they'll let you drive it," Bob said.

Tim needed some convincing but he eventually approached Buddy and Betty Elliott, a couple from Hildebran, North Carolina, sitting in their new car with all of three hundred miles on it.

Tim asked if he could race with it the following Sunday, promising to take care of it and not hurt it.

"Are you crazy?" Betty Elliott called out from inside the cab.

Buddy, however, was thrilled to be a second-party provider, promising to come back the next day without Betty to discuss matters. When he showed up, he and Tim painted the necessary letters and the number 90 on the side of his new car, and they did what they could to better reinforce the wheels. Come qualifying day, Tim would put the car on the outside pole, with the second-fastest time. The Elliotts had a good car, all right. Only Bob Flock would be faster among the qualifiers.

Red Byron, in a gleaming 1949 Olds supplied by renowned car owner Raymond Parks, would start third, next to Virginia mountain man Otis Martin, racing in bib overalls.

France reveled in having big names to promote; it was the way to bring in more fans, and nothing was more important than that. Sara Christian, "the leading woman stock car driver in the country" according to NASCAR press releases, and "sensational and beautiful" in the press, would be the only female among the boys. She'd be starting thirteenth in her husband Frank's 1947 Ford. Curtis Turner, the crowd favorite with the magnetic smile who had helped France promote many local Virginia races, had driven down three hundred miles from Roanoke with Paul Cawley first thing that morning, qualifying sixth in a 1946 Buick Roadmaster. Buck Baker and Herb Thomas, a tobacco farmer from North Carolina, had both made it in. And newcomer Lee Petty brought his family—including his son Richard—to watch him run in his stock car debut.

"We drove over there in the race car," Richard Petty recalled. "Daddy had borrowed it, a '46 Buick, from some of his buddies over at the service station where he hung around. It was a real fast car on the road. Our uncle went with us. And they pulled the car into the Texaco service station, put it up on the rack, changed the oil, greased it, checked the air in the tires, I mean after driving it to the race, we're getting ready *for* the race. I think they took the mufflers off, taped up the headlights, put a number on it, and it was ready to race."

Midwest driver Jim Roper would start twelfth for the race. The Kansas native was enjoying reading *Smilin' Jack* one day when he noticed word of the coming Charlotte race. This would be a chance, Roper thought, to test his mettle against some of the best drivers in the South. He and his friend Millard Clothier drove their sleek 1949 Lincolns one thousand miles without a break in order to qualify. Roper would run with Clothier's car on the sidelines as backup.

France was anxious, watching qualifying, in part because he was going into this race without four fan favorites: Buddy Shuman, Speedy Thompson, Ed Samples, and Marshall Teague. Each had been suspended for various infractions; most notably, Teague—NASCAR's original treasurer who had protested France's driver payment structure and then temporarily defected to Smith's NSCRA—was accused of a rather general, nonspecific infraction: "Conduct detrimental to the best interests of NASCAR." The phrase would in time become France's not-so-subtly worded declaration of power, a catchall for anything that riled him.

France observed a general sense of pushback among the racers, many of whom wished to drive for more than one organization. He made it clear, however, that card-carrying NASCAR drivers couldn't turn the wheel for anybody else.

The suggestion outraged drivers who weren't used to being told where to run and whom they could race for. But France had made these suspensions on the eve of what promised to be a welcome spectacle with a big payoff. And if he ended up being right about this strictly stock thing, where else would the drivers race?

First thing Sunday morning, Glenn Dunaway of Gastonia, North Carolina, knew where he'd be racing later that afternoon: in Charlotte, piloting moonshiner Hubert Westmoreland's 1947 Ford. Westmoreland had the right car but little experience. When Dunaway showed up at the track, Curtis Turner and several others convinced Westmoreland that a real driver would give his car a good chance at victory. Dunaway for his part volunteered to drive it for nothing. But Westmoreland agreed to pay him 25 percent of what he was sure would be some significant winnings.

*   *   *

France couldn't sleep Saturday night. His mind tossed through scenarios, possibilities, and memories. And then he thought about his dad. France had raced on a high-banked mile-and-a-half board track in Maryland in his father's Model T Ford in high school, getting the car back at the end of the day before his dad came home. His father never knew; all he'd do is complain that the tires wore out too fast. Then again, maybe he always knew his car-loving son was doing something and never let on, in case it all led the young man somewhere.

There was much for France to do at Charlotte Speedway that Sunday morning, but mostly it would be about the waiting. The gates were set to open at noon, but given the crowd, France opened early. People had come to town the night before, sleeping in their cars and searching for a breeze in the summer evening. The mercury would be high and there'd be no way to work enough calcium chloride into the dirt, which would rise as dust everywhere.

Race time was 2:00 p.m. Crowd estimates varied, but France would ultimately report more than thirteen thousand paying patrons coming through, all of them jammed into the stands, or the infield, or the sidelines. It was extraordinary stuff. France had advertised wherever he could, and the curious came from all parts of the country, eager to catch sight of gleaming new cars—family cars—racing on the track, just as he'd

hoped. Bob Moore, who'd later become one of the sport's most prominent writers, remembered his father coming back home after the race and
saying, "It was like a carnival."

The racers set up their cars with the standard preparations and
safety measures. They wrapped the bumpers and front ends with masking
tape. They climbed into their cabs and slipped inner tire tubes over their
shoulders, perhaps securing them to the driver's door. Others used ropes,
or even long chains, to tie themselves in place. They threaded their belts
or ropes or chains to connect the driver's door to the molding, making
sure those doors wouldn't snap open during a wreck. They put on some
makeshift helmet. Now they were ready for the call: "Lady and gentlemen, start your *engines*!"

The seventeen rows of cars on the starting grid made three slow
laps behind the pace car. Nine different car makes were represented in the
field, from Kaiser to Mercury, from Chrysler to Ford. There'd be something for everyone to see.

But after the green flag waved and the snarling engines picked up
the pace, the waves of autos slamming down the straightaway and leaning hard into the first turn, actually "seeing" the race quickly became a
challenge. Folks in the stands strained their eyes as the dust kicked up
and swirled.

Pole sitter Bob Flock felt the force of the wide turn shift him over
before the straightaway readjusted his body as he bore down, his new
Hudson like the head of a line of thoroughbreds, forcing the kicked up
dust backward. The dirt road offered rough going, and with each early
lap, Bob Flock could feel every bit of it. Had he been steering a Modified,
most of the punishment meted out to the car and the driver would have
been absorbed by a more comfortable coil of springs. But Flock would
have no such luck with something purely pressed out of Detroit, especially given how hard he was driving.

His instincts were right. Flock felt the heat climbing inside his car.
After thirty-eight laps, his Hudson had had enough, and he parked it finally in a pool of hot oil.

France's friend Bill Blair, a short man in a large black Lincoln, now had a commanding lead. It was, in fact, the spare Lincoln that Jim Roper had brought, borrowed now for the occasion. "That Lincoln," Blair later said, "would just mortally fly."

The heat, the bumps, it all took its toll, and Sara Christian lasted only to lap thirty. When she came in and parked, Bob Flock was ready to hop in and substitute for her.

By then, Blair appeared unassailable. He wondered how Roper's Lincoln managed to handle the heat. He couldn't be too far behind.

A third of the field was now stuck in the pits, victims of over-heating and other mechanical maladies. Halfway through the race, Lee Petty, with a suddenly cracked suspension, lost control of his bor-rowed Buick, which madly tumbled end over end several times before landing back upright. When he was able to open his eyes, Petty was thankful: He'd suffered only minor cuts for his trouble. His borrowed, beaten-up car was a different matter. Petty undid his seat belt, exited the car, and sat on a mound of dirt at the edge of the track, staring into space.

France watched to make sure that Petty was okay; halfway through the event and only one wreck. The racing, while hardly stellar, was safe. But as France patrolled the pits, he was warmed by a different kind of spectacle. Cars would come in, badly overheated and in need of repair, and regular people from the stands would rush to their own cars to get spare parts and tires to donate to the cause. This, France thought, was the ultimate validation: regular guys helping to fix regular-guy racecars with parts from their own autos.

The race now belonged to Bill Blair. He'd lapped the entire field and kept hitting his marks, making his way through the dust as sweat and dirt coated the back of his neck. The heat inside the car could suffo-cate, but there was $2,000 for the winner.

At almost 150 laps, the three-quarter mark, Blair taxied the Lincoln into the pits, and crew members began to work on it. One of them had had too much to drink, and in trying to deal with getting water into the radiator, he ended up breaking the lip off it. While the water could now get in, the cap wouldn't stay.

Blair screamed at the crew; there'd be no chance of winning now. Advised to go and run the thing till it blew up, Blair charged out. Five laps later, his car sputtering, Blair's day was done, thanks to too little oil and too much applejack.

Whatever traction problems beset all the other drivers, Glenn Dunaway seemed quite immune. All around the track, rising steam from engines cut through the dust, but Dunaway had no such problems. Behind him, Jim Roper's Lincoln now stood in second. As the laps ticked down, Roper could feel the ugly grinding under the hood; he slowed his pace, watching Dunaway pull farther ahead. There was nothing he could do about it but watch.

The checkered flag flew for Dunaway, whose 1947 Ford raced past it with a three-lap margin over Roper. Then came Fonty Flock—the only driver to make it the whole way without a pit stop—followed by Red Byron.

France had put on a memorable show. With ticket prices ranging from $2.50 for general admission to $4 for grandstand seating, it had been a profitable day.

* * *

Later on in his hotel room, France was basking in the glow, celebrating with Anne and some friends. With this race, he was convinced he'd leveled a decided blow to Bruton Smith, and plans were already in place for NASCAR's next strictly stock event in the center of France's racing universe: the Beach and Road Course in Daytona.

Then the phone rang early in the evening, and France's face became a mask of disappointment.

Al Crisler, NASCAR's first technical inspector, had conducted a post-race strip-down of the Westmoreland car that Dunaway drove so easily to victory. Blocks had been welded to spread the springs to better support the car, a typical modification for a moonshine runner. The only problem was bootlegging cars were not allowed to run in strictly stock.

France immediately declared over the phone that Dunaway needed to be disqualified, leaving Jim Roper the sudden winner of the race, along with the first-place money.

Westmoreland, the car owner, was beside himself; beyond the disqualification, he'd lost whatever he'd spent to bring the car and get it ready. And plenty of other racers were in his corner, wondering: What the hell was wrong with a simple modification? Dunaway had won the race fair and square, and no doubt his wasn't the only car with a few tweaks. "I think Glenn got a bad deal, I really do," Tim Flock said later.

The newspapers were especially complimentary to the race. And the NASCAR column in *National Speed Sport News* waxed poetic, boasting for all—especially Bruton Smith—to see. "The 150-mile Stock Car Race at the beautiful three-quarter banked speedway in Charlotte, N.C., proved to be another feather in the cap of genial Bill France who has a habit of coming up with the best," the column began. "With a publicity campaign second to none in the South, Bill had the satisfaction of drawing the largest crowd of any 1949 race with the exception of Indianapolis."

The column later went on to defend Dunaway. "Glenn Dunaway of Charlotte was disqualified when some bars were found welded on his Ford coupe to aid in handling. It was a tough break for Glenn who had never sat in the car until a few minutes before the race. However, the other drivers and car owners pooled a sum of money that reached $500 or more and gave it to him, one of the nicest sporting gestures in the history of racing."

Westmoreland was not so fortunate, and certainly not happy. He decided to sue NASCAR for $10,000.

France quickly understood that winning this lawsuit was as necessary to the survival of NASCAR as putting on a good show. A victory over Westmoreland would establish his reputation and send a hefty message to any driver not willing to run Strictly Stock fair and square.

France, as befit his talent, took his case to the people. In another racing article hyping the coming Daytona race, he reminded all potential drivers and owners that: "No souped-up jobs will be allowed, with only strictly stock automobiles of American manufacture of the years 1946 to 1949 allowed."

The first strictly stock season was all of eight races. Red Byron, who won two of those, ended up with the title, taking home $5,800 in winnings, along with the $1,000 Nash Dealer's Trophy given the following February at the start of the 1950 season. The purses were all good, as were the guarantees, but the drivers still bristled at whatever rules France insisted upon. Cawley remembered Curtis Turner routinely accepting appearance-fee money from non-sanctioned tracks, a practice frowned upon by France. Turner was a big NASCAR draw, and business was business.

"NASCAR banned that. Bill France wouldn't allow that," Cawley said. "Ain't no way you'd do that and walk into one of France's properties; you didn't have no rights. You couldn't open your mouth or anything."

On December 16, Judge Johnson J. Hayes heard Hubert Westmoreland's complaint. The car owner produced experts and witnesses to help his contention that his car had been illegally disqualified. Among the arguments Westmoreland listed was that the car had passed a prerace inspection. He also claimed in his charges that, "NASCAR has a monopoly on automobile racing in this area."

France sat patiently in court, listening to the talk and testimony and feeling confident, though anxious. But as it turned out, France's confidence was not misplaced. "The Court finds at the conclusion of the evidence that the automobile of the plaintiffs was disqualified under the rules of the race," Hayes stated. To add insult to injury, Hayes made Westmoreland pay for the cost of the action.

The case dismissed, France went about his business. The 1950 season featured nineteen races with fourteen different winners. Strictly Stock was also renamed the Grand National Series, meant to capture a sense of where France saw NASCAR growing. Stealing the thunder once again from a different racing promoter—this time, France's bitter rival Sam Nunis—the NASCAR founder agreed that the organization would be a part of the first-ever Southern 500, at the brand-new Darlington Raceway. It would be the first five-hundred-mile stock car race ever, featuring a $25,500 purse. And France kept steadfastly enforcing his rules, at one point stripping Byron and Petty of their total points for the season for running at non-sanctioned "outlaw" events.

The racing was exciting. Names such as Fireball Roberts, Curtis Turner, Tim Flock, and Herb Thomas thrilled fans with wild bangs and turns. With each new race and development, France further consolidated his power and gained confidence in considering all sides of an argument and then bending things the way he felt they needed to move. From the first moment, he held to the idea that acknowledging moonshining legitimized it. Asked late in his life by reporter Sylvia Wilkinson about whether or not car builder Red Vogt—who'd given NASCAR its name in the Ebony Room—was in fact a famed bootleg car builder, France replied that he had no knowledge of such a thing, adding that any good "tuner-upper" might end up working on such a car.

By then, France had long been regarded as the sport's "benevolent dictator."

"The customer comes to a NASCAR race; he is not only the promoter's customer, or NASCAR's customer, he's also a direct customer of the drivers and owners," said Bill France Jr., who eventually succeeded his dad as head of the racing organization. "He buys the sponsor's products, which lets them go racing. We're more like partners than we are players and owners. It's a neat structure as far as trying to maintain a sense of, 'Let's don't shoot the sport in the foot 'cause I got some of my toes on that foot.'"

Everyone felt involved, responsible, and charged with keeping the racing going. Drivers raced, promoters promoted, and the fans came in droves. France made money and he made the rules—and whoever wanted to be in the game followed them. Profit or no, NASCAR became the place you could go to get behind the wheel of a stock car and do the thing you loved.

"My dad, he started in '49 in the first race," remembered Maurice Petty, Lee's younger son, who would go on to build just about all of his brother Richard's winning engines. "Then it was NASCAR Grand National. You didn't know nothing else. That's all there was, man. You lived and breathed it."

Getting mighty close to the dirt track racing action in Atlanta during the 1950s.

Chapter Two
Feats of Clay

*"I enjoyed dirt more than I did asphalt. It takes a lot more skill to
drive dirt than it does asphalt. You gotta be able to handle a car better than the next guy because you're running sideways all the time."*

—JUNIOR JOHNSON

A T ASHEVILLE-WEAVERVILLE SPEEDWAY, MANY OF THE DRIVERS
leaned their bodies into the turns, as if they were on motorcycles, willing their cars to go faster. The track was like many
on the NASCAR circuit in the 1950s, a nearly perfectly cut half-mile dirt
oval etched years earlier into a piece of farmland. But people called
Asheville-Weaverville "the fastest half-mile track in the nation." It was
wedged into a chunk of property between Flat Creek Church Road and
Clarks Chapel Road, with the mountains rising all around it, and on September 30, 1956, Curtis Turner was leading a premier field of racers in
NASCAR's exciting new Convertible Division through the twists and
turns of race day.

Turner had started on the pole in this two-hundred-lap contest. If
he were to win, it would be his twenty-first victory in forty-six convertible
races, an astonishing record. With twenty-five laps to go, it was looking
good.

But for the 4,500 in attendance that day—sitting in the bleachers,
or standing in the infield—it was getting harder to see the action. The
day was hot and foggy, and there had already been a few crashes and
spins. And many of the top competitors would enter each turn on every

lap by sliding their cars sideways, gliding across the dirt surface, and sending up plumes of dust before righting themselves and dashing down the straightaway. Racing at Asheville-Weaverville was broadsliding at its best.

"That track could get real, real tough when it was dirt," remembers Humpy Wheeler, famed onetime general manager of Lowe's Motor Speedway in Charlotte. "It was sitting up on top of the mountain and I think the air was thinner and it was awfully difficult to keep these tracks together when they were racing in the hot sun. You had your hands full every time they ran there."

As the race moved toward its end, the air grew thicker with the residue of the brilliant red clay surface. It coated the cars and the drivers, drifted thinly, and flew into the fans' faces and onto their clothes. It seemed to cling to the air. The people loved the competition but even the faithful were overwhelmed by the voluminous rising tide. With the racers spread out at different points in their orbits, new plumes rose continuously, like a barrage of dust bombs.

"You couldn't see nothing and the only way you could drive that track, you had to count the poles," said "Tiger" Tom Pistone, the popular Chicago racer. "They had some poles on the inside of the racetrack. And when you got to that pole, you turned. That's how you could judge."

Turner led, but the competition grew fiercer, more charged. His best friend and Ford racing teammate Joe Weatherly hung in behind; short-track master Glen Wood and popular star Gwyn Staley were third and fourth, respectively.

With twenty laps to go, Jimmy Massey, a dark-haired North Carolina driver who'd won the week before on the paved track in Martinsville, Virginia, was arcing around the backstretch when the right front hub broke on his '56 Chevy. Right next to him, and swinging toward the curve, Possum Jones was startled by the jolting smack of Massey's car, and suddenly both autos came rolling and grinding into the third turn. Momentum carried them and together they bounded into a doughy dirt embankment, tumbled end over ugly end, and finally came to rest, each on its side, leaning together like some V-shaped roadblock.

Their wreck sent up fresh columns of dirt and the sun darted and gleamed through the thickening cloud. Clay mist very quickly masked the wreck.

What followed became metal-crunching slapstick. Art Binkley, driving a Plymouth, sailed into the smog and smacked the other cars. Then came Weatherly. And then Staley, Larry Odo, Larry Frank—*bang, boom, smack*—with the smells of exhaust, oil, and gas emanating from the haze-covered, car-swallowing wreck.

The only man past the action was Turner. Squinting at his rearview, he slowed, trying to decipher what was going on, as more autos were collected by the fog. All you heard were the cracking sounds, one after another, in succession. Pistone saw one driver leap from his car, cut through the haze, run off the side of the track, and hop over the fence to get away from it all.

"The only thing I remember about it is a big cloud of dust on the back stretch and I'm sitting over there watching Glen run head on into it," said Leonard Wood, who built his brother's race cars.

"I went into it wide open," Glen recalled. "I went by the flag stand and suddenly the flag wasn't [visible]."

When Glen disappeared in the fog, another sickening crash erupted. Leonard started screaming as loud as he could, running into the blinding mess. He found his brother sitting behind the wheel, his cheeks and lips covered in blood, the result of a broken nose.

"Scared me to death, you know, to watch your brother run head on into a car parked in the middle of the track. The track was high banked and very fast, you know?" Leonard said, to which he added, with typical Wood brothers respect, "But we liked running there. It was a nice racetrack."

The two-hundred-lap race was called after 181 circuits. All anyone knew was that the race—the only one in NASCAR history to end with a single driver still standing—was over. Turner had won. Weatherly, his '56 Ford a twisted heap, claimed second.

And dirt-track racing, upon which the sport had built its legacy, charm, and character, had yet another anecdote, one to be filed away by amazed fans who were there, and one to rile everybody from Bill France to the track owners to the people who felt stock car racing was too unrefined for polite society.

A race like this one became, in hindsight, one of a slew of final straws for dirt. In the late '50s and early '60s, the pace leading to the building of grand superspeedways became supercharged. Dust-covered fans symbolized an era of play at a time when a sport needed to define itself as a business.

Not that this changed dirt track racing's mythic appeal. Dirt races could be wildly unpredictable. And that was the whole point.

"We were running dirt tracks and we were doing everything possible to keep people away," says Wheeler of the sport's early races. "We coated them with dust, gave them lousy restrooms and terrible food. But they kept coming back and bringing people with them."

* * *

The joy of looking back now at old footage of dirt track racing—watching a wave of competitors sling their cars sideways into turns, tires tripping and bouncing on the dirt to recover momentum, before exploding back into the straightaways—is watching action miraculously free of orchestration.

"I saw a recent Las Vegas race and one guy got tagged in the left rear quarter panel," recalls Wheeler of current NASCAR Sprint Cup action. "It seemed like he went all the way through the corner, almost sideways, and never did crash. And everybody thought gee-whiz, what a fantastic job of driving he did. Well that used to go on all the time. That was just par for the course.

"People look at drifting now as something spectacular and new and different; that's all dirt track racing was."

During dirt track racing's NASCAR heyday in the 1950s, track lengths varied with the kind of artful carelessness you'd expect of facilities carved out of grass, and then graded and shaped. Quarter- and third-mile tracks had some dates early on, as did three-quarter and even a .9-mile track. But these weren't necessarily "facilities," places expressly built for auto racing. The stock cars were often an afterthought at that spot, when there weren't horses, baseball, or football, or perhaps even the circus.

Some of the tracks were disasters. Buck Baker, recalling one old dirt track in South Carolina, said, "It had holes in it you could bury a car in. They'd wet it down to keep the dirt down and it'd turn into a mud bog."

The best tracks were treated well, watered for grip, handling, and excitement, with a load of calcium chloride mixed in to help keep the dust from choking the field.

"Back in the days of the power slide, red-clay tracks, when prepared right, would get this sheen on them that looked like forty coats of clear lacquer and were slick, just like skating rinks," said Wheeler. "And that's the way you wanted them because you were trying to excite the fans. So on a lot of these tracks, you couldn't get the car totally straight; you were always turning right a little bit to go left. And it really required a tremendous seat-of-the-pants driver to be able to run fast on that because that was very much like driving on hard-packed snow. You felt like you were in control but you knew that you were right on the edge all the time and if you did anything really hairy you were probably going to crash. And if you let up a little bit, the whole field was gonna pass you. So you're sitting on that ragged edge all the time."

"I enjoyed dirt more than I did asphalt," said NASCAR Hall of Fame driver Junior Johnson. "It takes a lot more skill to drive dirt than it does asphalt. You gotta be able to handle a car better than the next guy because you're running sideways all the time."

The broadslide, as Johnson knew, had its roots in moonshine running, with drivers moving sideways into turns on local highways and town roads to help them elude the police.

Turner perfected a signature move that he'd used on some infamous liquor runs in the 1940s. He could work up a load of speed and then brake and turn the car around in a complete, tire-screeching 180-degree spin. It was a maneuver he'd once reputedly made on a rickety single-lane bridge in a run-in with the law.

Johnson, Tiny Lund, Weatherly, Baker, all of them could bring fans to their feet at the tracks. But nobody did it with the style of Turner.

"You'd have to say that he was either the best or as good as the best in any type of race: road course, superspeedway, dirt, whatever; he was just a great race driver," recalled Johnson.

Turner, also the sport's consummate partier, made a practice out of racing, and winning, after very long nights of camaraderie. As beloved as he might have been by his friends, Turner was feared, disliked, admired, and worshipped in equal measure on dirt by the NASCAR faithful. The sliding skills he used on Daytona's sprawling beach course were the wild extension of the centrifugal whipping turns he made on the half-mile dirt tracks that made up the majority of dates on the sport's top circuits.

"When Curtis Turner was on dirt—that was the greatest thrill. Oh man, could that cat drive on dirt! Good grief!" said Hal Hamrick, original manager of Bristol Motor Speedway. "It was poetry in motion."

"The first time I ever saw him driving on dirt, I was dumbfounded," said Ford's racing boss Jacques Passino. "He was amazing. He'd drive his car in a broadside skid all the way around the racetrack. And the crowd loved him. When he was going and his car stayed under him, he was wonderful."

"As far as controlling the car in the slide, keeping it from spinning out, holding onto it, of all the drivers I've ever known, ever heard of, ever worked with, nobody was better than him on that," said Leonard Wood. His brother, for whom Turner often ran, recalled, "We used to go watch him race before I started, and he was our hero back then. He was one of the most exciting race drivers that ever lived."

Wheeler laughs when recalling the outrageous dirt track battles between Turner and Johnson.

"When Turner and Joe Weatherly and Junior Johnson were racing, it was more than a show because Junior wasn't funny," he said. "There was nothing funny about Junior. If you saw him coming you'd either get out of the way or go into high defense. There's no playing around when he was there. So they had some interesting bangings."

Turner would often walk the tracks in the hours before a race, judging the dirt compound with a scout's instincts, observing the water-to-calcium ratio, looking for the best ways to hug the corners. At some tracks, drivers would mount wire mesh to the grills of their cars to help deflect the rocks and gravel that might fly up.

"I never will forget the first time I got in a race car down there in the Carolinas," recalled Paul Cawley. "The rocks were flying all over the place; rocks, gravel and stuff, man, it was flying everywhere. I thought I was in a rock storm, or a rock quarry."

* * *

Bill France was in a quandary in the late 1950s. Ten years earlier, he'd organized a sport that had very much needed a unifier, and he'd built a profitable business. But NASCAR now required an upgrade.

One August 1956 Grand National race in Oklahoma got one-third of the way through a one-hundred-lap contest before the thick dust overwhelmed the competitors. Lee Petty emerged from his car, squinted as he ran toward the flag stand, and waved the red flag himself to end the thing, mercifully.

One 1957 race was curtailed just past the halfway point; lots of crashes had reduced the twenty-two-car field to only four, and promoters stopped it where it was. A race later that season in Newberry, South Carolina, lured just nine hundred spectators. To be fair, the track was awful. As consummate NASCAR historian Greg Fielden reported, Mel Larson, who finished nineteenth in the field, said, "This is the furthest thing from a race track I have ever seen. And I've seen some dandies!"

Even a classy establishment like Darlington, one of the sport's premier paved tracks, was not immune to race-day issues. About a third of the way through the 1958 Southern 500, pole-sitter Eddie Pagan's tire blew, and the Ford driver barreled through the guardrail.

Pagan emerged with a broken nose; his car, however, was demolished. And the barrier he'd passed through was utterly destroyed. Race officials wondered if they'd have to call the race. Their solution: They warned the rest of the field to keep away from the upper groove in turn one. As it turned out, that spot was like a magnet. About fifteen laps later, a skidding Eddie Gray drove his Ford directly through the opening. He managed to come away in one piece.

But dirt tracks were the clearest culprits and something had to be done. In 1956, in an article for *Speed Age* about the future of NASCAR, France had written, "What is wrong with auto racing today? There is no need to hide our heads in the sand. We must face facts. Speedway operators in future years must improve their facilities."

Very much a self-made man, France doggedly followed a philosophy of effort and result. As he quoted to his friend Joseph Mattioli, when the latter was considering selling his Pocono Raceway in 1975, "On the plains of hesitation lie the bleached bones of millions who, when within the grasp of victory, sat and waited and waiting died."

By 1958, France was deep into building the Daytona International Speedway, which would open the following February and change the sport forever, a high-banked 2.5-mile facility offering incredible speeds. A year later, speedways of note would open in California, Charlotte, and Atlanta. They'd all experience growing pains but they each had large grandstands, and no plumes of dirt coating the crowds.

No figure in the sport represented the dream of what could be gained, and the cost of what was to be left behind with the loss of dirt tracks, more than Turner.

Many people had explored the idea of building a large paved track in the years since 1949 and Darlington. For Turner, who was a millionaire timber broker in addition to being a racer, the idea seemed good, sound business. He'd watched his friend Bill France put together Daytona with a Herculean effort, a process that took six years, with few guarantees of being completed. Knowing what he knew of France's struggles, and his own abilities to raise cash, Turner planned on building his own speedway, just outside Charlotte, in less than six months.

Turner and France had in years past developed a strong bond, promoting races together and teaming up for the first-ever Mexican Road Race in 1950. France, a racecar driver, turned out to be a much better businessman. Turner, a daring businessman, turned out to be better behind the wheel. An ease and a friendly competition existed between them; each man yearned to do what the other did, and better. Though France was fifteen years Turner's senior, it was easy to think the two could be brothers.

In Charlotte, the idea of building a racetrack also caught the imagination of Bruton Smith, the successful young race promoter who'd originally tried developing a stock car racing organization to rival France's. Both Turner and Smith announced their intentions to the Charlotte press on the same day. After weeks of grandstanding, the men realized there was going to be only one superspeedway in the Charlotte area, and in order to build it, given limited available funds, it made sense to unite their efforts.

They each played to their particular strengths in the project. Turner was the brash, determined president, flying his private plane from place to place, doing timber deals, and raising money for the track. Smith was the resolute general manager, throwing himself into organizing the construction and coming up with brilliant intuitive methods for bringing in the necessary cash. Without banks willing to put up the necessary loan money—a typical happenstance at the time—building a major track was a steep uphill battle.

Then disaster struck: Half a million yards of solid granite were discovered just below the surface of the track site. Unearthing that would be no small or cheap task. As Turner later remarked, "It cost $70,000 of dynamite just getting through the first turn."

"Bruton and Curtis made a giant mistake," said Smokey Yunick, the legendary car builder and engineer who fielded several rides for Turner in his career. "If they'd have searched North Carolina for the worst possible place to build a racetrack, that's where they built it."

When contractor Owen Flowe refused to allow his construction crew to grade the final stretch of track until overdue payment was made, Turner and Smith greeted Flowe with loaded guns, which convinced the man to listen to reason. Turner bought a small local bank that could lend only a maximum of $12,000 to any one person; he, however, borrowed $75,000. And when creditors demanded to see some guarantee of coming funds, Turner angrily showed them a cashier's check for $250,000—a temporary gift from a Mafia connection in Memphis. "It was drawn on the Bank of New York, and there wasn't a bank by the name," he later said. "But it was a nice *lookin'* check."

With incredible speed, the track was ultimately completed in time for the June 19, 1960, inaugural running of the World 600. The problem with that first race was the track surface: The asphalt had been put down too fast. Great chunks of it came up as drivers made their rounds during testing and practice. Trying to find the fastest line to run really meant making sure not to roll over potentially dangerous potholes.

While both men continued to try to raise the cash needed to keep the track afloat, creditors and board members sought to wrest control. Ultimately, after a vote by the new board, Turner, much to his shock, was unceremoniously shown the door. Smith, while also removed from his position of power, was retained by the track's new governing body.

In order to get the track back, Turner sought a loan offered to him from the Teamsters Union, then under the iron-fisted control of Jimmy Hoffa. The proviso for the loan was that Turner needed to organize the drivers into a union.

Turner was desperate. He had lost the speedway, which he'd grown to regard with enormous paternalism, a grand idea that he and Smith had seen to its conclusion. But he was now $200,000 in debt, and being sued for another $90,000. Worst of all, the new board at the speedway had posted a deadline: The place needed an $850,000 loan within sixty days in order to survive. With the loan money, Turner knew he could buy back the speedway, and the Teamsters were willing.

France was livid. In his view, his old friend Turner was attempting to throw a wrench into NASCAR in order to save his own track. What was worse, Turner hadn't detailed the entire plan with France before talking union with the drivers. "It actually hurt Bill France's feelings that he was not told that they were going to do anything like this," remembered racer Buddy Baker. "Then it became more personal."

France—and the friends in Washington whom he polled—believed that allowing drivers to unionize through the Teamsters could undo the hold he had over the sport. But Turner was already signing up drivers, including star racer Fireball Roberts and two-time NASCAR champion Buck Baker. Drastic measures were required.

* * *

Bill France announced that any union driver would not be permitted to participate in a NASCAR sanctioned race. At a drivers' meeting at Bowman Gray Stadium—one that Turner was not permitted to attend—he made his point to the drivers with more of an iron fist than usual.

"Make no mistake gentlemen: Before I have this union stuffed down my throat, I will plow up my 2.5-mile track at Daytona Beach and plant corn there instead," he told the assembled drivers, many of whom had already signed up for the union.

"After the race tonight," France promised, "no known union member can compete in a NASCAR race. I'll use a pistol to enforce it. I have a pistol and I know how to use it. I've used it before."

Secretly standing outside a slightly open window, listening to all the talk, Turner and fellow union organizer Tim Flock paced and waited, and grew more frustrated by the moment. At one point, France announced, "If this union you have was really such a great thing then I'd join it."

Outside, Turner reached into his pocket and thrust a card through the opening in the window. "Here's your application," he said.

France marched over, swiped the card, and slammed down the window.

In the ensuing months, he would also shut down Turner's NASCAR career. France, a proud man, was being made to look the fool. "Bill France, the NASCAR president, has been quoted as saying: 'No known union members can complete in a NASCAR race, and I'll use a pistol to enforce it,'" read a *Charlotte Observer* commentary. "Boy, think what this will mean to fans. You can buy a ticket to a track and not only see smash ups, but gang battles between pit stops."

France responded with his own published statement. "A recent newspaper story suggests that I might be some kind of rootin', tootin', hootin', shootin' cuss, waving a pistol and itching to shoot up anyone who might disagree with me," it read. "HONEST, I'M NOTHING LIKE THAT! But I am an American who believes in our constitution and laws—and bearing of arms to repel invasion is part of our great American Heritage. . . . WE HONESTLY FEEL THAT [NASCAR has] A RECORD OF SOLID ACHIEVEMENT AND PROGRESS FOR OUR MEMBERS AND FOR THE SPORT. AND WHEN, OUT OF A CLEAR, BLUE SKY, in a period of continuing growth and progress in the sport, I am suddenly confronted with the fact that a few of the boys who have grown to stature and respect in the sport as NASCAR members, and with the help and support of NASCAR over many years which have been good and profitable for them, engage in activity which is disruptive—and actually poisonous to the sport—I HOPE IT'S NOT TOO HARD TO UNDERSTAND WHY I MIGHT BE A BIT MAD."

The anger would not be quelled. "If early in the union situation, the two of them had sat down in the back room—the old cliché—and just screamed at each other, it probably would have been settled," said longtime *Observer* writer Bob Moore. "But soon it took on a whole different level."

France banned Turner—and Flock—from competing in NASCAR for life. Turner sued for reinstatement but was denied. Three years had passed since he'd promised a new speedway in Charlotte. Now he was without the track and his tie to the sport he loved.

NASCAR, meanwhile, continued its growth away from its ragged roots. Owners paved a succession of dirt tracks. Martinsville had been paved in 1955, followed by North Wilkesboro in 1957 and Asheville-Weaverville in 1958. Georgia's Augusta International Speedway would be paved in 1964, followed by the North Carolina speedways in Richmond and Hickory, and Occoneechee in Hillsborough. Bob Russo, *Speed Age* magazine's racing editor, insisted in the July, 1956, issue that, "Despite a history of breathtaking action and superb driving, the dirt tracks of the United States are today in danger of extinction. More and more, the critics of the dusters bring out the cry: 'Let's pave the dirt tracks.' *Speed Age*, however, takes the position, Let's *save* the dirt tracks!" And yet, the die had by then been cast.

"Paving the tracks seemed like the easy way to do it and the modern thing to do," says Wheeler. "I relate it to the floor salesmen that came through the south and put linoleum over those beautiful, old, hardwood floors."

Starting in 1962, the major auto manufacturers officially returned to the sport after a five-year absence, and competition and speeds increased. At the inaugural Daytona 500 in 1959, pole winner Bob Welborn had sailed around the track at an average speed of just over 140 miles per hour. Four years later, fastest qualifier Junior Johnson hit a blistering 165. Of the fifty-five races run in the circuit in 1963, nineteen were on dirt, a number that continued to dwindle, especially as richer sponsorship money slowly began seeping into the sport.

"It was very important for the race to involve big corporations to sponsor the cars, and the kinda people that run the corporations would not go to a dirt track because they showed up in suits and stuff of that nature," recalls Junior Johnson. "Sitting there with a bucket of red dirt in your pocket at the end of the day just didn't apply to 'em. And that's when asphalt tracks started coming about."

But beginning in 1964, France and NASCAR's fortunes fielded tremendous blow after blow. During a five-month period of racing, crashes ultimately claimed the lives of two of the sport's most popular drivers. Joe Weatherly died at the road course in Riverside, California. And Fireball Roberts succumbed to terrible burns suffered at a crash at Charlotte Motor Speedway.

Drivers were registering concerns and complaints. Johnson believed the cars were too fast for the tracks; popular star Fred Lorenzen considered quitting. Over the next several seasons, auto manufacturers staged season-long boycotts. By 1965, the racing facilities were looking better in NASCAR, but the fans were showing up less and less. "What we need is personalities," France told the Bristol, Tennessee, *Herald Courier* that May, after Chrysler had pulled out for the year. "If we still had Little Joe and Fireball, it wouldn't matter if they were all driving Fords." France had, months earlier, faced the indignity of being booed at his own track in Daytona.

In addition, fans began to miss the perennial excitement of dirt track racing. The smaller paved tracks didn't allow for the mesmerizing sliding that had brought thrills in the sport's early years.

"Asphalt was the way people thought you ought to go," says Wheeler. "And it was modern and convenient and it just seemed like the thing to do. And, of course, when the cars got on asphalt a lot of the races turned out to be very boring. People don't pay to see respectability—unless they go to the Kentucky Derby, and they can bet there and drink mint juleps."

Meanwhile, Turner had still been running in local races, often on outlaw tracks, mostly on the much smaller United States Auto Club circuit. He was clearly a top draw in the South, and fans regarded Turner races as showcases of his immense dirt track talents. They eagerly flocked to North Carolina's Concord Speedway by the thousands, just to watch racing the way it had once been, with Turner on a half-mile dirt track, nudging, knocking, popping, and pushing competitors out of the way, and running on to victory. Though he was now forty-one, and his legendary partying hadn't subsided, his skills remained undiminished and phenomenal. A public outcry, both from fans and reporters, for Turner's return was heard loudly and clearly by NASCAR's power elite.

But it took a self-appointed committee of track owners and promoters much time and effort to convince Bill France that the personality he needed to lure fans back to NASCAR was well within his grasp, and a phone call away. After a four-year "lifetime" ban, France grudgingly gave permission. And Curtis Turner was once again a member in good standing in NASCAR.

* * *

With Turner back, fan excitement was piqued. He was given a Ford factory ride with the Wood Brothers, and despite being out of shape, he prepared to ferry a good car in a race that he felt a little extra motivation to win: the National 400 at Charlotte Motor Speedway. Before the race, he threw the kind of party that indicated he'd lost none of his hosting skills either. When he arrived for practice the following morning, he promised Leonard Wood a fine showing.

"Don't worry, Pop," he told him. "I drive better with a hangover."

It would be hard to argue the point on race day as Turner nearly won one of the most spectacular, competitive races fans had seen in ages. He lost out only in the final laps to A. J. Foyt and eventual winner Lorenzen, the onetime young upstart—and now once again an admirer—who'd replaced Turner in the hearts of many fans.

"Curtis Turner is *back*," declared Lorenzen after the race. "His physical endurance is amazing. His reflexes and skills have not been hampered by age."

During the race, however, Turner had cracked two ribs. He'd lost his shock absorbers in the early going, and came to regret telling Leonard Wood not to bother adjusting his seat before the race. Ridges along the seat began gouging into him with each bump, making the going excruciating toward the race's end, and elevating his achievement still further.

The next race was the inaugural contest at yet another brand-new paved track, in Rockingham, North Carolina. Turner came to the race with taped ribs, a mean hangover, and an excellent Wood Brothers car. He napped on the hood of the car before the race and was ready to go.

The day, as it turned out, was relentlessly steamy. Racing five hundred miles would be hard enough; doing so with broken ribs that much harder. And the temperature in the cabs of the cars would be well over 100 degrees by race time. It was hard to imagine a fine Turner performance.

But he put on a remarkable show. The race came down to its final laps, with Turner challenged only by Cale Yarborough, a brash, thickly built rising star who, at twenty-six, was fifteen years Turner's junior. Everyone waited for the old man to falter.

But Turner held on. In the late going, he twice brushed the wall of the track hard and kept going, bounding forward as the thousands watching gasped and cheered one of the sport's few remaining original heroes. The temperature had climbed and the sun beat down at a harsh angle as drivers paraded around the turns. And when the checkered flag flew, Curtis Turner had captured the day, a dirt master taking the win in the superspeedway era.

As inspired a performance as it was, Turner's triumph would not lead to a lengthy return. A Ford boycott the following season curtailed his running for a while. And after a terrifying, soaring, flipping practice crash at Atlanta Motor Speedway—where he sailed high above Yarborough's car, missing it by inches—Turner's friend Yunick refused to give him another ride, famously saying, "I don't want to build the car that kills Curtis Turner."

So Turner became a journeyman, running the occasional NASCAR race and making his timber deals.

Asphalt tracks were in and that wasn't about to shift back. "The dirt tracks really were being squeezed out. I think my attitude is a good reflection of that change," remembered Bobby Allison, who helped usher in the new era, particularly through his incredible rivalry with Richard Petty. "My whole idea was, I didn't want to go run dirt because dirt was a different style than pavement and the big tracks were not going to be dirt. Pavement was going to be the future. And dirt was history."

But for Turner fans, who continued to pack tracks when an appearance was announced, dirt wasn't so much history as historic, and he continued to thrill on the surface.

In 1967, Don Naman, who would go on to manage Talladega Superspeedway, Bill France's second high-banked signature track, was operating Smoky Mountain Raceway, a half-mile dirt track in Maryville, Tennessee. The track ran a weekly racing series, along with two NASCAR Grand National races every year. During its regular weekly events, arrangements were sometimes made to bring in racing stars. Tiny Lund and Richard Petty were among the big names that Naman had contracted for appearances. But nothing rivaled one night when Turner came.

"We had advertised him a lot," Naman recalled. On the night of the race, "the car got there, but not *him*."

Naman was told that Turner was due to fly in. Adjoining the track was a small two-thousand-foot dirt runway that Naman wasn't sure would accommodate Turner's large twin-engine Aero Commander. Turner, who was busy with other business, had arranged for someone to come in ahead to practice and even qualify the car. When the racing came, he promised he'd be there.

Qualifying and practice came and went. Ten minutes to go before race time, with the drivers already behind the wheels of their cars, a nervous Naman scanned the large, fidgety crowd. A normal Saturday night event might bring in four thousand spectators; with Turner's name involved, twice that number had paid good money to show up, and they were loud. But above the din, he began to hear a faint, growing buzz; in the distant sky, looming larger, came the Aero Commander.

With no pause or undue calculation, the plane landed easily on the strip as the crowd burst into shouts and applause. A hatch opened and Turner bounded from within, ran across the field, vaulted over the guardrail, and stood for a moment with a smile and a wave.

"The crowd was cheering like crazy, just seeing him jump over the guardrail," Naman said.

Turner threw on a helmet and secured it as he got behind the wheel; he'd have to start in the back of the field after missing qualifying, but he was ready to mix it up with the track regulars who knew all the ins and outs of the place.

The green flag flew and Turner took to each of the track's curves with a style and skill unlike anyone else's. "Even the drivers who drove similar cars and were there every week couldn't take the turns with such skilled abandon. Turner's car was making the dirt fly the way a boat sends up a big plume in the back," said Naman. "The faster he went, the bigger that plume was. He was throwing dirt so far up in the air, I would estimate that if the normal car was throwing the dirt up three feet, he was throwing it up twenty-three feet. It was incredible."

Turner quickly pushed toward the lead among the thirty-five drivers in the field. But the harder he pushed the car, the more his tires began rubbing against the fenders. Turner wanted very much to win, but he also wanted to put on a show. Victory or no, he would need to be spectacular.

Coming back around the straightaway, eighty laps into a hundred-lap event and nearly in the lead, Turner suddenly blew two tires at once. He jerked and spun and the car slammed hard into the wall, now wrecked beyond racing use. A fantastic run had come to an end.

"But the people were just ecstatic," Naman said. "They were *standing* and *screaming*. They felt they saw something you only see once in a lifetime."

Turner navigated the now-broken car into the pits during the yellow flag, got out, ran across the track, jumped back over the guardrail, and returned to his plane with another wave. By the time the field was taking the green flag once again, he was gone, off into the night like a specter.

"A lot of people said, 'He can never take off on that little runway.' But off he went," Naman said. "And that was Curtis Turner. He was like a flash. The people just loved him, you know; he had a *name*. I'd heard about him but I never believed all that. I was a believer after that."

There would be more such exhibitions, but in terms of marquee major league NASCAR events, dirt racing grew increasingly rare. In 1967, fourteen out of forty-nine Grand National races were on dirt. In 1968, Smoky Mountain Raceway was among the tracks paved. Of the forty-nine NASCAR top-tier races that year, only five remained on dirt.

By then, Turner had become much more a businessman than a racer, starting one of the first-ever "driver experience" racing schools in the country and doing timber deals. He'd met a pretty brunette named Bunny Vance who became his second wife, and he dreamed of once again building and owning a speedway.

On Wednesday, September 30, 1970, NASCAR staged what would be its final dirt track race: one hundred miles on the half-mile State Fairgrounds Speedway in Raleigh, North Carolina. The contest was won by Richard Petty, with Neil "Soapy" Castles a distant second, some two laps behind. Turner wasn't in the field. He hadn't run a Grand National race in two years, since engine trouble knocked him out of a dirt race at Orange Speedway in Hillsborough, North Carolina. But a deal was now in the works for him to run two weeks later in a grand comeback at the National 500 at his home track, Charlotte Motor Speedway. Turner, it seemed, had nine racing lives.

The Sunday after the final Raleigh dirt track race, the NASCAR elite took to the field at North Carolina's North Wilkesboro Speedway. At around the same time, Turner was flying a friend back home to Pennsylvania, and planned to return immediately to North Carolina with golf pro Clarence King, so they could take their wives out to dinner. Twelve minutes after takeoff from Pennsylvania's DuBois Airport, the Aero Commander went into a mysterious spin. For unknown reasons, it was a spin that Turner, a pilot of notable skills, could not put right.

The plane crashed into the side of a hill, sending Turner catapulting some forty feet into the distance, killing him. By then, King, who'd suffered a coronary during the descent, was also gone.

Word spread among the competitors and with it came shock and disbelief. Hearing the news on his car radio, Glen Wood pulled off the road, shaking terribly. "It was a John F. Kennedy-getting-shot type of a pang in my stomach," he said. *Sports Illustrated* called Turner "The Babe Ruth of Stock Car Racing."

A year later, R.J. Reynolds pumped Winston cigarettes money into the sport, creating the Winston Cup Series, and the modern era of stock car racing began. The facilities were fast and, for the most part, modern. Petty, Allison, David Pearson, Yarborough, Bobby Isaac, Benny Parsons, and Buddy Baker would be among the drivers carrying the flag of competition, as the past slowly grew hazier, like a cloud of dust.

* * *

Dirt track racing has never gone away. The sport's best were bred on it. Jeff Gordon, Tony Stewart, Kasey Kahne, Mark Martin, the list of top racers whose careers were built, whose rough edges were smoothed on red clay, is lengthy. Stewart owns Eldora Speedway, a half-mile clay oval in Rossburg, Ohio, which is certainly among the most well-maintained dirt track facilities in the United States.

These tracks are related to a place like Asheville-Weaverville only as a modern racer is to some scruffy great-uncle. Today's dirt tracks are lean and hard packed. There are eight hundred of them in the United States, many with weekly racing series, the cars still thrilling fans. The dust rises, but not with the same plumes.

"How can you call it a dirt race when the tracks are so smooth?" asks Tom Pistone. "In our day you had to run fourteen-, sixteen-inch springs. You had to run the car seven, eight, nine inches off the ground. Today these cars are only two inches off the ground 'cause the track is so smooth. Our dirt tracks had big holes in 'em. Today it's just like asphalt. Back in our day, the guy who had the strongest car on a suspension was the one who was gonna finish. But the people like it. They like it. See, they like to see those cars sideways."

In mid-August 2008, Stewart, Kahne, and Dave Blaney competed in the Ollie's 360 Challenge Finale at Williams Grove Speedway in Mechanicsburg, Pennsylvania. Stewart, a huge dirt-track fan and veteran, was nervous that evening, making what were rare runs for him in a 360 winged Sprint car. Between practice laps, he stood off to the side, listening for the sounds of competitors running, while crewmen gouged out the rolls of dirt that had collected under the carriage of his car. Stewart's racing motto—"Experience Is Everything"—was plastered on the side of the car. Soon, he'd be going back out again on the surface he loved.

"The dirt was a little slick when we went out," he said. "I'm just trying to see when it starts to get a lot of grip in it."

Later that evening, the first time he took to the track in competition, Stewart spun in the first corner and turned around twice. The crowd roared at the sight of a top star finding his way through a learning curve. But by the end of the evening, he'd thrill the fans by being among the top finishers.

"To me, the appeal and the importance of that part of racing is not diminished," says Mark Martin. "I started thirty-five years ago and to me it's not diminished any."

What would be most impressive—and yet seemingly impossible—

is a turning back of the clock, and the running of a dirt track event in what is now Sprint Cup racing.

"I've been praying for that for six years since I bought [renowned dirt track] Eldora Speedway," says Tony Stewart. "There are variables that would make it very difficult but in a perfect world, I'd love to see it happen."

"This sport won't allow you to go do it halfway, and halfway would be the right way," says Martin. "And so it would be ridiculous. The engineering and the car and the hardware, it would take all the fun out of it. The thought is actually awesome but the competitive nature of this would ruin it and that's what would be sad about it. Racing's changed."

The business of racing certainly has. The instinct hasn't. It's the unpredictability, and a feeling of going back to one's roots, that keeps NASCAR stars returning to dirt races when they can. And it's what still appeals to die-hard fans.

"It looked like the guys were totally out of control all the time, which actually they were," remembers Wheeler of dirt track racing in the 1950s and '60s. "You had to be out of control to go fast in 'em and people *loved* that. We've lost a lot of that today. It was that kind of an atmosphere that people just loved because it's the unexpected that endeared people to dirt. That's what made it so exciting. You just never knew what was gonna happen next."

Officials keep an eye on the two most popular and powerful convertibles in NASCAR: the rides of Curtis Turner and Joe Weatherly.

Chapter Three

The Sky Was the Limit

May 6, 1961

"Convertibles were, I think, one of the most entertaining things rac-ing's ever had. People loved it; you could see the driver in action, crossing his arms up, seesawing in the turns."

—HUMPY WHEELER, former general manager, Lowe's Motor
Speedway, talking about NASCAR's Convertible
Division Series from the 1950s

THERE WERE SEVEN THOUSAND FANS PACKED INTO NORTH CAROLINA'S Raleigh Speedway front-stretch grandstand on that blistering mid-May afternoon in 1956. The place had history. It was the second-ever superspeedway built in NASCAR, after Darlington's 1.375-mile egg-shaped oval. Raleigh, meanwhile, was the definitive paper clip oval, a one-mile paved track with long, swift straightaways feeding into unforgiving turns and curves.

Raleigh was a big hometown stop, three hours east of Charlotte, straddling the center of stock car country. NASCAR's premier division, the Grand Nationals, ran its Fourth of July races there. During the sum-mers, when Bill France would take his family to spend the months in the Carolinas, his young son Jim would slide and tumble down the red clay dirt banks behind Raleigh's grandstand with other kids of NASCAR officials. It was at this track, in 1953, that defending champion Tim Flock ran his last-ever race with a little rhesus monkey in a tiny custom-made uniform and helmet as his passenger. The monkey, Jocko Flocko, was part of a publicity stunt, and Flock had been winning with him. At Raleigh, Jocko managed to undo his harness; he lifted a hatch that allowed Flock to judge his tire wear, was promptly beaned by a rock, and began screeching and bounding around the cab. Flock had to make an unscheduled pit stop to drop him off; he lost the race, and a memorable promotional stunt was mercifully over.

And on May 12, 1956, the fans at Raleigh got to see something else new and extraordinary that more than lived up to its billing. It was the speedway's first time hosting of the newest division in NASCAR racing: the Convertible circuit. For the faithful in the stands that day, it was like being backstage at a magic show while the magicians were putting together their tricks. Without the hardtops on the cars, fans could look into the cockpits while the racers drove by. Even at high speeds, seeing the helmets, the sweaty, grimy, grimacing faces, the arms and hands working the steering wheels, or perhaps the footwork, if you were lucky, was unforgettable.

By early May, Joe Weatherly had established himself as one of the division's brightest stars and most successful names. Ford Motor Company had hired Weatherly and his best pal, the determined, magnetic Curtis Turner, to be the first-ever factory-sponsored drivers in the division, recipients of the finest equipment the manufacturer could dole out.

Weatherly, an ebullient racer from Norfolk, given to great belly laughs, dazzling practical jokes, and memorable twists of the English language (explaining a wreck he once got into, he said, "I zigged when I should have zagged"), was the frustrated second fiddle between the two. "Little Joe" was the short practical joker; Turner, the taller, more serious charmer. Turner's success on the circuit was historic and mesmerizing. The pair were inseparable friends off the track and "the Gold Dust Twins" on it, beating seemingly anyone in their path and banging against each other on the way to the checkered flag. As the season wore on, they'd frequently finish one-two, with Turner almost always out in front.

At Raleigh, however, Turner was uncharacteristically good instead of great. Weatherly was better, starting third and keeping among the leaders. With fewer than twenty laps to go on the one-miler, he had a legitimate shot of catching race leader Frank Mundy.

And then just like that, it was all gone. Weatherly heard it: that distinct, brutal knock under the hood as he blazed down the straightaway, the sure sign of a blown engine, which was hardly a surprise in the 89-degree heat. But it was worse than that; the knock was a prelude. The engine hadn't blown so much as it exploded, and in seconds, fresh, biting, angry flames burst from the front of his Ford and curled toward the cab, threatening to surround him.

Weatherly could have slowed, pulled over, opened the door, and done a barrel roll to safety, especially given his fear of fire. But he was just odd and playful enough, and he had a flashback: There was a stunt he used to pull a few years earlier, when he was a prince of the motorcycle racing circuit, a move that could have been in a circus act. He'd get up to speed and stand on the seat. Suddenly, at Raleigh, it felt right.

The crowd had gasped at the sight of the flames and now they stood, quietly concerned, watching the fire and black smoke climbing. And then Weatherly, by now midway through the turn heading for the front stretch and the Raleigh crowd, and slowing down considerably, raised himself and stood on the seat, with one hand on the open-cockpit windshield and the other poised high, like a mythical charioteer, a specter on a platform of flame.

The place went crazy and Weatherly ate it up. Ralph Liguori, a journeyman from the Bronx, New York, making his only Convertible series start, who was already many laps off the pace, slowed behind the coasting Weatherly and, in a move that *Illustrated Speedway News* would call "a fine display of sportsmanship," pushed the fiery car past the crowd, toward pit road, amid the wild cheers. Weatherly ended up fourteenth in a field of eighteen, but he was richer by reputation.

The same could be said of the Convertibles.

"Convertibles were, I think, one of the most entertaining things racing's ever had," said Humpy Wheeler, among the most prominent and successful racing promoter in NASCAR history. "It was a wonderful idea. People loved it; you could see the driver in action, see him crossing his arms up, seesawing in the turns and all that kind of thing."

For NASCAR in the mid-1950s, the Convertible Series was a saving grace: a new division for a sport happily moving past its infancy, using an auto body type that had recently regained its cool cachet. It was, for a time, NASCAR looking ready for its close-up.

* * *

Bill France could see the future. By 1955, he was busily looking for the funding to build, in his hometown Daytona, a track to rival the country's definitive venue—the glorious, speedy expanse in Indianapolis, where the open-wheel cars created their own heroes.

France planned a 2.5-mile track, with banking in the corners as high as they could go, literally—the earth-grading machine had its limits even if France's imagination did not—and, hopefully, speeds to shatter records worthy of the land-speed challenges that Daytona had once hosted on its hard-packed expanse of beach.

At around the same time, France was busy making one other big move: He merged NASCAR with an Indiana-based race-sanctioning body that, among other things, put on convertible races.

In his book on the NASCAR convertible division, *Rumblin' Ragtops*, Greg Fielden quoted France's statement on the move:

"This new affiliation means that in 1956, NASCAR will sanction more than 2,000 auto race meets on more than 275 tracks. More than $2 million in prize money will be involved . . . I believe this move will have considerable bearing on making Daytona Beach the real speed capital of the world."

These two developments—the track and the division—would be competing, compelling events, playing out against the backdrop of a South happy to host the only professional sport available to see live in the region. For the Ford Motor Companies of the world, having another division meant greater opportunities to market and sell new cars. Everybody was happy.

The action began in earnest on February 25, 1956, in the first-ever NASCAR Convertible Series race: thirty-nine laps—160 total miles—on the 4.1-mile Daytona Beach and Road Course.

Curtis Turner started fourteenth out of twenty-eight competitors. But for Turner, being in Daytona for the weeks leading up to the start of NASCAR season was life as one big party. And his playground was this track.

Turner was a handsome, strapping, blue-eyed, tousle-haired Virginian. He was, for his good friend Bill France, the equivalent of a blue chip investment—his name a recognizable, guaranteed fan draw on any local flyer.

Given his success as a timber broker, Turner didn't really need to run. Throughout his timber career, he'd end up selling the land equivalent of 6 percent of the state of North Carolina. But racing was his passion and preferred pursuit. Plus, he spent much faster than he could earn, and the extra money came in handy: With the winnings and some timber proceeds, he held spectacularly memorable parties. Most famously, he'd get to Daytona every year in January, weeks before the annual speed trials, and he and Weatherly would rent out their "party pad," an apartment not far off the strip, where drivers, officials, friends, hangers-on, and plenty of beautiful women partied through the night, most every night, in a state of blissful excess. Weatherly would serve alcohol out of a converted fire extinguisher. Women occasionally danced naked on tables. And the moment Turner sensed an ebb in the action, he'd shout his motto atop the fading din: "If you don't like this party, don't worry 'bout nothin', folks. Another one's startin' in about fifteen minutes."

Weatherly won the pole and held an early lead, but it didn't take long for him and Turner to establish the two-man show that would define season one of the Convertible Series. Not long into the race, Weatherly's windshield blew out. But rather than create a problem, recalled fellow Ford driver Glen Wood, it made Weatherly's passage easier. "The windshield blows out, well, look how much less wind resistance you got," he said. "It's just a straight shot. It picked him up quite a bit!"

Turner remained tucked behind in second. To an envious Turner, this wasn't good enough.

"So Curtis gets his foot up there, trying to kick his windshield out!" Wood said.

Glen's brother, longtime crew chief Leonard Wood, added with equal glee, "He tried to kick it out and got a cramp in his leg!"

Six laps into the race, Turner passed Weatherly and was out ahead, with the competition now drifting behind considerably, and he could practice, solo, the art for which he was renowned: the power slide. Coming off the two-mile stretch of asphalt, then through the shaggy, barely navigable grooves of the dirt off-road, Turner caught hold of the smooth surface of the sand and took off, beelining down the beach, past the ebb and flow of the adjoining tide.

Chris Economaki, calling the race for fans at the track, worked by timing as much as by visual evidence, and when he sensed the favorite was midway down the two-mile beach trek, he'd shout, "It's time for TURNER!" and the paying spectators, hearing the call in the cone-shaped speakers, craned their necks for the sight of the sliding convertible.

Turner curled the car sideways at top speed, and the fans watched it glide, as if on some joyous ice dance, the length of several football fields, before Turner regained the throttle, and the car made its swift, choppy, diagonal correction and headed straight toward the highway. There are those who would happily argue that Weatherly practiced his slide with just as much style. To see the two of them doing it together, neck and neck, was to see stock car racing in all its synchronized beauty.

"The biggest thrill I've seen a lot of people get was Turner and Weatherly in convertibles races down there," said Bud Moore, NASCAR Hall of Fame car owner for Weatherly, Bobby Allison, and Dale Earnhardt, among many others. "When they got into them corners coming down the beach and going into the north turn, now I'm telling you they'd go in there so hard, the dirt and the sand was flying. The fans were just eating that up. And they'd go down the backstretch and sometimes, when they went off the pavement into the south turn, going into the sand over there, by the time they got them straightened up and got them gathered back up they were just about out in the ocean."

On that February afternoon in 1956, Turner outclassed the field. He crossed the finish line in front, the cheers of the 13,500 fans ringing in his ears. He'd won the race by almost five miles.

More important, as *Illustrated Speedway News* put it, the race "gave the spectators a 'goldfish bowl' picture of the drivers manhandling the wheel through the turns in their open-top cars."

* * *

Turner won the first few races of the Convertible season, but all was not well in the Ford racing camp. The manufacturer had come into the season with $2 million to be spent on all top stock car racing divisions for 1956. But Ford team manager Pete DePaolo's racing plant in Long Beach, California, was hit by a plague's worth of problems before the season began. Heavy rains caused flooding in the city and the headquarters suffered water damage. Things dried out just in time for the plant to be hit by a major fire.

Charlotte trucking company businessman John Holman was hired to run the NASCAR Ford operation, and after a few weeks of retooling, the company cars emerged plenty fast. There was no better showcase of their success than the Convertible Division record of Turner and Weatherly. In the twenty-eight races that remained in the first Convertible season, Turner won eighteen, including winning streaks of five and four races. Weatherly won four of his own, and in Turner's eighteen victories, Weatherly finished second thirteen times.

The Turner-Weatherly show, along with other big names—local Southern stars such as Bob Welborn, Glen Wood, Marvin Panch, Frank Mundy, and Gwyn Staley—brought in crowds averaging five to eight thousand on the smaller tracks, fifteen thousand and up on the larger ones. And Turner and Weatherly understood the vast allure of swift door-to-door action.

"For those of us who knew what was going on, when those guys got in a racecar, typically the convertibles, you could see they were just playing with each other," recalls Wheeler. "In the grandstand you'd hear, 'Man, *look* at that!' But they were playing with each other. They both were such good drivers that they could do that. You can't play in a race-car unless you're a really good driver, or you're gonna wreck bad. But when Curtis and Joe were racing on dirt, it was quite a show. I remember one night in Columbia, South Carolina, they really put on a dogfight and everybody enjoyed. And then you threw in 'Tiger' Tom Pistone and Tiny Lund and you could really have some good racing. These guys knew they were there to race but they were also there to put on a show."

Turner and Weatherly seemed to play that up in the series' return to Raleigh in August 1956. With their powerful Ford engines, they may have outclassed much of the field—especially the struggling independent drivers—but they didn't outclass each other. Weatherly won the pole and was chased down for the lead by Turner after five laps. The pair treated the lead like a tug of war after that, thrilling the six thousand or so packing the grandstand. Both men took pit stops and returned to the fight, watching while first Glen Wood and then Gwyn Staley were undone. For the final ten laps of the race, it was back to a charged grudge match between the Gold Dust Twins, as each man pressed and passed the other, and when the checkered flag flew, Turner was ahead by two car lengths. It was later discovered that only 149 of the 150 laps had been run, which lead to a scoring error that may have cost Weatherly the win.

Imaginative strategies were sometimes necessary to keep Turner or Weatherly—and, by extension, the wealthy auto companies—out of victory circle. Pistone won the race at his hometown Soldier Field in Chicago, before the largest crowd to see the convertibles in season one: 38,000. Though Turner led the first 194 laps in the 200-lap race, Pistone, despite a lap-165 spin, managed to catch and pass his friend and rival, with perhaps the most impressive use of a home-track advantage ever, during a caution flag stop.

"The only way I could beat Curtis is when we made a pit stop, all my buddies from Chicago blocked him in," Pistone says. "He couldn't get out. So I beat him. When Curtis and Joe and all the guys came in there, it was all factory-backed cars, so that killed the independents."

It didn't, however, hurt the interest in the new division, which posted competitive numbers in attendance, and sometimes outdrew the more established Grand National races. Bob Welborn, meanwhile, seemed forever in Turner and Weatherly's rearview through the season. With the sport's points system rewarding consistency above wins, Welborn ended up running away with the championship. While he won only three races—compared to Turner's twenty-two—he posted ten more top-ten finishes, and ran three more total races. The action was, to say the least, spirited, and made for a top first year.

But the crowd at Martinsville Speedway in Virginia saw a sign of things to come on October 28 at the "Mixed 400," the first of what would be known as Sweepstakes races that included both Grand National hardtops and the convertibles in the same field. It became instantly—and abundantly—clear that in terms of competitive speed, the convertibles weren't in the Grand National cars' aerodynamic league. When the checkered flag flew in the four-hundred-lap contest, Georgia racer Jack Smith had bested the field in a Carl Kiekhaefer Dodge. The top five finishers were Grand National cars. Weatherly, the leader among the convertibles, landed in sixth, six laps behind. By then, Turner had been out for one hundred laps, the victim of engine trouble, and Welborn, still running at the end, was in fifteenth place, some twenty-two laps off the pace.

There would be other Sweepstakes races and convertibles would even win some. But on the faster tracks, comparisons became quickly moot. The convertibles, on their own turf, could be dynamic. But against the Grand National cars, they couldn't measure up.

* * *

Even as Turner, Weatherly, and Welborn were keeping up their well-funded, exciting battles through the fall of 1956, there were bitter backstage issues that would threaten the way business was done at NASCAR.

Auto racing had been experiencing a run of tragedy in both open-wheel ranks and stocks, in the United States and abroad, with wrecks injuring and even killing drivers and, at times, fans in the seats.

Accidents, incidents, and scares, whether a result of speed, track conditions, risky moves, coincidence, or all these factors, kept occurring. The Convertible circuit experienced its share. At the season-opening race in Jacksonville, North Carolina, driver Mel Larson's gas tank knocked out in a crash, slid across the dirt track, hit a wooden guardrail, and exploded, setting the guardrail on fire. In another race, a loose wheel flew off one car, bounced, and hit a mechanic. These were near misses, which only stressed the need to curb the problem before it became chronic. In other NASCAR series, the incidents were worse.

Matters were pushed near the breaking point when the convertibles visited Darlington for the inaugural Rebel 300 in May. The day got off to a promising start as twenty-seven drivers took the green at one of the toughest tracks on the circuit, with Turner, Weatherly, Marvin Panch, Fireball Roberts, and short-track specialist Bobby Myers all jockeying for the lead in the early going. But twenty-nine laps into the race, Jim Paschal, behind the wheel of a 1956 Mercury, blew a tire in turn four and slid up into the track's favored groove. Buck Baker, with nowhere to go, smacked into Paschal. When both cars came to a rest, Baker's Chevy, sitting on the front stretch, might as well have had a giant target painted on it.

His eyes wide, Baker hastily unstrapped, bounded out of his car, and ran toward the infield; behind him, he heard a stomach-turning sound, and whipped around to the sight of Jimmy Massey's Plymouth boring into his car. Massey had nearly cut Baker's auto in two. Turner, Panch, and three others also skidded into the wreck. There were no injuries, but Baker was shaken, well aware of his fate had he not managed to free himself.

"It took them about an hour to get the show back on the road," remembers Wheeler. "I don't think there were but thirteen cars or so there when it was all over. It was quite a crash."

After another few incidents—one at a Grand National race involving an eight-year-old boy, among others, badly hurt when Billy Myers crashed through a guardrail and into an area where spectators had gathered—the Automobile Manufacturers Association met to discuss whether or not to withdraw all support from racing, to disassociate the organization from a sport that had become too dangerous. In the days leading up to the vote, at a convertible race at Asheville-Weaverville Speedway, Turner's Ford blew a tire, smacked through a picket fence, hopped an embankment, and landed in front of the grandstands, mere feet from the crowd. The AMA had pretty much had enough.

On June 6, the decision was made to discontinue all factory support. In NASCAR, Ford manager John Holman opted to get out of racing. A week later, looking over the free cars and parts left behind for him by the crew of DePaolo Engineering, Holman changed his mind and went into the auto ownership business, fielding cars for, among others, Turner and Weatherly in the convertibles. Holman now worked alongside a new partner, racer Ralph Moody, who'd bought into the business. Despite their incompatibility, the pair nevertheless offered a winning blend of savvy and smarts, and would go on to become one of the most successful ownership teams in the sport's history.

France helped matters somewhat by increasing race purses, and making sure the number of participants didn't drop to a ridiculous level. At times, France would rent cars at the local U-Drive-It, lend them to racers for competition, and return them later. On the track, the competition was no less fierce in the Convertible Circuit in 1957. There was a feeling of déjà vu: The ever-consistent Welborn won the title and Turner won eleven of the circuit's thirty-six races.

But the sport would be limping into 1958, and licking its considerable wounds. As bad as things had been at the Darlington convertible race, the Southern 500—the Labor Day Grand National event at "the Lady in Black," as the track had been nicknamed—was that much worse. Ever-popular racer Fonty Flock spun out down the backstretch and stopped at the crest of turn three. He looked up through his windshield to see the wide, terror-filled eyes of Billy Myers's brother Bobby, who came barreling toward Flock's prone car with nowhere to go. Myers's Oldsmobile smacked into Flock's Pontiac and, after additional contact from the equally helpless Paul Goldsmith, Myers went flipping errantly.

Injuries from the crash would effectively end Flock's career. But by the time track officials got Myers to the local hospital, he was already dead.

* * *

In 1958, the auto manufacturers, while needing to carry on the public impression of being removed from unsafe stock car racing, were continuing a practice of silent under-the-table support of teams and drivers. New cars might suddenly show up at a driver's garage, or parts would mysteriously appear. Early in the 1958 season, Glen Wood was running well, but barely managing to keep his cars competitive.

"Peter DePaolo called me and congratulated me on how we'd been finishing," Wood recalled of the Ford racing czar. "I said 'Well, I about used up the parts y'all give me, I guess I have to give it up.' And he said 'Well, what do you need for the next race?' And I said, 'The car is ready to go. All I need now is some tires.'"

DePaolo called Red Vogt, the famed car builder who'd been in charge of the Ford teams before John Holman, and said, "Red, roll Glen out six tires."

"So they did and we went to Richmond and won that race," Wood said. "From then on 'til now we've been with Ford Motor Company."

The battle that had gone on for years between the manufacturers to see which team could be more successful in racing had now turned into a form of covert warfare. Meanwhile, the automakers had lost out as well, giving up a rich marketing vein.

And with Turner's decision to concentrate in 1958 on the Grand National Division, the Convertible Circuit lost a lot of luster. Only nineteen convertible races were run, and Turner ran a scant five of them.

When the racers and crowds had gathered at the 1958 season opener on the beach in Daytona, it was a forgone conclusion that it would be the last-ever set of races at the stately course. Time and tide would literally sweep it away, with France having finally secured the necessary capital to complete the Daytona International Speedway. He'd had the foresight to offer wealthy Texas businessman Clint Murchison the use of his private plane when Murchison was in a bind. The grateful businessman then lent an especially open ear to France's plans and offered much-needed aid.

There were some fine racing moments in 1958, along with the professional debut, on July 12, of Richard Petty, the twenty-one-year-old son of Lee Petty, in Columbia, South Carolina. But fans of the convertible circuit, a division filled with vast promise and excitement only two years before, needed a reminder that racing could be joyous and raucous, a haven for hot, darting passes and "Did you *see* that?" moments.

They got it at Darlington on May 10, courtesy of the circuit's returning favorites.

Turner and Weatherly came to town for the second Rebel 300, in their shiny Holman-Moody Ford convertibles. Both cars had been anything but stellar in the days leading up to the race, and the teams worked long and hard to get the rides to work better.

As soon as the green flag flew, the crowd of 22,000 could see that all was right with the Holman-Moody autos. Turner started twelfth and Weatherly tenth, but after Cotton Owens sped quickly to the front, eyes were trained on Weatherly and Turner as they began making their way past other top cars.

Turner was mighty eager. He'd had a disappointing year. His plan to run the Grand National season had been foiled by, among other things, a dislocated disc that plagued him. This was only his third convertible race of the season; he'd won the other two.

But early in the Darlington race, Owens was growing bigger through Turner's windshield, and Weatherly was right there in his rearview. It seemed like old times.

After nine laps, however, the crowd got a sense that this one would be different.

Turner caught Owens heading into a curve, and gave him a sizable tap on the rear bumper. In one swift, fluid movement, Owns swerved, and Turner slid right along with him, with Weatherly yanking down hard on the wheel and skirting below the two, into the lead.

Owens and Turner were both still intact and unhurt, the damage minimal, and they were quickly back in the hunt. Turner's eyes were calm, dark, and fixed, looking ahead, lap after lap. For the next seventy-nine laps, Weatherly held his line and his lead.

After a run of pit stops, Weatherly was back out in front, with Turner now following him like an echo. He caught up quickly and nudged his friend on a straightaway and with Weatherly's wiggle, Turner took the lead for the first time all day. Weatherly clung to him for the next three laps as if on a string, and delivered loud metal slaps before passing his pal again.

It was Turner's turn: seven more laps of riding, getting closer, tapping Weatherly, both cars shimmying, before Turner nudged once more, dove down on the Darlington grid, and took the lead. In the stands, the people stamped and shouted; they could hardly stand it. The race was only halfway done.

Turner's lead lasted all of one lap. Weatherly charged ahead once more, out in front by a nose at the line, but Turner was right there, the side doors of each car grinding together until Turner was back in front. In the stands, the fans could see the straight arms of both determined drivers, the sweat glistening, the helmeted heads of each shifting and darting. It was magical.

Except for John Holman, who stood in the pits, growing angrier with each lap. These weren't Ford's cars anymore; they were *his* cars. And those cars cost money. And there wasn't any money to go around. And those two hooligans were killing his cars. With each bump making startling *pop* noises that were heard through the Raceway, Holman could only picture the ledger book and the tailspin of a convertible season with months left to go.

They kept shuffling the lead. Weatherly passed and whooped loudly; in the stands, the faithful could see him slapping his fist on the steering wheel. Then he held on helplessly as Turner, with seemingly the better car, passed, delivering one more punching nudge for good measure with a little shift of his hands on the wheel. It was a glorious game of bumper cars. For years, the friends would take out local rental cars and proceed to beat and bang them against each other down deserted roads for fun. Often they would vault one or both of them into the shallow ends of motel swimming pools. Throughout the South, rental companies had posted photos of the racers; they now refused to loan them cars.

Weatherly came in for a pit stop, his face a mask of grim determination. As much fun as he might be having, he had something to prove. Holman rushed over to his window, the deep red hue of rage coloring his face.

"What the hell are you two *doing* out there?" he shouted, as the tires were changed and the gas poured in.

"We're trying to *win*!" Weatherly shouted back, and peeled out.

With Turner's pit stop soon completed, the dogfight continued. Weatherly once again had the lead, this time by half a lap, and he held it for twenty-five laps. But there was no escaping Turner, who crawled back insistently, the visage of him hunched over the wheel looming larger.

With each lap, Weatherly passed the pits and saw that Holman had written something else on the chalkboard for his drivers to see. There were pleas to be careful, to go easy on the equipment, and to finish the goddamn race in one piece. But Turner was coming closer, and Weatherly planned to block.

With twenty-six laps to go, the Curtis and Little Joe show was about to begin full bore once again, and the crowd, on its feet, readied for the madness.

Holman, however, was madder still. He held up a chalkboard advising Weatherly to let Turner go past. The advice wasn't subtle. Weatherly squinted at the message, the curses scribbled with such force and ire that each "fuck" looked carved into the slate like a commandment.

Weatherly got the message—his car was no match for his friend's anyway and he knew it—and Turner sailed past. For the next twenty-six laps, Turner's Ford, by now incredibly dialed in, inched farther ahead. When he took the checkered flag, he was victorious by a whopping twenty-six seconds.

Emerging from his convertible, Turner saw Weatherly pull up with a squeal of the tires, noticing his friend's dark stare, and he put on an apologetic smile. But Weatherly suddenly laughed uproariously.

By the time Holman got to them, the friends were shaking hands and recounting every bump and run, as the shouts of the fans reigned upon them. In the weeks, months, and years to come, people would frequently refer to this as the greatest NASCAR race ever run. For the friends, it was another in a string of fine, memorable afternoons. This kind of thing between them wouldn't last forever—it wouldn't last much longer at all, in fact—but on that May afternoon at Darlington—for the drivers, for the fans, for the Convertible Series itself—it had lasted long enough.

*   *   *

The project that had first been hatched some six years earlier at the offices at 42 South Peninsula Drive in Daytona Beach, and had seen its groundbreaking in November 1957, was ready by the start of 1959: a glorious, majestic 2.5-mile speedway. The banking in the turns was a vertigo-inducing 33 degrees, steep enough so that when Curtis Turner climbed up to join his friend Bill France at the top of the Daytona International Speedway guardrail during a visit, he could feel it in his back, which was still sore from both his bad disc and two crashes over the summer, one of which had left him with seven broken ribs. Standing at so high a point, Turner could hardly wait to see what it would feel like to drive past that spot.

Among his fellow competitors, however, enthusiasm was mixed generously with fear. Lee Petty took his laps at the speedway and declared, "There wasn't a man there who wasn't scared to death of the place. We never had raced on a track like that before."

The trepidation came with good reason. At the 1958 Southern 500, Fireball Roberts had posted the fastest qualifying speed at 118.6 miles per hour. Drivers taking the track at Daytona were routinely posting speeds twenty-file miles faster than that. Along with that came the as-yet-unnamed phenomenon of drafting that was turning the racers into amateur engineers: Hardtop drivers found that you could be faster than your competitor, but you couldn't fully escape him. The principle of drafting was much like the idea of closely following a speedboat on a river. At Daytona, the car in front worked harder, breaking through the wind; the next car was carried along in its wake, keeping at a high speed with less effort.

As *National Speed Sport News* columnist Mace Benner wrote, "Bill France's high banked asphalt speedway promises to break every tradition and speed record in the world of auto racing. It's really worth chucking it all and going."

France had found success with the Showcase races that included both the hardtops and the convertibles. For the debuts at Daytona, he decided to hold hundred-mile races for each division on Thursday, and then combine both types of cars for the big "500" on Sunday. France was, in essence, making the first-ever Daytona 500 a big showcase race with both types of cars.

But something was amiss in terms of the speed difference. In the Grand National race, the fastest qualifier, Cotton Owens, went nearly 143.2 miles per hour. The pole winner in the convertible race, Glen Wood, hit 128.8 miles per hour.

The discrepancy was not lost on the press. Reporting on the two Thursday races, *National Speed Sport News* tagged Wood's "fast qualifying time." Of the "Searing . . . Sedan Race," the paper led with the words, "the larger and faster Grand National field quickly showed that the 140-plus qualifying speeds registered were not freaks as the 38-car field got off to a tremendous start."

Twenty convertible drivers made up a third of the fifty-nine-car starting field. But once Johnny Bruner stood on the track's apron and waved the green flag, the hardtop drivers sprinted ahead.

"They put the Grand National cars on the inside and convertibles on the outside," recalled Hal Hamrick, who was broadcasting the race that day. "By the time they got into five laps or ten, the Grand National cars, with the tops on them which made them a little more aerodynamically correct, were on the back straightaway, and the convertibles were on the front straightaway. They were that far behind. It was ridiculous!"

As the action continued, and the 17,000 fans gloried in the speed and the tight clusters of cars up front, the convertibles lagged, as if in some other race entirely. It was like watching NASCAR's past competing with its future.

"The aerodynamics of those open convertible cars on those high banks . . . forget it," recalled Hamrick. "It was like putting an extra brake on the car, or whatever they do to slow down planes. It was a built-in restrictor plate because the car just wouldn't get the job done."

If the convertibles were themselves clustered, it was in the middle of the pack, several laps behind. No open-top car led the race at any point, and they experienced a greater degree of attrition, as only seven convertible cars were still running when the checkered flag flew.

The big story at race's end was the photo finish between Lee Petty and Johnny Beauchamp. Without proper finish-line cameras, it took several days for France to declare Petty the victor, after calling in shots and videos taken of the close action.

The performance of the convertibles became a footnote to all the action. In the last paragraph of its race recap, *National Speed Sport News*, which reveled in the startling speed spectacle, mentioned, "As qualifying runs and the times and speeds in Friday's twin 100 milers indicated, the convertibles had a pretty hard time keeping up with the hardtops. Top finisher among the ragtop throttlers in the '500' was Marvin Panch of Charlotte, N.C., who wound up sixteenth in his '58 Ford."

The Convertible division, already something of a limping stepchild to the Grand Nationals, had taken a tremendous hit. The trend would now turn toward longer races on faster tracks. The writing was on the wall, and the money would be in even shorter supply.

"You've got to go back and figure out the stand from the manufacturer's view," recalled Ford racing's Jacques Passino. "At the time I started we were racing short track and had a short-track race on the East Coast and a short-track race on the West Coast, and we used to fly the drivers cross-country, and we had two guys that drove short track for us. We had the Convertible races, and you had the Grand National races, so you were preparing, in effect, six cars at minimum to race every weekend. And then it got to the point in the Grand Nationals, we were racing four cars, so now they had eight cars we had to prepare and it just got over-whelming. It got overwhelming from the standpoint of NASCAR, too. They couldn't get their arms around it."

* * *

The Convertible Series, a fascinating experiment, with a zealous following early on, and a lightning-fast ending, remained a happy curio for Bob Colvin, promoter of Darlington Raceway. Colvin, a good friend of Turner and Weatherly's, loved that the convertibles seemed to thrill like nothing else, and even after the division disappeared, he staged the Rebel 300 for two more years. Offering up the unique once-a-year convertible action made for an enjoyable, profitable day of racing at Darlington.

The second-to-last convertible-only Rebel 300 was run on May 6, 1961. A prerace party went on for several days at a local Darlington area hotel, with many of the drivers staying in or dropping in. Surveying the scene, one might have been excused for thinking stock car racing had turned into *Lord of the Flies*.

The "staying in" and "dropping in" primarily concerned the motel's pool in back. Drivers, guests, innocent bystanders, nobody was exempt from being tossed or pushed in. When Turner got out of the water at one point to refresh his drink, he looked down with a frown: His soaked leather shoes were making loud galosh-y noises with each step. Not that he was alone. "The pool turned whatever color it did from the dye in our shoes and socks," recalled Tom Pistone of the raucous affair.

Had the police come to the scene with any intent to break up the proceedings, chances are they'd first have to get the local tow company involved. A squad car was resting at the bottom of the deep end.

Not participating much in the action was Fred Lorenzen, the hand-some, young, sandy-haired second-year racer out of Chicago. Turner noticed the absence and was not pleased. Knocking on his door, however, seemed too refined for such a gathering. So he and Weatherly hopped into a car, and Turner, driving with pinpoint skill, smacked the front fender into the door jam of Lorenzen's ground-floor room, knocking the door practically off its hinges.

Lorenzen had cut his teeth in the Midwest USAC racing circuit, winning a championship, but keeping himself tuned into NASCAR. When he joined, he found success quickly, a tenacious standout now behind the wheel of a Holman-Moody Ford—one of Turner's old rides. He was young, pinup handsome, and, at the shop, a determined task-master who pushed his crew doggedly. And he emerged from his victories with the dirt and grime adding character and charm to a face dominated by gleaming teeth and a Hollywood-worthy dimple in his chin.

"He was the golden boy," says Wheeler. "He didn't look like your normal Carolina/Georgia stock car driver. Had all his teeth, looked good, and all that kinda stuff."

Like Ralph Moody, Lorenzen was also a Yankee, and the car owner took particular pleasure in helping his young charge beat the series regulars—especially Turner, a racer for whom Moody had tremendous respect. Few knew Turner's style better than Moody, and helping Fast Freddie win, and beating the best, would be especially sweet.

Turner was still a popular draw, but in 1961 he was no longer racing's young flamethrower the way he'd once been. Now thirty-seven, he watched while Richard Petty, David Pearson, and Lorenzen appeared poised to carry the sport. And Turner had other ambitions. He and Bruton Smith had already partnered up on building the grand but troubled Charlotte Motor Speedway, a facility to rival Bill France's Daytona monolith. Turner dealt constantly with creditors and board members, which left less time for the joys of racing. But the Rebel 300 carried a fat winner's share of $8,420. Given his and his track's debts, that would come in handy, and few could challenge Turner at Darlington. He'd be behind the wheel of a 1961 Ford specially prepared for the occasion by the Wood Brothers.

"Turner was a great racer," Lorenzen said years later. "He was the biggest man down there."

In the early going of the race, the two were among the stalwarts trading the lead, along with Roberts, Weatherly, and local short-track standout Ralph Earnhardt. It became clear early that this race had the earmarks of a classic, fitting for what would be the end of an era.

When tire trouble forced Roberts from the lead, Turner inherited it, and Lorenzen shadowed him, keeping to Moody's advice. "I was just the pilot; he was the radar gun," Lorenzen said of Moody. "Before the race, he just said, 'Look out for Turner during the race, 'cause he'll do anything to win. He'll run your rear end right out of the joint, so stay away from him. Stay ahead of him or behind him, but don't stay with him.'"

Lorenzen's Holman-Moody Ford seemed the better auto of the two, a fact that gained more credence as the day wore on. He wove past Turner for the lead and held it as the laps wound down, from forty, then close to thirty, with Turner sticking nearby. But then Lorenzen's plans had the worst kind of hitch at the worst time: With thirty laps to go, his car blew a tire, sending him spinning, and propelling Turner back into the lead.

Lorenzen went into the pits for a tire change. There were twenty-nine laps to go and he would be way off the pace.

"Just watch Turner," Moody told him, nodding, as Lorenzen took off again.

He went out and was back up to speed fast. As he passed the pits the first time, the tall, slender Moody stood like a pillar, holding up a chalkboard: "18 minus" it read. That's how many seconds behind Lorenzen was.

It was a lot, but Freddie was keeping his eyes fixed to Turner, reeling his man in, gaining seconds with each lap. The board's message changed at each circuit past the pits: "16 minus," "Catch him: two seconds a lap." The Holman-Moody team had the chassis adjusted just right and the car was working expertly.

It was soon down to seven seconds and seven laps to go. Moody wrote "T-H-I-N-K" on the board, pointing to his head as Lorenzen drove past. With each straightaway, he worked up high on the track, looking to eventually speed past Turner on the outside. With four to go, Lorenzen was back up with the master, who met his high pass attempt with a slam that practically spun him into the guardrail.

On the next lap, Moody stared incredulously and wrote, "W.H.T." for "What the hell are you thinking?"

Lorenzen needed to be patient, to beat Turner at his own game and calm his frustration. "My car was faster, and I was younger; I mean, young blood," he recalled. "The brain works the throttle and when the race gets close, the younger blood, the reflexes are better."

Lorenzen tried up high once again, keeping to his pattern. And again, Turner moved to block. With two laps to go, Turner felt assured of the win. The white flag would be flying soon and Lorenzen was working the high side once again.

Lorenzen could see Turner's hands working in his convertible, keeping his line steady. He locked his gaze there, waiting, as he kept his car hugging the high line.

The instant Turner's hands jerked slightly to the right for another block, Lorenzen veered left, sending his Ford swiftly to the bottom of the track. Turner looked back from right to left and shifted down fast, but Lorenzen was suddenly underneath and nearly past him, snatching the lead and barreling ahead of the off-guard and enraged Turner. It was the exact strategy the prescient Moody had insisted upon, and it had worked.

Heading back into turn one, Lorenzen felt the slap and the nudge from Turner's car, but he kept the lead going down the backstretch. In the stands, the 32,000 fans shouted loudly at this convertible contest of the ages, the popular veteran versus the fair-haired young charge. Coming out of the turn, Lorenzen built more momentum, leaning his entire body away from the curve. The white flag flew and Turner's red face grew that much smaller in the rearview.

One lap later, when the checkered flag came out, a victorious Lorenzen whooped through his deep exhale. "It was the greatest win of my career," he later said. "The race of my life."

But Turner was not ready for it all to end, and as Lorenzen cooled down, slowing as he passed the jubilant Holman-Moody pit stall, Turner hit him hard enough, it seemed, to drive his Ford right through Lorenzen's car. Freddie buckled, whipping his head back, but the momentum set him rolling again. He could feel no pain.

"The crowd came over the wall," Lorenzen remembered. "They went wild. I was the new hero. They wanted a change in the South, you know? I was the young kid nobody knew. They liked that. You like to watch somebody get knocked down off their own throne."

If anything symbolized the end of the Convertible Division, this was it: a changing of the guard, a bright young racer outdoing the circuit's best, the kid watching and learning from the handiwork of his onetime idol as they drove. Lorenzen's was a temperament for a new era of trailblazing, a transitioning time when money was usually in shorter supply than speed. The Rebel 300 was a fitting coda for the division.

Left behind were images of hands crossing over the wheel, of charioteers piloting fast autos in a suddenly more halcyon moment in motor sports.

"You could see the driver, and when he drove, I'm telling you," Passino said, stopping short and shaking his head with wonder. "They were beautiful, beautiful cars."

After an early wreck, Cale Yarborough would make back lap after lap during the 1979 Daytona 500. His last-turn tussle with Donnie Allison changed NASCAR history.

Chapter Four
The Evolution Will Be Televised

February 18, 1979

"We've seen a lot of tumultuous finishes here at Daytona, but I've got a feeling we're in for one today like we've never seen before."

—CBS TV announcer KEN SQUIER,
with forty-one laps remaining in the 1979 Daytona 500

NOBODY AT HOME SAW THE FIRST PUNCH.

The racers had been talking, arguing, all three spent and angry, as a small crowd gathered nearby in the muddy infield, everyone standing stock-still, expecting the worst.

It was your fault; no, goddamn it, it was your fault. If it weren't for you—hell, you started this whole damn *thing. You'd better watch your* damn *mouth.*

Too much talk; talk talk talk. Cale Yarborough had had enough. Donnie Allison stood by, his thick, puffy face looking sour, lips hanging, stunned. Bobby Allison sat in his Bud Moore Ford, resting an elbow on the door, looking all relaxed but spouting his big mouth. That fat god-damn mouth of his.

Yarborough, whom many considered to be the toughest driver in the history of the sport, lunged and swung, his helmet in his hand, and the helmet smacked Bobby Allison in the face. Bobby reeled back and blinked and then looked up; it was that stupid helmet of Yarborough's, with the big swirling "Cale" written in script, like something out of Hollywood.

Then Bobby looked down as the little drops of blood collected in his lap.

"And I said to myself, I've got to get out of this car and address this right now or run from him the rest of my life," he said afterward. "And I'd even say this with him sitting here: Cale didn't want to go and confront Donnie, but he felt that I looked pretty small and pretty light and not strong enough to withstand any kind of a person-to-person fight with him, and I felt like he was taking out his frustration on me. Well, wrong. You know, this blood says I got to get out of this car and address it."

Bobby likes to say he climbed out of the car, "and with that, Cale Yarborough went to beating on my knuckles with his nose."

He did climb out of the car and went clawing after Yarborough, who instinctively raised his foot, which Allison caught with his right hand, his left hand now extended. Donnie tried to stop him—Hell, this was supposed to be his fight, not Bobby's—but his older brother turned back to his prey. He grabbed Yarborough by the collar, and Yarborough's eyes registered something like shock followed by towering rage. Off-balance, he hopped, on his way to being forced to the ground as the guys in the growing crowd tried to grab on and separate them.

Donnie Allison moved around like a ref, getting closer, not knowing what to do. He forced his hands in, grabbing at the fire suits. Even in his own anger and disappointment, he had more presence of mind than either of these guys.

"Bobby!" he shouted at his brother. "Bobby, we're on television!"

The scuffle continued, as people tried to pry the men apart.

"*Bobby*, we're on *television*," Donnie yelled again.

And that's about when the people at home started watching, when the cameras had found this fight and picked it all up. The viewers saw the hop, the momentum of the movements, the forcing of Yarborough to the ground. They saw frustration and anger increased to some distant boiling point.

"They're disappointed; they know they have lost," said CBS TV motorsports anchor Ken Squier, sounding exhausted and conciliatory from the booth, reporting on the melee.

What could you say to something like this? The first-ever live flag-to-flag coverage of a race in NASCAR history, and it's the Daytona 500, the most important race of the year . . . and it ends with a fight?

Across America, people were glued to their screens. And it wasn't some modest crowd either: An unbelievable storm had dropped as much as thirty inches of snow on spots stretching from the Midwest to the eastern seaboard. Millions with nothing to do were at home, taken in by the curiosity of this spectacle, and now mesmerized, full of questions. *Do all races end like this in NASCAR?* many wondered—the one thing nobody in the sport wanted them to wonder. Damn it all to hell.

The camera flitted back and forth, from the infield to victory lane to some long shot of the track taken from the blimp overhead. And after a moment, one could almost see the collective squint of everyone watching at home, followed by that one vexing question people understandably had to be asking themselves: *Wait—who won again?*

With one punch, a sport that had fought to suppress its savage past, and gain corporate respectability, had unveiled it at the biggest moment possible. It was damned embarrassing, *damned* embarrassing. And it was a beginning.

* * *

Almost four hours earlier, the Allison brothers, Yarborough, and the rest of a prize stock car racing field coursed around Daytona's majestic track—at a top speed of about sixty miles per hour.

It had rained the entire night before and most of Sunday morning in Daytona Beach. When it finally stopped, the track driers were sent out in full force. By the noon start time, the track was close to dry, and the forty-one cars took lap after lap at caution speed. It couldn't be helped: CBS had a schedule to keep, and at 3:45 p.m., come hell or high water, the nation would get NBA Basketball, featuring the Washington Bullets and the Seattle Supersonics. As they weaved around the 2.5-mile high-banked oval, the racers could see the infield was a sloppy, muddy mess. "It's terribly, terribly wet," said racing commentator David Hobbs, standing next to Squier in the booth. "And that inside safety apron is so wet that if a car slides off, it's gonna take off like on a skating rink."

The weather was as disappointing as it was surprising. The long-time humorous axiom in the sport was that Bill France could control the weather, especially during the February running of the Daytona 500.

But what nobody at the track fully realized was that as bad as things were in Daytona, it was a blip compared to the storm that had hit the rest of the country. Anyone wondering later on, *How bad was this storm?* could post this obscure answer: For the only time in recorded weather history, snow fell on the Sahara Desert, in equatorial Southern Algeria. It lasted thirty minutes, like a mirage, and was quickly gone.

CBS had made a May 1978 agreement with NASCAR to broadcast this first of five live flag-to-flag runnings at Daytona, and they were going to do things right. Cameras had been set up all over the track, in the sneakiest of places, which would provide wild race shots. The Goodyear blimp soared slowly overhead. The network installed an in-car camera—a first for the sport—in the Oldsmobile of 1975 winner Benny Parsons. In the booth, Squier—who'd begun announcing at age fourteen, owned Vermont's Thunder Road International Speedbowl, and loved few things more than the drama of auto racing—sized up the field. Hobbs, a world-renowned racecar driver who had led two laps of the 1976 Daytona 500, was ready with additional commentary.

Cameramen stood at their vantage points, waiting, training on the cars that veered back and forth as the drivers warmed their tires, the anticipation building until finally the signal came. Popular character actor Ben Gazzara waved the green flag wildly, and the field took off with a mad groan.

The contestants had waited too long for this. The field fled in some wild lockstep. The recently resurfaced track proved extraordinarily speedy. One year before, Yarborough gained the pole at 187.5 miles per hour. For the 1979 500, Buddy Baker qualified first at better than 196 miles per hour.

But Donnie Allison jumped out to the early lead, his car moving effortlessly up front. After two green-flag laps, he passed the start-finish line, thrust a hand out the window, and pointed a long, darting finger, seeming to say, *Watch this*.

The field clung together, and Squier made the play-by-play as if this were the Kentucky Derby instead of a long day in Daytona, calling out many of the top drivers and action in a short, feverish sprint. Parsons made a climb toward the front, his in-car camera catching the view. "There's Parsons, and you can see the windshield already spattered as he flies down the back straightaway," Squier said, his voice full of mad urgency. "Into turn three at over 195 miles per hour, you're riding with Benny Parsons." No move forward among the leaders, no bit of jockeying was ever lost on him.

"He made you feel like you were in a movie theater, and you were watching *Ben-Hur*," said current Fox NASCAR commentator Jeff Hammond, who was then a mechanic and tire changer for Yarborough's Junior Johnson–owned crew.

"*Look* at that Oklahoma land rush back there," Squier said. "Inches apart at over 190 miles per hour, back they come through the straightaway, here they come, screaming down two at a time, back into the banking they go."

It was the Allison brothers, Yarborough, Parsons, Indy racing regular A. J. Foyt, Darrell Waltrip, and an up-and-coming rookie driver named Dale Earnhardt all looking for an early shot at some Daytona glory.

* * *

The slide seemed to go on forever.

The field had been green for all of thirteen laps, with five lead changes, and Donnie Allison back out in front, when his brother decided to have another go at him.

With Donnie on the high side heading into turn one, Bobby went low, making the pass. But the draft of cars was strong, and Donnie, now with Yarborough in tow, quickly regained the lead.

Bobby drew off the throttle, trying to wedge back into second, yet Yarborough was right there, pulled along with Donnie and asserting his place. Bobby would need to squeeze back in just right.

As the cars headed out of turn two, gaining speed, Yarborough touched Bobby like a whisper on the back bumper just as Bobby tapped his brother's left-rear fender. And at about 190 miles per hour, that's all it took.

Donnie Allison spun to his right and Bobby clonked his brother hard, lifting Donnie's back tires off the ground. Donnie spun halfway around and now they were, for an instant, side-by-side, driver's side to driver's side, their faces perhaps an angry foot apart till Donnie spun around again. And by now, the momentum carried Bobby, Donnie, and Yarborough, all facing forward, on the apron and into the muddy infield, sliding at close to two hundred miles per hour.

Yarborough kept incredible control, gliding straight along the grass for the better part of a mile, through puddle after puddle, the still waters shooting up like giant waves. Bobby slid sideways like Curtis Turner taking on Daytona's old Beach and Road Course, but here there was nowhere to go except hard into the dirt bank separating the racers from Lake Lloyd, which sat in the middle of the Daytona Speedway infield. And Donnie took his own path between them and slid to a stop, feeling his tires spin, gripping nothing. A man who was dressed more like a fan than a NASCAR track official came over and started pushing on Donnie's trunk to help. The Oldsmobile jerked forward but when the man stopped pushing, the car ground back in. "C'mon!" yelled Donnie, motioning wildly with his right hand, and the man shrugged and began pushing again. Frustrated as hell, Donnie was seeing his best chance to win the race that mattered most to him slipping away.

"Donnie feels that I was very much to blame for the spinout, you know, very much the one that made whatever error it was that caused it," Bobby Allison said later. "I don't remember that part of it being like that. I felt I was kind of the victim. At any rate, Donnie got his car going, and Cale and I each lost [several] laps."

The caution flag came out, and Yarborough sat in the infield, stuck no doubt like any number of regular guys on some freeway in the Northeast at that very moment. The leading cars came into the pits, followed by each of the Allisons. It took a wrecker's help to unearth Yarborough from the muck, and by the time he got to his pit stall, he and car owner Junior Johnson were plenty angry.

"There was mud all over it," recalled Johnson. "And we had to get that mud off and put new tires on it and stuff to get it back on the race track. And we lost four laps."

Yarborough kept returning to the pits during the caution, having more mud gouged out of the underside of the car.

Amazingly, dirt aside, his Oldsmobile remained stout and fast. And while both the Allison cars were knocked around, Donnie's appeared aerodynamically sound enough to return to the center of the action. Bobby would not be able to make up the lost laps. This race—and perhaps his own eagerness—ended up biting him.

Many of the other cars or drivers were dealing with their own issues. Darrell Waltrip discovered engine trouble early and had to fight it all day long. Richard Petty, the sport's undisputed king who'd already won five Daytona 500s, was also a little off, but he had health issues to deal with as well. During the off-season, seemingly routine ulcer surgery had led to the removal of almost half his stomach. Petty really shouldn't have been in the race to begin with, but Daytona had too much history, starting with the first running in 1959, and a photo finish won by his father, Lee. Besides, it was just stomach surgery.

"I've driven with broken ribs, broken shoulders, broken feet—both of 'em broke at different times—and broke legs, tore up knee, you know, you just went," he said later. "It's sort of like a football player playing hurt, they tape him up and send him on out there."

Plus, in 1978, Petty experienced an indignity he hadn't suffered since 1960: a winless season. He was hungry.

As the green flag waved again following the infield slide, Squier and Hobbs made note of the rookies and other young drivers competing well at Daytona, many of whom were now winding their way toward the front as more experienced drivers limped. Daytona was the seventh-ever start for Terry Labonte, the debut Cup run for Geoff Bodine, and the start of only the second full-time season for Ricky Rudd.

And for Dale Earnhardt, a guy who'd made only ten previous Cup starts, with no real kind of continuity, it was hard to imagine that he could be this good. Granted, he was the son of Ralph Earnhardt, the late short-track legend, but this was the swift superspeedway of Daytona. As Earnhardt kept the pace in his No. 2 Rod Osterlund Buick, Squier and Hobbs began wondering if a rookie might win the Daytona 500 for the first time.

In the pits, reporter Ned Jarrett—who'd won NASCAR's Grand National championship in 1961 and '65—was asking Osterlund if he'd expected his new kid to be this competitive.

"We sure did," Osterlund said. "He's a very gutsy guy, very dedicated, and he's got that little natural instinct that you know about, Ned."

"He looks like a professional out there," Jarrett said, with a touch of admiration in his voice.

Osterlund nodded and smiled as if in possession of some secret weapon. "Right now, he probably feels like one, too."

A. J. Foyt wrestled the lead from Neil Bonnett and sped on ahead. The leaders nearly kissed the walls in the turns, and Earnhardt blazed out in front, leaning into each curve.

"He's not intimidated out there," Squier said.

Buddy Baker, meanwhile, chugged slowly back into the pits. His car was operating on seven cylinders instead of eight. His Harry Ranier team had changed all of Baker's spark plugs to no avail. Another year, another disappointing Daytona 500.

Baker's car, which had been swift all week, had failed him at the worst time. This track owed him, as it did too many others. The year before, Bobby Allison had won this race in his fifteenth try; several of them had been heartbreakers. And he'd won only because Baker's engine had quit during the very late going for the second time in six Daytona 500s. And Baker had been in front by plenty. Within the sports world, winning the Daytona 500 held a stunning individual cachet, much like movie stars winning an Oscar. And Baker had felt the snub yet again in 1978. "I felt like crying," he said afterwards, and added, "What have I got to do to win?"

Baker climbed from his Oldsmobile, removed his helmet and goggles, gave a quick quote to Jarrett, and scratched his head discontentedly. He was thirty-eight years old, and he sensed that great opportunities at this hallowed place wouldn't be around forever. He had no way of knowing that one year later, his Daytona 500 luck would change dramatically, and that he'd win the race at the fastest-ever speed in Daytona 500 history, on what would be his twentieth try. He'd pull into victory lane and talk and talk, hardly able to contain his joy, nearly embarrassing himself in his relief and glee.

But at the 1979 race, after starting first, he'd end up finishing second to last. He walked slowly around and stared under the open hood of his beaten Olds; then the sound captured him, and he turned to watch the cars go blazing by on the track. He grew wistful for a moment, then glanced back under the hood before walking away.

* * *

The Big One, a sweeping wreck of all wrecks, was almost inevitable at every Daytona race. The cars were driven too fast, the field was too tight, "No room for error, no room for the pressure to come off," as Squier kept reminding the millions at home, who were stuck in rapt attention at hurtling cars so close together that you could hardly stick a toothpick between. And then Waltrip and Kansas racer Bruce Hill spun and the rows of drivers collected behind them, spinning and viciously banging.

Moments after the cracking of the metal subsided and the plumes of haze began to dissipate, David Pearson stood in the infield chewing gum, his thumbs tucked into his belt loops, surveying the damage. In the seven-car wreck that came just past the quarter-mark of the race, Pearson got smacked around both in front and back. He pulled himself easily out of his Wood Brothers Ford and stood by, glancing at the crumpled PUROLATOR stretching across the driver's side doors, after crashing out of his second Daytona 500 in a row.

Told on camera that he was taking this well, Pearson said, "Well, you don't need to cry about it. I feel bad for Leonard and Glen [Wood], and Purolator."

Donnie Allison kept making his rounds on the track slowly, having done his best to put that early wreck out of his mind. He was heading back toward the front.

Doing so meant avoiding still more wrecks. Ten laps later, Bonnett and two rookies, Labonte and Harry Gant, had a grisly crash in turn four, with Gant hitting the inside wall, ricocheting back onto the track, and barely being missed by the onslaught of other drivers. It was a shocking, ugly-looking wreck the type of which many at home had never seen, but Gant climbed out of his car looking fine. Questioned afterwards about what it felt like to go into a wall at 190 miles per hour, Gant smiled and said, "Seemed like it was going 200."

With the caution flag out, Donnie Allison raced back to the start-finish line and regained his one lost lap. It was a useful tool of the sport: see the caution flag, and if you're fast enough, race past the leader, beat him to the line, and you gain back a full circuit.

The debris now cleared, the cars prepared for another restart. High above, a flock of some eighty seagulls hovered. There'd been a time, twenty years before, when they'd gotten to watch the action from a distance closer to home, on the famed Beach and Road Course that had been the roots of Daytona racing. But now, as the cars took the green flag at the speedway, the gulls, as if on cue, moved off clockwise, mimicking the field but heading in the opposite direction. And when the cars hit the curve, all the dirt and sand that had held ground on the track, seemingly blown in from the past, scurried up the banking to make way for the swift machines. Watching at home, the camera angles capturing the action made it look roughshod, without organization. The cars were coming at the screen in gangs.

The lead changed hands again and again. For perhaps three quarters of the race, the field never spread out too far as packs remained together up front. Some Daytona 500s had been won by as much as a lap or two; this one would be different. "It's a demolition derby out there," Squier said. It was one thing to hype the spectacle for the new people watching at home; it was quite another to have something this spectacular and fast to hype. Two-thirds into the race, Squier said, "We now only have *eighteen* cars on the lead lap."

"Is that all?" Hobbs said with a chuckle. "Oh, how boring."

"Take a look at what it's like as they come into the tri-oval, just barely turning the wheel at 190 miles per hour," Squier added. "Turn that wheel about two inches and you're through the tri-oval; turn it three, and you could be through for the season."

Donnie Allison was running either with the lead or near the front. And every time a caution flag came out, Yarborough stood on the gas like a swiftly flying ghost in Allison's rearview mirror, drafting behind him down the backstretch before using the air and momentum to slingshot past and then beat him back to the start-finish line. Allison wasn't putting up much of a struggle; he had a fine car. But Yarborough kept doing this déjà vu move until he'd regained all the laps he'd lost. Down two full laps with seventy-five to go, Yarborough was caught up and in second place forty-one laps later.

"Cale is one of the most incredible characters I've ever met," Hobbs said of the racer who'd won the previous three Winston Cup championships in a row. "He still enjoys a Sunday afternoon of duck hunting or fishing or catching water moccasins bare-handed. He's quite a guy."

Donnie Allison took the lead back from "that young lion" Dale Earnhardt. Leaders began to fall away. Parson's cooling system problems—at times, his engine was hitting 270 degrees—forced him several laps down. A green-flag pit stop took Earnhardt off the lead lap. And when Donnie Allison and Yarborough finally fell together for a two-car draft, it became clear which autos were best in the field. The gap between first and eighth place had only recently been less than two seconds. Now the two leaders were widening away.

Waltrip and Foyt, along with Petty, began a classic tussle for third, fourth, and fifth. But the distance separating them from Allison and Yarborough quickly ballooned to nearly half a straightaway. With twenty laps remaining in the race, the top pair opened a whopping nine-second lead on the field. For the first time all afternoon, the race seemed a little less exciting, except for the anticipation.

Donnie knew all this. He wasn't the long-admired racer that his brother was. Bobby, with his determined mien, was a ruggedly handsome, dark-haired Alabaman with clear brown eyes, a square jaw, and a handsome smile. "He looked just like Gregory Peck," said Humpy Wheeler, then the General Manager of Charlotte Motor Speedway. And he'd been the subject of long profiles in *Sports Illustrated*, detailing his one-time on-track tussle with Richard Petty, as well as other struggles and victories.

Donnie was built more solidly, and had a less stubborn character than his older brother. He'd won plenty of races but didn't bleed for racing in quite the same way Bobby did—except perhaps when it came to this race. He'd never won the Daytona 500 but, like everyone else, he desperately wanted to, and he'd be damned if he'd lead the final laps and then lose it on the last one.

Yarborough remained tucked in behind Allison. If he could stay there, he'd get one good chance to slingshot past him again, just as his car owner Junior Johnson had advised, and win his third Daytona 500.

"There wasn't no use to us being in a big hurry to try to win the race before the end," Johnson recalled. "And we just sat there and rode him till it was time to go."

The laps counted down, the gap between the pair and the rest of the field grew to be the better part of a full lap. "It all comes down to this," called Squier as the white flag waved, with Yarborough weaving behind Allison.

"We knew we had the car that should win the Daytona 500," said Hammond of Yarborough. "We were just hanging on Donnie's back bumper and Cale was very satisfied that he was going to make his usual move down the back straightaway right off turn two like he'd been doing all day long. And I remember as it happened, I was thinking, *man* we're going to win the Daytona 500, this is gonna be cool, and everybody's getting excited. I mean everybody *knew*."

*   *   *

From where Hammond and the rest of Junior Johnson's crew were situated, there was no way to see the two leaders as they came around the final lap. "He's gonna pass him!" crewmembers were saying excitedly, as they listened to the echoing race call by the track announcer.

"Cale Yarborough makes a move to the inside," the call came. "And they touch! They're hitting, banging each other down the back straightaway!"

"And we're standing there like, 'What?'" Hammond recalled. "And we're thinking, okay, they're banging on each other, but surely we're gonna come out of this thing, we're still gonna win this race. And we're waiting and we're waiting and the crowd is just screaming at the top of their lungs and we're looking at each other like, 'What's going on?'"

Yarborough had made his move once again; this time, Allison steered down the track toward the apron, keeping him at bay. Yarborough went still farther, making his way right aside Allison's Hoss Ellington Oldsmobile, and between the metal and the determination, the two autos clapped, came apart, and clapped again like some attention-grabbing ovation. Together, Allison's and Yarborough's cars curved slowly up toward the wall, bounced off it, and headed, still locked together, back down past the apron, coming to a rest in the infield.

Hammond and the crew were still waiting. "And we knew Cale was late; he should have been back, we should have seen him," he said. "And all of a sudden here comes Richard with Darrell and A. J. in tow, and it's like, 'Oh . . . my . . . God.' You know you go from the highest high and all of a sudden your stomach just drops? We had no clue exactly what happened. All we knew is they wrecked."

Meanwhile, Petty, exhausted from racing not long after his surgery, was doing his best to secure third place. When the caution flag suddenly came out, he knew it would be a race to get the best position possible. Waltrip passed Foyt but the trio was half a lap off the pace, some twenty seconds behind and not even on the same straightaway.

"Whoever got back to the start-finish line was gonna win that particular little race we was in," Petty remembered thinking.

It was only when he'd gotten through the backstretch and into the corner that Petty saw the two cars in the infield. He couldn't race any harder, but now it was Waltrip who would try the slingshot move to pass the king for the win.

Waltrip rolled back and forth, searching for the right line and an opening, and made one dashing, desperate move to get in front of Petty. But Petty was too crafty and smart, and knew this place better than anybody. It would be close, but when they came around for the checkered flag, it waved once again for the king. Richard Petty had won his sixth Daytona 500.

There was jubilation in the Petty racing pit, and shock everywhere else. Allison and Yarborough remained in the infield, and emerged from their cars looking stunned. Noses, jaws, whole faces had been broken for lesser reasons than this. What had even happened? Had Donnie thrown too much of a block? Had Yarborough taken advantage? Did it even matter?

Bobby Allison took the checkered flag in eleventh, three laps off the pace. Then he turned the car and headed toward the wreck in the infield. If Donnie's car was badly damaged, he might as well be there to help out.

He pulled up to find Donnie and Cale out of their cars, each talking to their own crew people. Bobby stopped by Donnie.

"Do you want a ride to the garage area?" he asked his younger brother.

Donnie looked dazed but anyone could see he was crushed. "No, go ahead," he said. "I'll get a ride."

Bobby looked up: Yarborough was eyeing him menacingly.

"This is all your fault," Yarborough said. "You caused that wreck."

Bobby answered and the two of them kept talking, the words getting more and more bitter. If anyone knew any better, they'd think the last lap confrontation had been between Yarborough and the other Allison. The sound of the Petty crew cheering in victory lane was like some distant call from another town. TV cameras were trained on the winner, and Petty was all smiles. He looked a little wan but plenty happy.

There in the infield, it was Yarborough and Bobby Allison. Talk talk talk. Bobby wouldn't stop. And Cale Yarborough had had enough.

* * *

Jeff Hammond never had a ride home like that one. He sat squeezed into a van with five other crew guys, heading back to North Carolina, going straight up 95 out of Daytona Beach after the race. It should have taken about seven or eight hours but there was snow everywhere. It took more like eleven hours.

The whole way, you couldn't turn on the radio without hearing someone talking about the last lap. "Not so much about Richard Petty winning his sixth Daytona 500," said Hammond. "It was about the attempted pass by Cale Yarborough and the subsequent fight between him and the Allison boys."

At every truck stop they pulled into, any restaurant, from Daytona to Charlotte, that's all anyone wanted to talk about. And when Hammond got home and turned on the TV, particularly CBS, he couldn't believe the attention it was getting.

That next day, Humpy Wheeler was scheduled to speak to the Charlotte Rotary Club about ways to increase local business. "This was a conservative, austere group of guys that wore dark, navy blue pinstripe suits and black Oxford shoes and who went to the Presbyterian Church and didn't particularly like NASCAR," he said. "I had prepared this speech very, very carefully, about stock car racing, the popularity increase and the reasons behind it and where I thought it was going. And when I got there I found out they didn't want to hear a damn thing about that. Forget whatever I wanted to talk about, what I needed to talk about was *the fight*."

Given the storm across the country, the race did whopping numbers, earning a 10.5 Nielsen rating and bringing in 15.1 million viewers. During the last half hour, the ratings hit 13.5. Not until 2001, and the start of NASCAR's behemoth TV contract, would the ratings be that high again.

The fight put NASCAR on the national map. The race had been perfect. Practically from start to finish, the on-track action produced an exciting maelstrom, with cautions, lead changes, rookies battling veterans, attempts at redemption, tight racing, and an unpredictable finish. And all, for the first time, live from start to finish on the grand stage of television.

But to NASCAR execs, hungry for the presentation to be a showcase of a fine-tuned, respectable, corporate-friendly sport, the way the 1979 Daytona 500 ended was like showing up to a big affair wearing a tuxedo and a black eye. Officials were livid, and fines for "conduct unbecoming" were delivered to the Allisons and Yarborough.

And yet, there would now be no stopping the interest from fans. As much as the sport's ruling body disliked the method, it had to secretly embrace the madness.

"NASCAR fined us $6,000 apiece," said Bobby Allison. "And I've always said they used the money to make commercials [about the fight]. Now, that may not be totally accurate; they did refund us some of the money, but I never got all of it."

CBS had bought into the idea of NASCAR being a sophisticated, growing business that, several years earlier, had welcomed Winston as title sponsor, along with sponsor companies such as Anheuser-Busch, Hawaiian Punch, STP, Purolator, and Gatorade adorning top cars. And the crowds were formidable; at Daytona, the packed stands held, at the time, 120,000 fans. The sport had moved far away, it was argued, from its moonshining, gin-soaked roots, an era when champions such as

Buck Baker won with the motto, "I didn't go to a racetrack to make friends."

"There was a lot more fights; tempers flared," recalled Richard Petty's car-building brother Maurice in 1999, speaking of NASCAR in the 1950s. "They still flare, but with the big money in it and with the sponsorships, you sort of have to keep your cool."

"Even though there was a fight in the infield, it went from being a roughneck sport to all of a sudden there was a few white collar people around there," said Donnie Allison. "And it's progressed since then to the enormous thing it is now."

"That fight spelled the end of an era and also the start of a new one," said Humpy Wheeler.

And the cameras being there set the stage for the transition.

"Television gave people a chance to see what it's really all about," says Darrell Waltrip, the two-time NASAR champ turned Fox TV racing analyst; Waltrip followed the pioneer Ned Jarrett and then Buddy Baker and other star drivers/crewmembers into the TV announcing booth. "NASCAR's the thing that they say is just a bunch of cars going around in circles, but it's a bunch of high-strung emotional drivers driving those cars going around in circles, too. And it doesn't take very much at the end of the day for someone to push somebody, or somebody to shove somebody a little bit and you've got a little ruckus on your hands."

For the people involved in the ruckus in 1979, however, it remained an unforgettable sore point. Deep down, the race is not "historic " to Donnie Allison or Cale Yarborough.

Two weeks later, the NASCAR tour moved to Rockingham for the Carolina 500. Nine laps into the race, Donnie Allison and Yarborough tangled while fighting for the lead and collected each other in a wreck. Both drivers maintained that the incident had nothing to do with Daytona. But it did fan the fire.

The fire continues to this day. "When I talk to Cale about it he still feels like Donnie did him wrong," says Hammond. "He just really feels like Donnie knew he couldn't outrun him and rather than let Cale win that race, he'd wreck him."

"Donnie knew what he was doing and he has said since then that he [wrecked] rather than let Cale win the race, which is kinda stupid because second is better than nothin'," adds a still bitter Junior Johnson. "If we didn't think that Donnie would be fair about the thing, I'd have just had Cale spin him out going down the straightaway. We coulda wrecked him without wrecking ourselves. That was just absolutely foolish."

For Donnie Allison, who maintains the wreck wasn't his fault, it's hard to really care much about what anybody else thinks. This was the Daytona 500, which he never ended up winning.

"That particular day was very, very, very hard on me," he said decades later. "Because it was the third time I should've won the Daytona 500. And I didn't. And I tell everybody, forget the appeal of NASCAR and what happened with that and everything else, it's hard to wreck a guy from in front of him. I did not run into Cale; he ran into me first. It was really sad for me that day. I was so hurt when my car stopped. Up till that time, I'd never been that hurt in my life."

The NASCAR tour continued in 1979, the fan base built, and more new sponsors entered. The top drivers—Bobby Allison, Yarborough, Pearson, Baker, Waltrip, Parsons, and Petty—stayed dominant. Petty won the title for the seventh and final time in 1979. And that year, the stars were joined by Dale Earnhardt, who'd win Rookie of the Year, followed, in 1980, by the first of his own seven titles. On the way, he'd get criticized left and right for rough driving by his fellow competitors, earning the nickname "the Intimidator," and some warnings now and then from NASCAR officials. He, like the sport, would continue to run the tightrope between rough riding and respectability. Stock car racing still treads that tightrope today, but to a much lesser degree.

"You gotta remember, corporate sponsorships have changed our sport, but the Allisons and the Pettys and all that group, all those guys had to stand up for themselves, too," said Buddy Baker in 1999. "Once you put 180,000 people in the grandstands and you represent major companies, you just can't do that anymore. That was the time and it served its purpose at that time. It got people excited about the sport.

"Every sport's gone through that. They used to have fighting on the fields in football; you hardly ever see that anymore. You do that in our sport and you get to watch a lot of it. You get an opportunity for eight or nine months to sit there and wonder how much money you'd have made if you hadn't made a fool of yourself. It's funny how money can control your temper."

Fred Lorenzen, one of the most popular racers of his day, pilots the stalwart No. 28 LaFayette Ford en route to a 1964 victory at Atlanta International Raceway.

Chapter Five
Twenty-Eight

"There's just something about certain numbers that do grab fans. I mean, Rusty Wallace made number 2 famous. People liked that. And every time I see 2 today I have to pinch myself to say, 'Hey now, that's not Rusty, that's somebody else.'"

—HUMPY WHEELER, former general
manager of Charlotte Motor Speedway

THE LAST SEVERAL LAPS OF THE 1992 DAYTONA 500 WERE PLAYING out the way so many others had, with two worthy combatants —a swift leader and a patient follower—waiting for some final-turn fireworks.

It was Davey Allison in first with Morgan Shepherd in second. The race offered at least one nice guarantee: The winner would represent something important and historic in the sport. Shepherd was driving the No. 21 Wood Brothers Ford; if he could slingshot past Allison, he'd be the fifth different Wood driver to win a Daytona 500, after Tiny Lund, Cale Yarborough, A. J. Foyt, and David Pearson.

Allison, who steered the No. 28 Robert Yates Racing Ford, was rich in racing blood. His father, Bobby, who had won three Daytona 500s and the 1983 Winston Cup championship, was a founding member of NASCAR's famed Alabama Gang, along with brother Donnie and racer Red Farmer. Davey was the inheritor and leader of what Donnie dubbed the Peach Fuzz Gang. In 1988, Bobby had won Daytona with Davey tucked in right behind him in second.

"To win that race at age fifty and to have the best young man in racing be second behind me and have that young man be my son has got to be the greatest achievement that anybody could hope for," Bobby said years later.

But in 1992, it was Davey Allison who had the car to beat. He'd led all but five laps in the race's second half. Losing would be heartbreaking, of course; winning would seem like fate: the perfect start to what many thought could be Allison's first championship season.

Shepherd tried to foil that plan in the final lap. He pulled back, he moved in close, he looked low and went hard for a spot on the inside, but he couldn't compare to Davey that day.

Davey took the checkered flag as his crew, led by young crew chief Larry McReynolds, celebrated and prepared to join their driver in victory lane.

Davey was wildly beloved by the fans. It wasn't just that he was an Allison—that alone would have been plenty—but he was also a thoughtful, respectable driver, a smiling hero in his prime, now just nine days shy of his thirty-first birthday. The fact that he looked like a rail-thin warrior with intense brown eyes, dark hair, and an unpretentious kid-next-door grin didn't seem to hurt either.

The car may have been as loved as Davey was; they seemed inexorably linked. It gleamed in bright black, with a swirling blue-and-white Ford logo out front. Fittingly, a big red-and-white star—the insignia of chief sponsor Texaco Havoline—blanketed the hood. And also on the roof, and on the driver's door right, the familiar, unmistakable bloodred "28" was painted. You couldn't miss the 28 of Davey Allison.

His proud dad joined him after the win. "That second place is still the most special day of my career," Davey said of the 1988 race. "This is the biggest victory of my career but it's not as special as finishing second to my dad."

The celebration, sadly, would be short lived. In 1992, which easily ranks among the greatest seasons in the sport's history for white-knuckle competition, no one would stand out more than Davey Allison, in ways both good and bad.

"We won the Daytona 500 and we were on a pretty good roll," McReynolds recalled years later, beginning his comments about the season. "But we were on a pattern: We would wreck one week, we would win one week."

That would be Davey's story in 1992, a season for which the adjective roller-coaster now seems woefully inadequate. It would have its victories, but those triumphs would be more than offset by enormous tragedy, startling crashes, and great physical and emotional pain.

Everyone watching the year unfold, from race fans to competitors, would come to respect Allison's fount of strength, and his single-minded pursuit of both victory and solace inside his racecar.

"There just was not a more determined individual on earth than Davey Allison," says McReynolds.

Strangely enough, this wasn't the first time 28 represented such qualities. It has borne many drivers through the generations of the sport, some of whom showed an uncanny ability to ply their trade with a resolve several levels deeper than most, and frequently in the face of great distraction.

It is a number that has produced winners, and yet it has also left fans—and some of those who've been behind the wheel—wistful and hungry for what might have been. As one study of the history of the sport's car numbers summarized, "Ten of NASCAR's forty winningest drivers have driven it, but a car carrying No. 28 has never won a NASCAR championship."

But it will always be associated with Allison, and a promise left unfulfilled by his all-too-brief life. Like Dale Earnhardt and his number 3, the continuing history of 28 will be dominated by the number's past and its legacy.

"You definitely sense its importance," Ricky Rudd once said of the 28 car, a number he drove—and won races with—from 2000 to 2002. "I think whoever is in that car, there's a little extra pressure to make sure it does well."

* * *

When Lee Petty decided to compete in NASCAR for good in 1949, he did so in his own 1949 Plymouth. His license plate number began with a four and ended with a two; for that reason, he decided to paint the number 42 on the side of his car and drove with it whenever he raced. Ten years later, his twenty-one-year-old son Richard began to race more regularly, and chose the number 43. He said, "So me and Daddy could be like a team." For much of NASCAR's history, it's hard to imagine a more beloved image than Richard Petty's 43 car, painted bright "Petty Blue," heading for victory lane.

"Stock car drivers made their own numbers [back then]," says Humpy Wheeler of the sport's early days. "Buck Baker was 87, but that never went down as a number that got fans enraptured. Twenty-two did. That was Fireball Roberts's number. That number just endeared him to fans."

Roberts also owed at least some of his car number's popularity to the power of paint. He hooked up with famed car builder Smokey Yunick in 1959, and in time, Yunick applied a brilliant black and gold scheme to Roberts's 22 car. "It really made the car stand out," says Wheeler. "And people jumped all over it."

Roberts was one of many Southern stars of the sport. But two years later, the racing folks at Ford found themselves fielding a car for the complete national marketing package: Fred Lorenzen. He was a different sort, an Illinois-born racer who'd made his name on paved tracks in the Midwest and who came to NASCAR as a good-looking, well-spoken, erudite outsider—in essence, the Jeff Gordon of his day. It was Lorenzen who first put the number 28 car on the NASCAR map.

"Freddy was kinda unique when he first come in," says Junior Johnson, who raced against Lorenzen. "He was young and attractive and popular and that's basically what made the 28 popular for him."

"He was just somebody we hadn't seen before," recalls Wheeler. "He was the golden boy, he was Robert Redford driving a stock car, the women loved him; we'd seen Northern drivers but he had a style and a flair and he had that great smile and the good looks. He gave us Hollywood when we needed it.

"A lot of the guys he was running against were pretty ugly-looking guys. This was back in the days when to drive the car was so different than it is today. There was no power steering, there were no power brakes, it took a man to drive this car. These were guys with big forearms and big necks, a lot of dirt, and they usually looked dirty when the race was over. So if they weren't very good looking before the race started, the competition didn't endear them to the modern day salon. And Fred, he even looked good when he was dirty."

Lorenzen was a particular favorite of Ralph Moody, the racing brain behind Ford's premier Holman-Moody team. And like Yunick, Moody understood the power of the brush: The 28 car was painted pearl white, the finish shining almost like metal flakes had been brushed on it, with a blue "28" and gleaming, matching pearl white wheels.

"That car," says Wheeler, "was just pristine."

And it visited victory lane frequently, and on particularly marquee afternoons. Lorenzen never competed for a title, running mostly at the higher profile tracks. In 1963, running only twenty-nine races—about half the Grand National schedule that season—he came away with six victories, and a third-place points finish on the way to becoming the first driver in NASCAR history ever to earn $100,000 in a single season.

Lorenzen succeeded because of a strict single-minded approach to his craft. At a time when the going was frequently raucous—with Curtis Turner and Joe Weatherly running races and then parties—Lorenzen had a regimented approach to racing.

"On Friday and Saturday nights guys like Weatherly liked to party," Lorenzen recalled. "I didn't go to that stuff. I stayed away from the parties, see, that's why I had the edge on them. The next day I'd be fresh, I'd have eight, nine, ten hours of sleep, they had four, five, six hours of sleep, and I was ten years younger than them. So that's how I had my hidden horsepower. Age and sleep."

Lorenzen was famous for not suffering fools on his race team either.

"You make your crew good, you know? The driver has say-so, and that's what Ford felt when they hired me," he added. "I was tough on the crew. I got in one day, it was seven o'clock in the morning. Lee Petty comes up to me and says, I wouldn't work for you, you're like a mule. I says, 'Yep, and what do you bet I'm going to win the race?'"

Lorenzen won plenty, with probably no victory more memorable than his Convertible Series triumph over Curtis Turner in the 1961 Rebel 300. On the final lap at Darlington, he brilliantly snuck past Turner for the win. That day, the twenty-six-year-old Lorenzen pulled off the seemingly impossible by outsmarting the man many considered the sport's best at a track no one figured him to lose.

"To me, Lorenzen dented the veil at Darlington when he knocked Curtis aside," said Max Muhleman, a top NASCAR reporter for the *Charlotte News* during the 1960s.

In fact, Lorenzen had gotten into NASCAR hoping one day to race against these men whom he considered heroes. Beating them was the goal, and an honor.

"I used to listen to it on the radio in the backyard of my house," Lorenzen recalled of stock car racing. "Curtis Turner in Darlington, Joe Weatherly, and Fireball Roberts. Some of the best."

* * *

The 1964 season was awful and tragic. Every driver on the circuit felt the pain of it, and the events worked double on Lorenzen.

Five races into the season, the tour returned to the formidable road course in Riverside, California. By 1964, Weatherly had long emerged from the shadow of his best friend Turner, who'd been banned from the sport by NASCAR president Bill France, the penalty for attempting to form a drivers' union under Jimmy Hoffa's powerful Teamsters banner. Weatherly had won the 1962 NASCAR Grand National championship, driving for Bud Moore. In 1963, he'd managed the feat of winning a second-straight title in journeyman fashion, driving for an incredible nine different owners.

After wrecking early at Riverside, Weatherly ran into transmission trouble. The insistent champion hurried his Bud Moore crew to replace the part. With the red flag out and NASCAR cleaning debris, the crew swiftly did the job. Once back out on the track, Weatherly was only two laps down, driving hard to make it all up through the eleven snaking turns.

Weatherly cascaded through the esses. But after a hard left followed by a hard right into turn six, Weatherly suddenly lost control of his Mercury. He was not going fast—only about sixty miles per hour in the turn—when his car hit the retaining wall. But Weatherly had no window guard in his car, and he wore no shoulder harness. The angle and force of the blow jerked his head, slamming it hard into the wall. Weatherly was killed instantly.

Lorenzen, some fifteen car lengths behind, found the image of the crash frozen in his mind.

"I saw that happen, right in front of me," he said. "His head came up out the window and it snapped his neck. . . . I didn't know how bad it was. I know he didn't have a shoulder harness on. We wore harnesses then. He didn't. Neither did Fireball."

Weatherly, like many racers, including Roberts and Turner, professed to be most afraid of fire inside the racecar. Without a shoulder harness, they theorized, it would be easier to escape.

Lorenzen was already having another season for the ages. In his first nine races, he'd earned five consecutive wins. He qualified second for the May 24 Charlotte race, pumped by great expectations for making it six in a row.

Seven laps into the race, Lorenzen was in a pack of several cars running near the front. As he later recalled, the battling felt particularly heated at so early a period in a six-hundred-miler; sensing things could get out of hand quickly, he wanted to steer clear. He was moving toward the front when behind him, Junior Johnson, attempting to pass Ned Jarrett, wiggled in turn one and accidentally tapped Jarrett's left-rear quarter panel, sending both cars spinning. As Jarrett slid down the track, he collected Fireball Roberts, with both cars hitting the inside retaining wall.

Jarrett's impact was hard; it burst the gas tank and flames enveloped the car. Roberts's slam was worse: His Ford caught an opening in the inside wall as he headed backward, which sent it flipping onto its roof. The car was now also on fire. All too quickly, billowy trails of black smoke rose up from both cars, with Roberts trapped inside his.

Jarrett managed to climb out and ran over. He found his longtime friend frantically working to free himself.

"Oh my God, Ned, help me, I'm on fire," Roberts called.

Jarrett plunged in his hands, helping to pull Roberts out, and together they ripped off as much of Roberts's fiery jumpsuit as they could. But he was burned over 80 percent of his body.

The much-admired Daytona Beach driver improved somewhat in the short run but the burns ultimately proved to be much too severe. After a month and a half, pneumonia and infection set in. At thirty-five, Roberts was dead.

The deaths of two of the most popular racers in quick succession devastated the sport. A number of safety measures were either instituted or improved upon, including, in time, fuel cells to prevent the kind of fire that claimed Roberts.

The losses of Weatherly and Roberts hit Lorenzen hard. A year earlier he'd been considered the sport's great young future champion.

Now, at twenty-nine, he was suddenly lacking the same killer instinct that had made the 28 car a victory lane fixture.

"After Joe Weatherly and Fireball died, Fred Lorenzen quit," said Jarrett, who also retired unnaturally early in 1966, weeks after his thirty-fourth birthday. "He had a lot of money and decided to get out before he got hurt."

Lorenzen retired in April 1967 but grew bored and questioned his move. He attempted a comeback in 1970 but was out of his regular ride and found limited success. Whatever thrill there had been was gone for good. The 28 car, like its driver, languished.

"The thing is, I perfected it; it all came too fast, too quick, and I got tired of it quick," Lorenzen said of racing. "But [retiring], that was the worst move of my life."

* * *

"When Cale was driving it, it kind of built the name for that car number," remembers Andy Petree, who was Dale Earnhardt's crew chief during his 1993–94 championship seasons. "It didn't matter who drove that car, it seemed like it was extremely fast and to the guys in the sport, the insiders, that car was always considered to have more power under the hood than any other car in the garage for so many years, especially when they'd get to a big track."

Ranier had designs on competing for a title again beginning in 1987, and he found the ideal driver for his 28 car to be a young, serious, committed racer with the instincts of a winner. For this opportunity, Davey Allison rewarded Rainer with what would be the greatest rookie seasons in NASCAR history.

Davey had been born to the sport, an adoring boy hoping to gain some attention from his father, whose eyes seemed perennially looking down the racetrack. It fueled the young Allison's ethic.

Bobby, meanwhile, had finally seen his almost nomadic career pay off with a championship in 1983, and was gruffly determined that his son learn the ropes with limited help.

"In his first part of his career, I didn't think he'd make it," Donnie Allison said of his nephew Davey. "He wrecked and he wrecked. We had a pretty good conversation one night, Bobby and I. And I said, 'Why don't you give that boy a car, a piece of equipment that suits him?' And he said, 'No, he's doing all right.' Well, I gave Davey his first good race-car. And he put it together, raced it on Friday [in a local racing series], and won his first race. Then he went Saturday night and won again. His father come home on Monday and said, 'Maybe you're right.' That's the way the boy was."

By the time Davey graduated from more regional stock car series to Winston Cup, the next generation of racing stars was solidly in place, with Dale Earnhardt, Terry Labonte, Rusty Wallace, Bill Elliott, Ricky Rudd, and Kyle Petty now competing for wins and titles. Benny Parsons, Buddy Baker, and Cale Yarborough were soon to retire, but a few older veterans—Richard Petty, Darrell Waltrip, and Bobby Allison—were not quite done. And Davey came in strong.

In twenty-two races in 1987, Davey won two—the first time that a rookie had won more than once in twenty-two seasons—and with the Texaco Havoline star on the hood, became a much-loved fixture in the series. When Davey finished second to his father at the 1988 Daytona 500, it seemed a new chapter in racing mythology was destined to be written.

But four months later, Bobby Allison blew a tire on the first lap of a race at Pocono. As he tried to get to the pits, his Miller Buick was broadsided in the driver-side door by Jocko Maggiacomo. It was a terrifying hit, and Allison's head trauma, among other injuries, was severe. When it was clear that he would survive, it also became evident that he'd need a great deal of therapy to regain his strength.

Davey watched helplessly as the towering figure he revered was reduced to a shadow of what he'd once been. Davey would now need to be the leader of the family.

Through 1988 and the next several seasons, he alternately succeeded and struggled. Robert Yates had bought the Harry Ranier team at the start of the 1989 season, selling his house and most of his possessions to do so, even at Ranier's fair price. The commitment meant a great deal to Davey Allison; he promised to align himself with Yates for the rest of his career.

While Davey had some success with Jake "the Snake" Elder as his crew chief, the chemistry clearly improved when Elder was replaced by Larry McReynolds after the mid-March 1991 race at Atlanta. Driver, owner, and crew chief were kindred spirits, and Allison and McReynolds formed the kind of rare driver–crew chief bond that always leads to success and frequently championships.

"I don't know if I've ever been around a more focused individual than Davey Allison," McReynolds says. "Whether it was driving that racecar, playing with his kids, spending quality time with his family, or playing a game of cards. Whatever he was working on at that moment had his 110 percent attention. When he was eating lunch, there was no sense in trying to carry on a conversation with him. He was very focused on eating his lunch.

"And Davey Allison did not like to lose. He didn't want to lose a race, a practice session, or a qualifying session. He did not want to lose a game of one-on-one basketball in the driveway."

The Allison-McReynolds team scored eight top tens in the following eleven races in 1991, including three wins. And Allison finished the year with two victories in the last three races. "We absolutely hated to see the season end because your big fear is, 'Gosh, we hope we don't lose this momentum we've got right now,'" McReynolds recalls.

But the 28 team began 1992 with a Daytona 500 win. All the cards seemed to be lined up just right.

* * *

The oil broke loose on the 28 car; Allison felt the clang and he winced when he swerved hard into the wall at Bristol Motor Speedway. It was the sixth race of the 1992 season and he was leading in the points standings but it would now be a little harder with a bruised shoulder and a couple of cracked ribs.

"I took a pretty good shot," he said afterward.

The next race was at the .625-mile short track at North Wilkesboro and Allison was feeling poorly, to the point where Virginia driver Jimmy Hensley was brought in to qualify the car, and to be on standby for what seemed like an inevitable substitution.

But Allison started the race and hung around near the front for a good part of the day and, despite one small wreck and a spin with Kyle Petty, he moved into the lead just past the three-quarter mark. As he continued making the tight circuits on the track, Rusty Wallace crept in behind, challenging him. Allison's left leg began to hurt, then his right one cramped.

Allison's 28 car crossed the finish line in front, two car lengths ahead of Wallace, the driver feeling bowed and achy. But he was ahead in the standings by eighty-six points.

North Wilkesboro was a true NASCAR town, its track a fixture on the schedule since the sport began. After the race, the grandstand gates opened and the faithful came down to mingle with teams. With the 28 crew going through postrace inspection, McReynolds scouted around for his driver.

"I just happened to look up on pit road, which wasn't that far from the garage area. Somebody was up on the back of a pickup truck and there were tons of people surrounding it. And the closer I looked, I said, 'That's Davey.' He was sitting in the back of his pickup truck with broken ribs, just had run a four-hundred-lap race, in victory lane he couldn't even stand up, he had to sit beside the racecar, and yet here he was on pit road signing autographs until there was nobody else left."

The topsy-turvy season would continue. A week later, in Martinsville, a blown tire sent Allison hard into the wall, bruising his already beaten ribs. Another week later, he won the race at Talladega.

The tour then moved to Charlotte, for the Winston All-Star race, followed the next week by the Coca-Cola 600.

To pump up the excitement, the format for the All-Star race had been changed to allow for a final ten-lap shootout after two thirty-lap segments. It worked. On the last lap of the ten-lap final dash Dale Earnhardt, Kyle Petty, and Davey Allison were jockeying for the lead and the $300,000 payout. As Earnhardt pressed Petty ever lower on the racetrack heading for the final turns, Allison waited, scouting for an opening. He was in his favorite of all his No. 28 Fords, a Thunderbird that the team had nicknamed "007." In five races at Charlotte Motor Speedway, the car had produced four wins and a second-place finish; the victories included the Winston he'd won the season before. As Earnhardt righted himself and Petty got off the gas a touch, it left a perfect opening for Allison on turn four, with the checkered flag looming in the near distance.

Allison made his move to the inside and sped to the front with Petty right behind him. The two nudged and banged and momentum took them toward the checkered flag, with Allison ahead by inches. But the force of motion continued, and Allison swerved helplessly into the outside wall. The beloved 007, now suddenly a massive wreck, slowed to a stop, silence coming from the car.

"He won the race but I'll tell you, he sure paid the price for it," Buddy Baker said from the TV booth.

Allison sat unconscious inside his car for several minutes. When he'd been removed and brought to the hospital, doctors found he'd suffered a concussion, bruised lungs, and bruised legs. A victory was a victory but Baker was right: The cost was great. And the 007 was damaged so badly, Yates had it demolished so he'd never have to look at it again.

Incredibly, Allison was back on the track the following week, finishing fourth in the Coca-Cola 600. He healed up through the spring, got a win at Michigan, and held a slim points lead as the summer months came, and the tour headed back to Pocono.

With Pocono came bad reminders of Bobby's wreck. But on July 19, Davey seemed poised to clear out some of the bad taste left by the track.

He'd earned the pole and led 115 of the first 139 laps. But as dominant as he'd been, a long pit stop sent him back in the pack. There were about fifty laps to go, leaving ample time to grapple for the lead, provided he got there quickly.

Allison began winding past competitors, and he pulled up close to Darrell Waltrip, hoping to make a pass. Waltrip was stout; passing him would be hard, and the pair jostled. As the 28 cut below him, Waltrip's Chevrolet touched the back of Allison's Ford. Davey swerved low on the apron, his tires jutting onto a patch of grass, and suddenly the 28 car was off the ground in silent, perilous flight.

For a moment it hung there, but momentum was carrying it the wrong way, into what amounted to a backward spin, the car moving in on itself. A spin like that creates terrible force, and when the car smashed back down to the ground, it leapt forward, barrel rolling mindlessly—as if falling down a flight of stairs, nine, ten, eleven times—vaulting over a guardrail before finally landing in front of a line of safety vehicles, its metal shell in tatters.

The safety crews approached the car cautiously; they took their time, carefully removing Allison from the wreckage, and while he was alert, he soon had to be airlifted to a hospital. Doctors treated Davey's head injuries and performed surgery on the broken bones in his right forearm, collarbone, and wrist, which required a pin. He also had a fractured skull. No wreck that he'd suffered earlier in the season had been as bad as this one.

McReynolds was there at the hospital later that night, and Allison seemed alert and aware. In time, the conversation drifted to contingency plans: The race the following week was the DieHard 500 at Talladega, the Alabama Gang's home track. A substitute driver was most certainly needed.

Allison listened until he couldn't stand it anymore.

"You sonofabitches, quit standin' around here moanin' and groanin' about me, get home and get my Talladega car ready. I will *be there* and I will *race* that racecar."

It all seemed unlikely. Bobby Hillin Jr. was brought in as a backup; he qualified the car third, and Allison, by now out of the hospital but hurting, got in and practiced the car.

"The driver has to start the race to get the points," McReynolds said, regarding NASCAR's points system. "And NASCAR told Robert [Yates] and I, 'That boy's not gonna run many laps. We will accommodate him starting this race but we're not gonna tell you the first caution; we're just gonna tell you a few laps to start this race and then Bobby Hillin or whoever has to get in that racecar.'"

Allison had no mobility in his right hand and wrist; in order to allow him to shift gears, the team Velcroed his glove to the shift lever. Allison started the race, holding steady but in great pain. And then, as if on some cosmic order, Talladega, Alabama, in the midst of a hot July day without a cloud in the sky, had a ninety-second rain shower during lap eleven. NASCAR threw the caution and Allison was removed from the car. Hillin ended up running third in a stellar showing. Allison led the Winston Cup standing by a single point.

* * *

Bobby Allison had been making progress in his recovery. Slow as it still was, he had renewed optimism. Despite Davey's pains, he was competing for a title. And both father and son were helping Davey's brother Clifford get his own NASCAR career started.

Davey had been born to work; Clifford, on the other hand, was always about play. "He had a way to finagle around and get out of work; he was a very, very good lad but he was shrewd," remembered his uncle Donnie. "And I think this hurt him later in his racing, because the opportunities that he had, there were some very good ones that he didn't take advantage of because of the work ethic, I think."

But that had changed. And if the brothers weren't as close when they were youngsters, it had taken till now—with Clifford finally focused, embracing this chance to race as seriously as anything he'd ever done—for them to be on the same wavelength. That was also a boon for Bobby.

Bobby had gotten Clifford a ride with new team owner Barry Owen, and two weeks after the Talladega race, Bobby and Clifford were in Michigan, with Clifford testing his Busch car in the days before Davey would run in the Cup race.

"Clifford was very good at helping to enthuse me, assimilate me, get me going," Bobby said of his sandy-haired twenty-seven-year-old son. "We were there, adjusting the car, and they made one more little adjustment and Clifford said, 'Dad, we're gonna get 'em.' And he pulled out."

Clifford made a good clean lap, the car responding very well. Then suddenly, Owens, who was standing in the pit area next to Bobby, took off his radio headset and threw it to the ground in frustration. "He just crashed," Owens said.

Bobby waited a second. "Well, is he okay?" he asked.

Owens picked the headset back up. "Clifford, are you all right?" he called into the mouthpiece. "Clifford?" There was no answer. Bobby watched as the safety crews headed out of pit road, turning to the right. Normally, they went in the direction of race traffic. They took this shorter route only if the crash was bad.

Bobby began walking toward the crash scene in turn four. The closer he got, the more his heart crept into his throat. A NASCAR official ran up to him with a palm raised.

"They don't want you to go over there," he said.

"That's my son. I'm going."

"Okay," the official said. "But I'll go with you." And he walked with him, bracing him. Bobby's daughter Lisa, Clifford's sister, quickly climbed a fence, scratching herself up in the process, and walked with him as well, until they got very close. And then she stopped in her tracks.

Bobby moved out to the car as a crewman tried to undo Clifford's belts. When he pulled back out of the car, Bobby Allison looked straight in, up close. And he knew.

"I could see Clifford was dead," he said. "And it was an incredible pain that gripped me. Agony."

Allison had hit the wall at about the worst angle possible, and he'd been killed on impact. Thinking later on about the scene, Bobby remembered he'd seen a cut on the side of Clifford's face, without any blood. "That's pretty instant," he said.

After hearing about the crash, McReynolds and Yates flew immediately to Michigan, met with Davey, and began the familiar discussion of contingency plans.

"Davey, what do you want us to do?" McReynolds asked his driver. "We've got a couple of options."

Allison shook his head, his face steady with resolve. "My brother was killed today," he said. "And my heart is crushed. But I'm up here to do a job and I'm up here to do the best job that I can to try to win this race, and try to win this championship. We'll leave here Sunday night and we'll go home Monday and we will mourn the loss of my brother and we will bury him."

"Here's a guy, he's lost his brother, and he's picking *us* up," McReynolds remembers.

Davey soldiered on. Three days after Clifford's crash, he was back in the 28 car full time, starting the race in third and finishing fifth. Two weeks later, he was running in or near the front for much of the day at the Southern 500. Having won earlier that season at both Daytona and Talladega, Davey needed to win this Darlington race in order to secure the Winston $1-million bonus. But rain came to Darlington with sixty-nine laps to go. NASCAR officials called the race with Davey in fifth.

After a string of subpar finishes in the fall, Allison was locked in a tenacious battle for the championship, swapping leads with Bill Elliott, with owner-driver Alan Kulwicki creeping up behind. After a win at Phoenix on November 1, Allison took the points lead away from Elliott going into the season's final race. He'd need to finish fifth or better to guarantee his first championship, with Kulwicki now thirty points behind and Elliott forty off the pace.

The Atlanta race would be a changing-of-the-guard occasion as well. Richard Petty, the King of Stock Car Racing, made his final NASCAR start at Atlanta; Jeff Gordon, the kid from California, made his first.

Allison led briefly and remained among the front pack, feeling healthy and being careful not to do anything to jeopardize his chances.

But three-quarters of the way through the race, with Allison running in fifth, Ernie Irvan spun out on the circuit's swiftest speedway with Allison right behind. No amount of turning or swerving would save him and he knew it.

Irvan collected Allison's car and both headed for the wall. The drivers were okay; the cars were not. While the Yates crew went through swift repairs to get Allison back on the track, the driver understood it would take a miracle to win the championship, and he wasn't going to get it.

The miracle worked, however, for Kulwicki, who finished the race in second behind Elliott. Elliott had led 102 laps during the race; Kulwicki had led the most laps with 103. By virtue of that single extra led lap, Kulwicki earned another five bonus points, and won the Winston Cup title by ten points in what was then the closest finish in the sport's history.

* * *

Allison finished the year in third, sixty-three points off the pace. The long season over, the events caught up with him, filling him with disappointment, dejection, and pain. The injuries would take time to heal. Losing a championship—well, there'd be other years. Losing a brother, however, was the bitterest blow.

Thoughts of Clifford left Davey racked with guilt, and regret that perhaps he could have done more to help his burgeoning career. Who knows what would have happened. His father had that sense twofold, and Davey had to steer Bobby clear of it.

Until his wreck, Bobby Allison had seemed indestructible; now he was permanently scarred and altered. And another wreck had wiped Clifford away. Davey felt the need to shoulder it all. He would have to be all things to all people. A husband to his second wife, Liz, and a father to their two children. An unwavering crutch to his dad. A racer and a teammate.

The tragedies and his own injuries energized Davey's faith. They also put into stark relief the notion that things can happen like this, incomprehensible things. Some direct hits have no warning shot off the bow at first. Such an idea may have once seemed unbelievable. Now it was a thing to live with on a daily basis, and then put out of his mind if he was going to place one foot in front of the other, and then find his release in a racecar. And so Davey trudged on.

"He was my role model," says McReynolds. "When I get down and out and start thinking I can't handle this, I think about Davey. He's my inspiration even today."

The season's finish made the 28 crew clamor all the more for the start of 1993, and while there was no repeat win at Daytona, a March victory at Richmond justified everybody's confidence. Still, focusing entirely wasn't easy.

One month later, the sport was rocked by more tragedy: A private plane carrying Alan Kulwicki and four others crashed in a field a few miles short of the runway at Tri-Cities Regional Airport in northeast Tennessee. In the blink of an eye, the defending NASCAR Winston Cup champion was dead.

It was an unimaginable, gut-wrenching turn for the sport and everybody who ran in it. It was hard to accept that so committed, respected and stalwart a champion would perish like that.

Kulwicki's death brought everything back to Allison. It would be that much harder for drivers on the Winston Cup tour to continue to race, as much as the driving might be a welcome distraction. Allison turned even more to helping his father—and by extension, himself—get better, and attain a measure of solace in the wake of loss. It could all be gone in a moment; you had to do the things that made you happy, and live every moment to its fullest.

In 1993, Earnhardt was quickly threatening to run away with the season; a championship would be his sixth, and that much more welcome after a subpar 1992. Just past the year's halfway point, Davey finished third at the first-ever Winston Cup race at Loudon, New Hampshire, and was mired in fifth place, more than three hundred points back.

He'd traveled back home from Loudon with his father, and they'd talked openly about all the things they were facing, and the great comfort of going through it together. They discussed the early days, and the fact that they were, happily, now closer than ever as father and son. There was openness and acceptance.

Davey, like his dad, had long loved to fly; of late, taking a craft into the air had come to be one of his favorite escapes. His latest toy was a Hughes 369HS helicopter, and a few days after the Loudon race, he and Red Farmer—another inaugural Alabama Gang member—took the short sixty-mile flight from Hueytown, Alabama, to Talladega to watch Neil Bonnett's son David test for his Busch Series debut. He didn't have many flight hours yet with the craft; he needed as much time in it as he could get.

The wind blew steadily as Allison approached his landing patch, a fenced-in parking area in the Talladega infield. He brought the craft downward, getting within one foot of the ground, but in a sudden, jarring motion, the front lifted upward some twenty-five feet. The ride quickly grew turbulent, with Allison losing control. As he struggled to regain it, the helicopter shook, spun left, and hit the blacktop below, with Allison's body taking the full brunt of the force.

Farmer was upside down and injured, calling out to Davey. Neil Bonnett, running over from nearby, was able to help the sixty-one-year-old racer undo his belts. Farmer, with a broken collarbone and fractured ribs, implored Bonnett to help get his young friend out; there was a full tank on the helicopter and it could blow. Allison was unconscious, and

Bonnett couldn't reach him. It took medics longer to remove him, and he was brought to Carraway Medical Center in Birmingham, with critical head injuries.

Larry McReynolds soon got the call telling him that his friend and driver was critically injured. He shook his head, as if he knew where this was all leading. "You know what? That's enough," he said out loud. "I don't need this anymore."

Doctors performed surgery and the family gathered and waited. It all felt familiar and awful. Bobby Allison prayed hard for a miracle and fought against the unthinkable. But come early the next morning, Davey Allison, so bright a star, immeasurably talented, and all of thirty-two years old, was dead.

After the funeral, the 28 team met at Robert Yates's house to mourn and contemplate their future together. The first decision was to forgo the race on Sunday in, of all places, Pocono. It wouldn't be fair for any replacement driver to be serviced by a team whose members had tears in their eyes all afternoon. And yet, McReynolds was convinced that somewhere, Allison was looking down on this decision saying, "You weak sons of bitches. I can't believe y'all are not racing at Pocono. What the hell do you think you're doing?"

Earnhardt ended up winning the race that day. He met his crew at the start-finish line where they all knelt in silent prayer. Danny "Chocolate" Myers, Earnhardt's longtime friend and gasman, said, "I've never seen Dale Earnhardt cry until today."

Earnhardt took a flag bearing the rich red number 28, and waved it as he drove around the track in Kulwicki's famed reverse "Polish Victory Lap" to honor both racers.

"When we lost that championship in '92 I was pretty crushed, but you know what, I took the attitude that maybe the old cliché—you gotta lose one to win one—is gonna kick in to play here," McReynolds says. "Early April of 1993, I kind of felt like maybe I got the answer to why we lost that championship to Alan Kulwicki because Alan got killed. Unfortunately on July 13 the answer that I got in April became a little foggier when Davey was killed.

"People ask me all the time how many championships do I think he would have won, how many races. You can go to palm readers but I don't believe in those things. Davey made a huge mark in the sport. And he would have made a much huger mark."

* * *

It wasn't going to be easy for anybody. The week after Pocono, Robby Gordon took the wheel of the 28 car at Talladega; he crashed early on and finished last. And veteran driver Lake Speed sat in for three races.

Yates wanted the ride to go to Ernie Irvan, whose raw talent was matched by a reputation for overaggressiveness. He'd earned the nickname "Swervin' Irvan," and had once, two years earlier, apologized to his fellow Cup drivers for his metal-bending impatience at a televised prerace drivers' meeting. And it was Irvan's wreck in the last race of 1992 that had led to Davey's losing any chance he had at a championship.

Though Irvan was under contract with Morgan-McClure Racing, the 28 ride was a step up, with a title-ready team. It would take a firing and a lawsuit settlement but Irvan was in Yates's car by the Southern 500 on Labor Day weekend at Darlington. He started tenth and finished fifth, and though McReynolds still felt the loss of Allison keenly, he also began to think things would be all right. With Irvan, some stability felt achievable.

"Ernie knew he was stepping into a car that had a very strong legacy," McReynolds says. "There were a lot of people that were not very high on Ernie Irvan being put in that racecar. I don't even think Bobby Allison was that high on it. Davey and Ernie had had on-track encounters. They certainly didn't hate each other but they didn't love each other either. But Ernie said, 'You know what? I'm not here to replace Davey Allison. I'm here to make this car run good with Ernie Irvan.' He wanted to make sure that he didn't walk in the shadows of anything with Davey. He didn't want anything that looked the same as Davey's uniform and I think it was more out of respect to Davey.

"But I think everybody, especially the naysayers, were sayin', 'Are y'all going to be able to be as successful in this 28 car now that you don't have Davey? I don't care who you put in it. Are y'all going to be able to recover from what happened?' I'd never been to victory lane with anyone other than Davey and I think maybe I had those questions myself. Nobody knew what to expect with this deal."

If anything was going to guide the tide of public opinion it would have to be Irvan's performances on the track, and very quickly, his runs were startling. In the season's final six races, Irvan had wins at Martinsville and Charlotte, with two additional top fives.

At Martinsville, he'd dominated from start to finish. Starting on the pole, Irvan led 402 laps out of 500, gaining a victory in only his fourth start in the car.

Crossing the finish line, taking the checkered flag, he rode his Ford along the half-mile oval, his fist raised high, soaking in the screams of the sixty thousand fans in the stands. McReynolds, meanwhile, felt a tempered flow of satisfaction, and a measure of relief. Maybe this win would bring about some closure.

He had no idea how much so. As Irvan rolled the 28 car slowly toward pit road, McReynolds spotted a lone figure waiting there; it was like some dusty scene near the end of a Western. The figure, he soon realized, was Bobby Allison. As Irvan came closer, Bobby raised his thumb to greet and honor his son's replacement.

Irvan passed Bobby and made his way to victory lane. When he emerged from the car, he pulled down the top of his uniform and tied it around his waist to reveal his T-shirt, which read, "In Memory of Davey Allison." He'd been wearing it each Sunday, hoping to break it out for a win. And the ovation erupted from the Virginia crowd.

"I think those two things right there brought [answers] to all the questions around Ernie Irvan driving the 28 car that Davey Allison had been in," recalls McReynolds. "The rest of 1993 and on into '94, we worked with fire in our eyes."

Irvan finished the 1993 season in sixth place, with Earnhardt winning again. In 1994, with Irvan in the car full-time, the success would be phenomenal.

He began the season with wins at Richmond, Atlanta, and Sonoma, and an incredible ten top fives in the first twelve races, numbers that propelled him into the points lead. But no date was more important to the team than the May 1 showing at Talladega. McReynolds knew old bitter feelings died hard for fans. As well as Irvan had been doing, there was no gauging crowd reaction at the Winston Cup home of the Alabama Gang, the track where Davey Allison had made his name.

"Of all places, thank the good Lord we didn't have to go there [with Irvan after Allison's death] in '93," says McReynolds. "We were carrying the 28 car to Alabama with a guy that people didn't really have a lot of good things to say about and we're gonna go to Allison country? So in '94, when he went out on the racetrack to practice, we didn't know if they'd coat the car in beer cans and chicken bones. We had no idea what to expect."

Irvan took the car out to qualify in the days leading up to the race. Normally, there's not a huge, vocal crowd for qualifying. That day, McReynolds got goose bumps standing in the pits, listening to the incredible roar of the crowd. "You could hear the cheers and see all those fans standing up as the car qualified and how much better could it be scripted that we went out and sat on the pole?" McReynolds says.

Watching Irvan slow after his blistering qualifying effort, hearing the cheers, McReynolds felt these years blend together for a moment. Like everyone else, he couldn't take his eyes off the car.

"With Davey, there was a large Davey following, a large Allison following, and something of a 28 car following," he says of Allison's popularity. "When Davey got killed, so many [more people] became 28 fans. . . . When Ernie drove off pit road to go qualify, those fans went crazy. That's when I realized: After Davey's death, it wasn't ever about who was in the car. It was about the car itself. The fans used that car to still have a link with Davey."

* * *

Less than a week after the Talladega race, that link would grow deeper still, and in ways that would bend any fan's resolve. Irvan was leading the Winston Cup points when the tour headed to Michigan. During a practice session the Friday before the race, Irvan's right front tire deflated as he headed swiftly into turn two. His car barreled into the wall at about 170 miles per hour.

Irvan's hit nearly killed him. At the hospital in Ann Arbor, the doctors categorized his head and lung injuries as critical, and he was given only a 10 percent chance of surviving the night. Yates, McReynolds, and the 28 crew sat an all-too-familiar vigil.

Irvan hung on for one day, then another. The pressure of watching him and trying to work to get the car ready was immense. Kenny Wallace was recruited to drive the 28 while the addled team tried to dig in and hold on.

Wallace would have the wheel for the remainder of the season. Meanwhile, Irvan, despite so dire a prognosis, made small but steady improvements. Within a month, he was breathing on his own; a month after that, he was moved to a rehabilitation facility closer to home in Charlotte.

Yates kept going. He hired Dale Jarrett to drive the 28 car during the 1995 season. And Irvan's miraculous recovery continued.

At the start of the 1996 season, Yates proudly fielded two cars: the 88 car driven by Dale Jarrett, and the 28, once again motored by Ernie Irvan. The latter punctuated his return with a victory in one of the 125-mile Daytona qualifiers and ended up starting second at the Daytona 500 next to Earnhardt.

Irvan would gain some success that season and the next, but he'd never again come so close to winning the championship. Meanwhile, Jarrett was taking the 88 car to more vaunted stops on the way to what would be Yates's only Winston Cup championship, in 1999; the title would come with the 88 car.

Irvan left Yates at the close of the 1997 season. In 1999, on the fifth anniversary of his horrific crash, back at Michigan and behind the wheel of his own Busch series car, he once again crashed hard into the wall. It was a sickening scene of déjà vu. His head and lung injuries were much less severe but they were too strong of a reminder. Days later, Irvan announced his retirement from the sport.

By then Kenny Irwin inherited the 28 ride, a promising rising star who won Rookie of the Year honors in 1998. But after a less-than-stellar sophomore season, coupled with some communication issues between him and teammate Jarrett, Irwin was released from his contract and began racing for Felix Sabates. Midway through the 2000 season, Irwin was killed when his Chevrolet went hard into the wall during a practice run at Loudon's New Hampshire International Speedway. It was a tremendous blow to the sport in the midst of too many tragedies. Two months earlier, Adam Petty had been killed during another practice run at the same track.

Ricky Rudd brought the 28 car back to prominence during three seasons, gaining three victories and placing as high as fourth in the overall standings in 2001. But after the 2002 season, a year after the death of Dale Earnhardt and the seeming retirement of his famed No. 3 car, Yates decided he'd had enough of the brittle feelings related to a car he'd loved so much. Texaco Havoline, the longtime sponsor of the 28, switched to Ganassi Racing and the 42 car of Jamie McMurray. Yates decided he would field the 88 with Jarrett, and take up the 38 car with Elliott Sadler behind the wheel. NASCAR, he figured, would put the 28 number on a shelf and leave it be.

"We are all challenged in our lives to do something different, and that's what we are going to do," Yates told *Charlotte Observer* reporter Scott Fowler at the time. "I'll miss that number 28 and it's very special to me, but it's time to wrap this up and try to make a new name for ourselves. Some things are just not forever.

"Am I too old to brand another number? I don't know, but we're going to find out. We're not going to try and live up to someone else's standards anymore, we're going to try and create our own new standards. I went to work with the team in 1986. I bought it in 1988. I'm giving it up in 2002."

"I've got mixed emotions about it," said Bobby Allison of the decision. "It was Davey's car without a doubt even though a lot of other people drove it. It still was Davey's car. Now Davey's gone." And when other drivers took the wheel afterwards, with less success? "They'd say,

'You're not driving Davey's car good enough,'" Bobby said.

McReynolds, by then a popular Fox TV NASCAR commentator, asked Yates about the decision at Indianapolis later in 2002. "Davey's been gone nine years," Yates told him. "Maybe it's time to start something new and fresh."

"Robert Yates is a far better businessman than I am," Bobby Allison said. "If he thinks it's time for something new, I have to accept that."

* * *

At the close of the 2007 season, Dale Earnhardt Jr. was bitterly parting company with Dale Earnhardt, Inc., the organization that his father had built, and moving to Hendrick Motorsports. From the time he'd come into the sport, he'd driven the 8 car, a tribute to his grandfather Ralph who'd used the number throughout his career. But DEI had control of the number, and Junior's relationship with his stepmother Teresa had frosted.

"He really wanted to take that 8 number with him," McReynolds says. "I say this with confidence: Teresa Earnhardt would have burned that number before she let her stepson have it."

So Junior, looking for something similar, and a number with its own winning tradition, requested the 88 from Robert Yates Racing; they obliged.

Doug Yates, another well-known scion of a racing family, was about to take over the newly renamed Yates Racing from his father. Still very much in place was the deal that Robert Yates had made with Jack Roush to supply engineering, cars, and advice. And Doug Yates and his partner Max Jones saw a good opportunity—for sponsorship, for fan support, and perhaps for Yates's own bent of nostalgia—to resurrect the number 28. The car would be ready with limited sponsorship heading into the 2008 season. After five seasons away from the sport, here was another chance.

"Hopefully, we can do the things we used to do with it," Doug Yates said in November 2007. "We hope it brings back the good times we had before. It's always been a number we've been fond of."

Travis Kvapil, the 2003 Craftsman Truck Series champion was brought in to drive the car made famous by Fred Lorenzen and, a generation later, Davey Allison.

"There are a couple of numbers in the sport that have a special meaning behind them and there's a lot of fanfare, and the 28 is definitely one of them," Kvapil said. "When I was growing up, I'd think of the 28 as Davey's car. He kind of started a new generation of Cup drivers. I looked up to him.

"And now, it's Yates Racing turning the page and starting fresh and along with it they brought their old number back and it's pretty cool."

But fortunes had changed for NASCAR, Yates Racing, and the country. It's accurate to suggest that Yates chased sponsorship for the car as doggedly as Kvapil pursued the competition. Kvapil's car sported, at various times throughout the season, an astounding eighteen different major sponsor logos splashed on the hood—anyone from Zaxby's Restaurants in the Southeast, the California Highway Patrol and Academy Sports Outdoors, to Dish Network, FreeCreditReport.com, and Carfax. For the race at Darlington, Lafayette Ford, which had famously sponsored Lorenzen's car, signed on. And at the season-opening Daytona 500, and several other weeks in 2008, the hood went blank, with a prominent SPONSORYATES.COM logo on the side. One week, the Yates team painted a huge 11 MILLION on the hood, signifying the average NASCAR TV viewing audience awaiting a fortunate sponsor.

Despite the uncertainty and challenges, Kvapil managed to be both focused and competitive. It wasn't only the four top-ten finishes, and the pole at the fall Talladega race and the ten laps he led there. Kvapil was in the thick of the running on many other occasions, and a mid- or late-race threat, as his good working relationship with veteran crew chief Todd Parrott paid dividends. He finished the year a highly respectable twenty-third, four spots on the final grid ahead of his teammate David Gilliland.

But Doug Yates felt the company needed to expand in order to be more competitive, adding a third Cup entry for 2009 in Paul Menard, whose lucrative family business would serve as a top sponsor. And Bobby Labonte's Hall of Fame Racing entry was also to be run out of Yates Racing. It behooved management to move the points that Gilliland and Kvapil had accrued to Menard—whose sponsorship was secured—and Labonte.

The move put Kvapil in an incredible ditch. There was sponsorship for a few races from Golden Corral restaurants but nothing remained after the spring race at Bristol, where Kvapil ran strong and finished eighteenth. Suddenly Kvapil and his car were out of luck.

It was an ignominious end. The 28 car had never produced a loss of faith; it was undone by a loss of funds. In some ways, Kvapil had managed to pull it off. But the team was victimized by an economic climate that had swept through the sport and the nation.

Kvapil waited through the year, returning to the Truck series briefly, and hoping for a call from Yates that didn't come.

"Obviously I want to be racing," he said not long after the Bristol race. "I don't like sitting on the couch. And if there were other opportunities that came up, we'd have to look at them.

"But in a matter of two or three days we could probably be ready to go to the race track," he said at the time of the 28. "We'd have to hire a few people back right away, but a number of people we had on the 28 came from within the company already, so they're there. They took my handful of racecars and pushed them over in the corner. The 28 is ready to go."

* * *

In one sense, the demise of Dale Earnhardt Sr.'s No. 3 seems now symbolic of the departure of a time when numbers inspired a rooting interest in a car, a manufacturer, a team, or a racer. They no longer hold so much sway.

"Dale Earnhardt Jr. could run quadruple number zero, his fans don't care, all they care is Dale Earnhardt Jr.'s driving it," says Larry McReynolds.

But McReynolds, like many of the sport's longtime fans, wishes that were not the case. He still pines for a day when the 28 rules the speed charts.

"That number, that car, is what put Larry McReynolds's career on the map," he says.

His son Brandon began racing in 1999, at age eight. In the many divisions he's run, he'd always sported the number 8 ("He loves Dale Earnhardt Jr. to death," McReynolds says), and that includes several years in the Allison Legacy Racing Series. In 2008, he joined the United Auto Racing Association; in the UARA series, the 8 wasn't available, and his father looked over the list of non-taken numbers and asked Brandon if he wouldn't mind considering the 28. "That's cool," his son said.

Davey Allison and his wife, Liz, were Brandon's godparents, just as Larry and his wife, Linda, were godparents to Davey and Liz's son Robby. Both boys had been baptized together.

In 2008, Brandon's 28 car was sponsored by Scully Boat Builders; the company's paint scheme was black, with a fluorescent red-orange number on the door. It practically made his dad's heart jump out of his chest.

"You talk about heartwarming," he says. "Every time I was at the racetrack seeing that car go, that meant a lot."

McReynolds was in Michigan that August to cover the Cup race and missed it when Brandon took the checkered flag in Franklin County, Virginia, scoring his first-ever UARA victory. But a picture from that weekend remains ingrained in McReynolds's mind. It is Brandon, holding the checkered flag, standing next to the 28 car owned by his dad. It was yet another image on the loop of continuity that the sport offers through its generations.

"I still get chills just thinking about it," McReynolds says.

Dale Earnhardt, Terry Labonte, and the moment that decided the 1999 Night Race at Bristol, which fans voted the top-ever moment at the storied track.

Chapter Six
It's Just Bristol

August 28, 1999

*"I wasn't gonna wreck him.
Meant to rattle his cage, though."*

—DALE EARNHARDT, after the 1999 Goody's Headache
Powder 500 at Bristol Motor Speedway

ANDY PETREE COULD FEEL IT: THE STRAINING IN HIS BICEPS, THE exhaustion in his shoulders. He was about to have a heart attack. Petree fought it as best he could. His arms—thick from years of turning screws, and those long days of swiftly carrying tires on championship racecars—stood tight against the pressure. What a gorgeous day, he thought, sitting here on a beautiful boat in the Bahamas; it would suck to have a coronary.

"I can't do it!" he shouted, as a tired, drunken chuckle finally broke from his throat. Behind him, more laughter flowed, as the large fishing pole in his hands arced out, seemingly ready to snap from the force of the two-hundred-pound shark trolling the open seas. Petree dug his heels in and swiveled to look back. There stood Dale Earnhardt, master of his fishing boat, his arms crossed. He was squinting at Petree as if he was some kind of pussy. And Petree let out a laugh.

"Reel it!" Earnhardt shouted with frustration. "*Reel* it! *Reel* it!" The seven-time NASCAR Winston Cup champion paced around, trying to be encouraging, but more than anything just wanting the sumbitch shark on his damn boat.

They'd been in ugly spots before, uglier than this. Petree, Earnhardt's good friend, had been the crew chief on Earnhardt's black No. 3 Good-wrench Chevrolet for the two championship seasons of 1993 and 1994, before moving on to become owner of his own Winston Cup team. Here they were, five years later, and the Man in Black was still testing him.

It had all started off so well. A few spring days in the Bahamas during an early season break in the 1999 Winston Cup season. Petree, driver Terry Labonte, Earnhardt, and their wives, on Earnhardt's yacht, sailing and enjoying the lulling surf. But now the men were on *The Intimidator,* Earnhardt's fifty-foot fishing boat. They'd caught a dolphin, and Earnhardt knew from instinct and experience that when you have your prey on the line, you've got to reel it in instantly, come hell or high water. But it hadn't happened fast enough: A shark had gotten hold and seemed to be making a meal of the dolphin. That made Earnhardt mad. As he stood with his drink and peered over the side at the battle going on, Petree felt like saying, "Hey, that's okay, you just relax, Dale."

"Don't try to catch 'em both, Petree," Earnhardt said, as if readying to slap him on the head. "I just don't want that thing eating our damn fish."

Labonte watched the action with a wide smile. He and Earnhardt weren't the best of friends but they got along well enough and enjoyed the fishing. They'd come into Cup together, two pillars of a terrific 1979 rookie class. Earnhardt had won Rookie of the Year but Labonte later won his own championships in 1984 and 1996. They'd had their tussles over the years on the track but there were no grudges. He wouldn't be here otherwise.

Labonte figured Petree had tired the shark out by now. It was a perfect time to take over the fisherman's chair and bring this thing in.

Petree eagerly made the transfer to Labonte, still feeling the echo of the effort stretching through to his rib cage.

Labonte sat and immediately understood he'd erred big time. But he hadn't earned the NASCAR nickname "The Iceman" for nothing. He kept his composure, the physical torque apparent on his pressed lips and the slight shiver in his cheeks. It was the kind of look you'd wear while strangling somebody, except without people laughing and whooping behind you.

"C'mon, Terry!" Petree shouted, more relieved than anything else.

Labonte was methodical as he always was on the racetrack. Pull and reel, pull and reel; maybe he'd gotten the rod at the right time, like getting four fresh tires toward the end of a race, and pulling in rivals on a rope.

The shark was closer now, growing larger. But there would be no grabbing the thing out of the water. Earnhardt kept peering, his anger growing till finally he took a few steps back and reached down for a bat he just happened to have onboard. This shark was not going to win. Not against the Intimidator.

"He was *mad*," Petree later remembered with a riotous laugh. "He was mad because this shark was getting our fish."

"Swing 'im round, Terry," Earnhardt shouted. The shark, right on cue, now rode beside the boat, and Earnhardt leaned down, gripped the side, and began calmly whomping it with his bat, "beating the fire out of that thing," Petree remembered. "And he's laughing, looking around."

"This is *my damn dolphin*!" Earnhardt yelled, an angry wrinkle creasing his nose.

Petree was doubled over.

"What the *hell*?" Labonte called out, laughing.

Petree looked back until he caught sight of the captain Earnhardt had hired to steer the boat. He got the man's attention and pointed down at the shark.

"Why don't you just *shoot* him?" Petree yelled. "Heck, if you wanna kill him just shoot him. Don't you have a gun?"

The captain looked over with a squint and a calm shake of the head. Waving Petree off, he pointed instead at Earnhardt.

"Do you really think I'm gonna have a gun on a boat with *him* on here?"

The struggle went on. Earnhardt switched to a gaff, jabbing at the huge shark whenever it got close enough, to no avail. And the only thing this fish tale would net is a good story.

A few months after this trip, the NASCAR tour returned for its annual late-August Saturday-night race at the famous bowl-shaped half-mile speedway in Bristol, Tennessee. Labonte—methodical, determined, ready to spring at a moment's notice—found himself in prime position to win what many fans and drivers consider the most grueling, magical yearly stop on the tour. Earnhardt, driving a hard-to-handle Chevy on a frustrating night, would do his level best to ensure that didn't happen, ultimately working his racecar with all the subtlety of a club flying at the head of a shark.

"That's one of the things about Dale and this Intimidator thing that he had; that label," Petree recalls now of Earnhardt's gritty nickname. "I mean he really was kind of mean on the racetrack. His attitude was 'whatever it took,' you know? That little grin of his was genuine. If he didn't have a good enough car he was going to find a way to beat you. And most times he'd figure out a way to do it."

The battle between Labonte and Earnhardt that August 1999 night produced one of the most infamous finishes in modern racing history, an ending at once both astounding and infuriating, and one that left experienced television announcers and 141,000 fans in the stands dumbstruck. And yet, what may be most fascinating is that the ending had only so much to do with Labonte and Earnhardt. It had just as much to do with what happens in NASCAR every year on a particular late-August Saturday night in the Eastern Tennessee mountains.

Ask any Cup driver and they'll say the same thing. They'll grin, shake their heads, and, to a man, utter three words, like some familiar NASCAR mantra: "It's just Bristol."

For many drivers, it's an important, useful phrase. It is both an explanation for the things they've done, and the perfect excuse for the things they've yet to do.

Many incidents had occurred at the track previously; all told, that Saturday evening in August 1999 was even relatively tame for a place that's normally a magnet for mayhem. But because of its finish, that race gave birth to a gloriously gritty new era for Bristol, the small speedway with a huge and ever-growing crowd, a place where anything could happen, and could also be explained and condoned. And plenty has happened since.

In a sense, it's never anybody's fault, really. Bristol will do this to you.

* * *

"At Bristol, the speed is so fast, it takes you forty laps of going around the track for your head and your instincts to catch up," says Dale Earnhardt Jr. of the adrenaline rush of racing there. "We go to tracks like Daytona, you've got a long straightaway to prepare for the corner. At Bristol, the high bank is so fast, by the time you get out of one corner, you're getting ready for another corner and it takes awhile for your brain to realize what your eyes are seeing."

Laps at Daytona International Speedway stretch for 2.5 miles; it takes almost fifty seconds at top speed for the leader to make his way back around to the start-finish line. At Bristol, a lap takes an astonishingly swift seventeen seconds—that's about four seconds for each turn and each straightaway. And in a Cup race, there are five hundred of those laps.

Bristol is a tiny .533-mile oval with a slender forty-foot-wide racing surface that often seems not nearly big enough to fit forty-three racing cars going, at times, three-wide. (The only other half-mile track on the circuit, Martinsville Speedway, has a fifty-five-foot track width.) Pit road is also lean and is inconveniently split in half, with drivers pitting on either the front or back stretch, depending on how fast your qualifying time is. And pit stalls are snug enough to almost suggest parallel parking.

But it's the pace that will produce a kind of temporary insanity, allowing for no relaxation during runs.

In 1992, Bristol's track surface had been changed from asphalt to concrete, making a swift track that much faster.

The result—the speed shifts, the mountainous 36-degree banking, the endless turning, the fighting through traffic to pass lapped cars— might make a driver feel like he's spinning in circular loops with no respite, until an inevitable wreck brings out a caution.

And cautions bring out bad blood.

The 2002 night race is where five-time Cup champ Jimmie Johnson, after being wrecked by Robby Gordon, stood on the track and waited for Gordon to return so he could show him the contours of his middle finger—perhaps the only time Johnson has made such a gesture in NASCAR competition. His teammate Jeff Gordon earned his only NASCAR probation period in 2006 after a Matt Kenseth bump late in a Bristol race sent him spinning, dropping him from third to twenty-first place. After the race, Kenseth came over to apologize and Gordon shoved him harder than fans and detractors thought he'd had it in him to shove.

And these were minor incidents. There was Kevin Harvick angrily climbing over the hood of a car in order to get into Greg Biffle's face after an on-track incident. Jamie McMurray admitted he was being "an idiot" when he angrily banged into Kenseth's car after a 2004 Bristol race, in retaliation for Kenseth's bump and run on the last lap.

"I never get mad, but I was mad," McMurray said afterward. "That's just what Bristol does."

Which is why McMurray had to shrug it off when the unflappable Kasey Kahne—who'd been knocked out of the race earlier by McMurray—angrily promised to get his revenge at a later date.

And Ward Burton was leading the 2002 night race when Earnhardt Jr. bumped him hard enough to end his night. Burton waited on track for Earnhardt to return, took the heat shields off his shoes, and threw them at Earnhardt's open window. Later, the part-time conservationist regretted that he'd not had something to "shoot" through the window instead.

"Since we're out there driving on the track in that altered state or that desperation or urgency, when something does happen, you're so close to the boiling point . . . that you fly over the boiling point," Johnson told writer Dustin Long of the *Virginian-Pilot* (Norfolk, Va.) several years ago.

And there are plenty of people to watch when that happens.

In early January 1996, famed track owner Bruton Smith, who'd co-built Charlotte Motor Speedway with legendary racer Curtis Turner, added Bristol to his Speedway Motorsports, Inc., empire. The track cost him $26 million. He quickly began an improvements campaign, spending more than twice that amount to add seats and skyboxes, and by August 1999, a mere three and a half years later, seating at the track had nearly doubled, from 71,000 to 141,000. Smith did it by adding ring after ring of rows. While the racing surface remained not much larger than a football field, Bristol now had three times a stadium's seating capacity, as the gap between track size and racing spectacle grew all the more disproportionate. With that many people watching, everything was ramped up.

"It is so loud at Bristol, you don't actually know you've said anything," says Matt Borland, team competition director at Stewart Haas Racing.

To watch the race from the top rows meant climbing to a spot twenty stories in the air, making the track one of the tallest buildings in that area of Tennessee.

And climb they did: The night race at Bristol is a perennial sellout. Twice as many people who will witness the average Super Bowl descend upon this spot in the mountains for race day. The crowd that now attends the race is more than six times that of the actual population of the city of Bristol. It has been said in the past that the opening ceremony of the Olympic Games is the only sports ticket that's harder to get.

The place has been called a bullring and a hippodrome, and it's been compared to the old Roman Colosseum, where Christians were rent to bits by lions. Watching the action from the sky at night, the cars circling in a tight, mad twirl, it looks, for all its size, like a claustrophobic exercise. The track is somehow reminiscent of the *Close Encounters* alien mother ship, which must have been designed on a computer. But this is Bristol Motor Speedway, with the night settling in over the Eastern Tennessee mountains.

"After being in the sport almost thirty years, I still get excited every race week. But there's three times a year when the hair stands up on the back of my neck," says Larry McReynolds, famed crew chief turned Fox racing analyst. "One is at the Daytona 500. Second is at Indianapolis. And the third time is when it's not night, it's not day, it's dusk; and those forty-three cars take that green flag at Bristol in August on Saturday night, and it looks like one million flashbulbs going off. It sends tingles up my spine."

*   *   *

Forty-five drivers attempted to qualify for forty-three spots in what would be the aptly named 1999 Goody's Headache Powder 500 at Bristol Motor Speedway, set to run on August 28. It would turn out to be the closest qualifying field in NASCAR history: The one-lap time separation between the fastest and slowest cars among the qualifiers was a quarter of a second. The gap between the top three qualifiers was nine one-thousandths of a second. Only Dick Trickle and Rich Bickle missed the cut.

Among those climbing into their cars that Saturday night was Robert Pressley, who'd qualified to start twelfth in his No. 77 Jasper Engines Ford, his second-highest starting spot of the season, after his eleventh-place start at the year's first Bristol race. It was Pressley's fifth year racing in Cup and it was a season of struggles, one where talk of his past achievements in other racing series and his reputation as a guy who could get a lot out of a car was being plagued by second guesses; he was in danger of being regarded as less of a good bet and more of a journeyman. He was no longer young—the spring Bristol race had come two days after his fortieth birthday—and although experienced veterans were coveted in 1999, they were not in short supply.

But Bristol was a favorite; short tracks were in his genes. And any track, on any given week, was an opportunity even for drivers on lower-budget teams to exceed expectations, if luck allowed.

"This is," said ESPN commentator Bob Jenkins at the start of the TV broadcast, "the kind of race where you can get caught up in someone's troubles easily."

Tony Stewart, so far winless in his rookie season, was strapped in tight as he pulled out first behind the pace car, having earned the pole for the race. Stewart was calm behind the wheel, which felt like a respite from his dogged daily frustrations. When would he—the previous year's Indy Racing League champion—finally win a race in Winston Cup? Stewart had already gotten six top-five finishes and wondered what he'd need to do to stop knocking on the door.

Stewart's crew chief, Greg Zipadelli, did his best to talk good sense to his driver over the radio, to remind him that patience was key to a good showing at Bristol, much as impatience might seem shrewd. Stewart and the rest of the field warmed their tires behind the pace car, weaving back and forth. Rusty Wallace, winner of the spring Bristol race and a perennial threat, would start second. His weaves came close to Stewart's car, in a little prerace metal trash talk.

The green flag waved and Stewart could feel his wheels spin slightly—just enough to allow Wallace to dart past him into the first turn. Wallace knew exactly when to take advantage of such things: In thirty-two previous Cup races at Bristol, he'd won six times.

Starting side-by-side in row thirteen and coming back to the line together after one lap were Dale Jarrett and Dale Earnhardt. Compounding the less-than-stellar showing in qualifying, they'd now need to pit on the back stretch pit road, a distinct disadvantage at Bristol. Drivers starting in the back half of the field needed to wind their way past the front-half pit stalls, and make the pit road turn to pods on the second straightaway, which invariably added a few seconds to one's stop.

Jarrett finished third in the spring race, but as he began coursing around Bristol's tight turns in his No. 88 Yates Racing Ford, he could tell his car was not nearly as commanding as he wished. Now, two-thirds of the way through the season, he had a 314-point lead over Mark Martin in his quest for his first championship, and a chance to match his dad, Ned—presently up in the announcing booth—as a champion. It was unlikely that anyone could catch him. He'd been stellar at almost every race all year. But at Bristol, two laps into the night, his grip on the wheel became more tense as the back of his Ford fishtailed around the turns.

Out his window, Jarrett watched Earnhardt begin to move ahead more easily. In front of Earnhardt was Jimmy Spencer, a stocky ten-year veteran who frequently led laps at Bristol and usually did well. Farther ahead were the three Bodine brothers, Geoff, Brett, and Todd. Chances were good that Earnhardt and Geoff Bodine wouldn't be going fishing together anytime soon, seeing the number of times they'd been brought together to the sport's disciplinary hauler. For Earnhardt, passing these guys would be tough.

In the opening laps of a Bristol race, everyone is trying to get up to speed; at the start of the second lap, the careening takes on a mad character, and because of the momentum off the high banking, 130 miles per hour looks much swifter. Drivers need to keep their line. A little jerk left or right, as everyone else is trying to go straight, can be disastrous.

Pressley felt the comfort of his groove, but he was on the high part of the track. He drifted down going into turn one, hoping to merge in ahead of Ken Schrader, who'd started a row behind him. Schrader was moving around the curve, hoping to stay in front, and his Skoal Chevrolet tagged Pressley's left rear bumper, sending the No. 77 car hard into the wall at a dangerous angle.

Pressley buckled and bolted in his seat, feeling a twisting jerk in his neck upon impact, his belts gripping tight against his chest as he slowly steered the car down toward the inside apron. He could hear the hard breathing in his helmet as he felt the bump of his flat tire and imagined the considerable right-side damage. It would require a lot of work to get the car back into the race. He hadn't even lasted long enough to watch dusk turn to darkness.

Moments later, while the rest of the field continued their weaving behind the pace car, Pressley was preparing to talk to the press. He knew the drill: Thank your team owner and main sponsors and talk about how the Ford would get 'em next week.

ESPN trackside reporter Bill Weber may be a typically melodramatic presence with a mike, but he hit the nail on the head when he said, "This is why this track will break your heart. It will tease you in qualifying and crush you in the race."

Meanwhile, the pace car made its veering turn to pit road, the green flag waved again, and now forty-two cars growled and groaned, as Rusty Wallace led the field back into the dizzying, merry-go-round blur of Bristol.

* * *

The day had peaked hours earlier at 85 degrees; now in the low 70s, and dipping slowly toward 64 degrees, each degree change in the night played with the way the cars chose to roll, as well as the grip of the Goodyear tires on the concrete, which was now blackened by laid-down patches of thin, hot rubber. The cooler the temperature, the harder it would be to go through the corners. Wallace felt a tightening in his Ford, the car going from invincible to now suddenly vulnerable, and Stewart and Gordon quickly passed him. Until Wallace came in for a pit stop, he'd have to ride it out.

Joe Nemechek had started forty-first in the BellSouth Chevrolet but he'd been on the move ever since, so when Tony Stewart crept up to his back bumper, pride took a certain hold, along with a thought about the executives over at BellSouth. Falling a lap behind would be a distinct disadvantage, so he blocked Stewart's path for a lap or two, just to let the rookie know that he wasn't the only driver with a fast car. Behind Stewart, Gordon kept creeping forward. Nemechek was upsetting the flow through the turns and he knew it. After two laps, he let Stewart get underneath for the pass. Things like that aren't quickly forgotten.

For Jarrett, a car that began the race troubled started to improve as the cool air floated in. He moved up to seventeenth and began running some of his best laps of the race. But seventy-eight laps in, Jarrett came off the corner and felt his tires begin to shuffle. He jammed the wheel over, trying desperately to correct his line, wobbling errantly. He moved to safety on the apron, or so it seemed, but the car spun again, drifting back up onto the track. Competitors with suddenly nowhere to go rammed into him and each other, with Bill Elliott, Jeremy Mayfield, Hut Stricklin, John Andretti, and Elliott Sadler collected, and Jarrett taking all the slams like a favorite target in bumper cars, they had to roll there and wait for the action to end.

"I got a big hole in the right door," Jarrett said over his radio, his voice wan. "It's my fault; I got down too low on the apron."

Twenty laps later, contact with Jerry Nadeau would knock Jarrett out of the race for a long time. His team, understanding the wild variables of Bristol, had prepared an entirely new rear-end assembly to replace what had been broken on the car. But even after returning to the track many laps down, Jarrett would end the race climbing only to thirty-eighth place, which would no doubt cut into his points lead considerably. Up in the ESPN booth, analyst Ned Jarrett grew worried and subdued.

A 150-lap stretch produced four cautions. Every time Earnhardt came in to pit, after continuously battling a tight car, he had to deal with the back pit stall. By staying out when other drivers pitted, and vice-versa, he managed to gain some ground. As the race went on, the strategy paid off big time. It brought him into the top ten and then, after one more caution, a second-place spot, behind Terry Labonte.

Labonte, who'd started the race ninth, had been hovering near the lead all race, but the cautions allowed him to change his pit sequence as well. And three-hundred laps into the race, he inherited the lead from Gordon.

After the caution, Labonte and Earnhardt now awaited the green flag at Bristol. There were two hundred laps left in the race. In 1995, four years earlier, the pair had finished the race this same way, one-two. When Labonte took the checkered flag, a frustrated Earnhardt slammed him into the wall. Labonte's crew had to come push the wreck, and the smiling driver rode slowly to victory lane, as water generously poured from the car's busted radiator.

* * *

Earnhardt's horsepower carried him out of turns and into straightaways, his Chevrolet wearing a circle of ground-in rubber on the right door, the panel almost entirely dented, playing further aerodynamic havoc with an already uncooperative racecar. No adjustment seemed to be helping much. And yet he was reeling Terry Labonte in.

In each turn, Earnhardt's No. 3 car bottomed out, producing a shower of sparks. The traffic that he and Labonte needed to slog through at 130 miles per hour was thick. As Earnhardt tried to pass his teammate Mike Skinner, he rubbed too close and the two bumped hard and deflected away, as if anti-magnetized. Earnhardt's car became instantly worse.

"I think I knocked the right front fender onto the tire," he called out over the radio, sounding almost apologetic. Crew chief Kevin Hamlin gave a quick "ten-four" but both wondered the same thing: Could that shred the tire and send Earnhardt into a wall at any time?

Earnhardt waited two laps, and realized all was well—he'd dodged a bullet. But the tire rub was a wake-up call to move faster. Adrenaline flowed through him. As he and Labonte fought through the endless line of traffic, Earnhardt finally faked high and went low, passing Labonte. With 120 laps remaining, he held the lead for the first time all night.

Jeff Gordon, whose No. 24 Chevy rode much more smoothly than Earnhardt's, passed Rudd and moved into third, now 1.5 seconds behind.

Cautions were inevitable in this place but they were the last thing Earnhardt wanted to see, knowing that a wreck would cost him the lead because of his pit stall. But Dave Marcis, who at fifty-eight was the oldest racer on the circuit, hit the wall, bouncing against it again and again before settling between turns one and two, bringing out the yellow with eighty-nine laps to go.

Labonte came out of the pits first, followed by Gordon, then Earnhardt.

"This place will erupt if Dale wins the race," Bob Jenkins told the TV audience.

Earnhardt had won seven Winston Cup titles, tying him with Richard Petty, but his last had come five years earlier, in 1994. He'd famously—and finally—won the Daytona 500 to start 1998 but he hadn't scored a short-track win in four years. The proffered word was that he'd been losing his edge. For a driver with that much pride and success to be seen this way was galling.

Wayne Estes, then the director of communications at the track, had by then made his way from the press box to the turn-three crossover gate, a perch that afforded him a prime view of the back straightaway action.

The growing excitement of the crowd over Earnhardt being in the hunt filled the air. "Bristol was an Earnhardt place," Estes now recalls. "They talk about North Carolina but the capitol of Earnhardt country may be here. He owned this crowd. He won his first race here and plenty more. I'm pretty sure people would lie down in front of trains if he asked them to. He had that kind of power over the people who came to the races at Bristol."

But as Earnhardt got back into rhythm behind Labonte, his car was still way too tight. Despite being a lap down, Geoff Bodine wasn't going to make it easy for Earnhardt to pass him once again, and the pair rubbed and tussled coming out of turn four.

Labonte, Gordon, and Earnhardt moved like locomotive cars through the pack, and when Earnhardt, as if by force of will, managed his way around Gordon, the 141,000 spectators erupted.

"Don't tell Earnhardt that pitting on the backstretch is a disadvantage because it just makes him meaner," Jenkins said. Then, not wishing to be misinterpreted, he added, "Not in a physical sense; *determined* is perhaps the correct word."

It took Earnhardt twenty laps to completely fill Labonte's rearview. No one liked the vision of Earnhardt's piercing blue eyes that close. John Andretti once recalled seeing Earnhardt behind him after he'd already *won* a race, and the memory haunted him. "It would have been better had it been anybody but him," Andretti said. That's part of the reason Earnhardt insisted on wearing his open-face helmet. He happily cultivated his lore.

Earnhardt tried setting Labonte up, rolling toward the outside and then the inside. Then he gave a couple of bumps, first soft, then more insistent, and the lead was once again his, with Tony Stewart now in third and closing.

Three laps later, Labonte passed Earnhardt again with hardly a glance, Earnhardt's car floating too high out of turn four, as if Labonte had invited the first pass to play possum. Only thirty laps remained in the race, with Labonte running very smoothly.

But Earnhardt suddenly found a new gear, with twenty-two laps to go.

"Earnhardt is not that far back," Benny Parsons told the TV audience. "One little slip by Labonte and he'll be all over his back bumper."

The slip was coming. With thirteen laps remaining, the transmission erupted in Bobby Labonte's, Terry's younger brother, No. 18 Pontiac. Plumes of smoke filled Bobby's cab and he was all but blinded, his spotter guiding him through the turns over the radio. Bobby had entered the day third in the standings, having won the previous Sunday in Michigan, and was looking to capitalize on what would turn out to be the worst finish in Jarrett's incredible season. When he finally made it to pit road, his team, fire extinguishers at the ready, had to immediately douse the flames that had grown beneath the car.

Drivers blinked at the sight of the smoke and many checked up. Jeremy Mayfield lost the handle of his car and went hard into the wall, spinning around.

The yellow was out now, and Terry Labonte saw it and took his foot off the gas just a touch—or a touch more than Darrell Waltrip, who was right behind him. Unbelievably, Waltrip plowed into him and turned him around.

Labonte, stunned and breathless, sat in his once-perfect car, now up near the wall, stretching halfway across the track, as Earnhardt, Stewart, Gordon, and Mark Martin passed him by, before he steered down into the pits, lividly shouting and cursing over the radio.

Earnhardt may have been leading the race but he was not happy. He knew Terry Labonte would get four fresh tires and come out fast and angry. There was no way he'd win without new tires of his own.

"I need to come in," he called out over his radio to Hamlin.

"Ten-four—*stay out*," called back Richard Childress, Earnhardt's team owner and one of his closest friends. "Dale, you are the seven-time NASCAR Winston Cup champion. You can *do* it."

Earnhardt smiled and nodded. Yeah, he was that. But the Iceman would now be hard to stop.

The field was set up, with Earnhardt first, followed by Stewart, Gordon, and Martin. Terry Labonte was now in fifth. The green flag was out and the flagman waved it. There were now five laps to go—

it would amount to only about eighty seconds of racing.

"Is Dale Earnhardt going to win this thing?" Jenkins yelled.

"Looks that way," shouted Parsons.

As if hearing this and getting only madder, Terry Labonte was quickly on the bumper of Mark Martin, who'd gone in the pits for two tires but had come out with his car inexplicably worse than when it went in. Labonte jostled and passed him on the inside as they got to the scoring stand with four to go.

Labonte's eyes were strained with focus. Half a lap later, he was easily bumping Jeff Gordon, who gave way on the next straightaway. Labonte had third place with three laps to go, proceeding as if his car were somehow juiced.

He was practically on top of Stewart by the time they entered turn one, and passed him underneath with a little more than two laps to go.

"He's gonna catch him; can he pass him?" Ned Jarrett shouted.

Earnhardt, with two laps left, shifted his gaze from the windshield to the mirror, rolling hard into turns, protecting the bottom. Labonte, now in second, came right to him, punching his rear bumper once, then again, going low with robotic insistence. Earnhardt guarded the line, forcing Labonte down two-thirds onto the apron of the track, but Earnhardt understood that Labonte was ready to punt him off the track—and he had the car to do it.

The No. 3 rose up just enough and Labonte ran beneath him, taking the lead as the flagman waved the white flag—there was one lap to go. Earnhardt's car, half out of control, swerved right, slamming hard into Labonte, whose own car hardly buckled, and then was away.

Earnhardt, his eyes dull and steely as a shark's, trailed Labonte into the turn-one corner, the only place left where, veering sharply and slamming hard on the gas, he could really reach his old friend.

And reach him he did.

Earnhardt gave one choice nudge in turn two, and Labonte slid and spun sideways as a billow of smoke rose now from his fresh tires. Labonte had held his lead for all of six seconds. As his No. 5 car came rolling down, again covering half the track, Earnhardt slowed and timed his pass, barely missing Labonte's front fender. And he was away.

"Oh! and Earnhardt—" Jenkins practically groaned, stopping to figure how best to put it. "He spins him out!"

In his rearview mirror, Earnhardt watched all the carnage: Stewart, Ricky Rudd, Martin, and Sterling Marlin each ran into Labonte, or each other, or both, in a crashing crescendo.

Earnhardt kept running as if escaping the law, with Jimmy Spencer now smelling blood and fighting to catch him. But there was only one turn left in the race. The checkered flag came out and Earnhardt swept below the stand in improbable victory. Several car lengths past it, Spencer, wearing his nickname "Mr. Excitement" with pride, smacked the back of Earnhardt's bumper. Earnhardt wobbled big, but kept his car heading forward, and on a path that would take him to victory lane.

Up in the announcing booth, Benny Parsons still had his hands raised in amazement. He finally dropped them to his side. He'd seen Earnhardt pull such a move plenty of times, and had been on the track to see it and feel it as well. But no, not ever like this. He watched the Intimidator slow through the cool-down turns, soaking in his seventy-third victory. As it turned out, it would be Earnhardt's last-ever win on a short track.

"Wow!" Ned Jarrett called out with a heavy nod. It was hard to reconcile this finish in a few seconds. Cars, some looking well, most needing welding, coursed around the track slowly. That's when Jarrett shrugged. Only one word could sum up a night like this. "Bristol," he said.

* * *

They were a study in contrasts, two men who'd been sure of one outcome, only to be shocked by so sudden a shift.

The cameras followed Terry Labonte, who walked silently toward his hauler, wiping a sleeve across his nose, looking angry yet resigned. What on earth could he do, and what could he have done differently?

"They're going to talk about this one for a long time," Jenkins said.

Earnhardt made his way to the checkered flag platform at the center of Bristol's victory lane. As is the rite of all winners, he exited his car and stood upon the driver's side window ledge, his fists raised in victory as fireworks shot up all around. But when only murmuring came from the crowd, Earnhardt quickly realized he'd miscalculated his joy. The quiet lasted only a couple of seconds, as most of the 141,000 people realized that Earnhardt was being audacious enough to celebrate.

Jenkins was right: The place was very much ready to erupt over his win—but in anger.

As Earnhardt got set to step down, his arms at his sides, the fans roared their immense disapproval, the boos coming loud and strong. Bristol may have been the capitol of Earnhardt country, and the fans had seen him win races this way before, but in this case, the condemnation was everywhere. In the stands, some folks were peeling off their Earnhardt T-shirts and tossing them over the fence. Earnhardt took a swig of Coke and jumped off the car, looking nonplussed. Then he turned to J. R. Rhodes, his friend and trusted PR man. "Watch my back," he said.

"I was gonna get back to him and just rattle him," Earnhardt said about Labonte, in his post-race interview, still more than a little thrown by the crowd's anger. "I wasn't gonna wreck him. I got to him and just turned him around. Didn't mean to really turn him around," he said. And then, with a mischievous grin he added, "Meant to rattle his cage, though."

Ricky Rudd, Jeff Gordon, and Tony Stewart followed Jimmie Spencer to round out the top five. Officially, Labonte would be tagged in eighth, one lap down.

A moment later, Labonte was at his hauler, graciously answering questions. He tried to smile, to somehow put on a good face. Asked by Bill Weber to explain what had happened, he said, "Got wrecked, so then we got fresh tires and came back out and I got wrecked again. It just wasn't my night."

Weber understood he was asking for trouble with the one question he needed to pose to Labonte, but he said anyway, "Obviously he said he planned to get up to you, had no intention of taking you out."

Labonte turned to Weber, his bile rising. He stared incredulously.

"He never has any intention of taking anybody out," Labonte said, his voice breaking. "It just *happens* that way."

Deputies from the Sullivan County Sheriff's Department, providing security for the race, were also there in victory lane. It was traditional to see a few of them standing near the winning car, with their brown shirts and their badges, keeping things in order, "on the outside chance someone will throw a fist or two," Wayne Estes says. "But on that night, I think everybody in the sheriff's department showed up in victory lane."

The deputies formed a wall around Earnhardt, and he climbed into one of several police cars for the short ride to the track's Tower Five elevator. The race winner would ride that elevator up to the third-floor press box for more postrace interviews.

A crowd stood near the elevator, waiting to catch a glimpse. The great majority of them were exceedingly unhappy.

"All these people were screaming and yelling right where the tower was," Estees says. "I can't say it was a huge angry mob but it was a mob."

The deputies were smart enough to not put Earnhardt in the first car, just in case. But Earnhardt emerged from the second car and, along with Rhodes and Estes, he strode ahead confidently. "And yep, he had that little half grin of his on," Estes remembers.

When the elevator door opened, Earnhardt walked in and sank against the back wall. After Rhodes and Estes, everybody else taking the ride up was wearing a brown shirt, with a badge, and a gun. With the deputies in a state of alert, the enclosure was reduced to silence.

Earnhardt couldn't contain himself. Energized by an adrenaline rush and by the victory, and recognizing the relevance of the moment, his famous smile grew broad as he listened to the angry shouting continuing from outside.

"Man, that's my music," he said. Immediately, the tension was eased inside the elevator.

"He was eating it up," says Estes. "He loved it. He made no apologies for anything that happened. He was happy to have the win, happy to have the moment, and happy to have people all stirred up."

Meanwhile, throughout the grandstands, the majority of the crowd remained standing at their seats for a long time, scanning the track and the haulers, perhaps waiting for some massive scuffle to break out. The temperature had cooled considerably and a nice breeze played in the air. The night sky was bright; it was only two days past the full moon. Perhaps it had come too early.

* * *

Two days after the race, Larry McReynolds was on a plane with Earnhardt and the Childress Racing team, heading out to St. Louis to test the new Chevy Monte Carlo. The driver was feeling conciliatory about the race, wishing for a different path to the same result.

"I just wanted to do the bump and run on him and get him upset a little bit and out of the groove," Earnhardt told McReynolds. "The last thing I wanted to do was wreck Terry Labonte to win that race."

"But still, his attitude was, 'It is what it is,'" McReynolds recalled years later. "And that was Dale. When he was outside that racecar, you couldn't meet a guy with a bigger heart than Dale Earnhardt. When Dale buckled himself into that racecar and buckled that chinstrap, he'd wreck his mom or his wife to win a race."

A year and a half after the 1999 race, NASCAR began the first season of its new six-year, $2.4 million broadcast television contract, ensuring that every race would have a greater number of fans at home watching, with the sport gaining a more prominent place in the nation's collective consciousness. The drama of the 1999 race guaranteed the Night Race at Bristol would remain a popular draw, even among a newer slew of fans. The 2001 Bristol night race was seen by 3.5 million viewers at home. By then, seating capacity at the track had increased further, to 147,000, on the way to its current total of 161,000.

The numbers astound Darrell Waltrip, who practically owned the track during his driving heyday; he won seven straight Bristol races at one stretch in the early 1980s.

"Do you know how many people showed up there in 1985? About

thirty-five or forty thousand; that was a sell-out crowd, standing-room only," he recalls. "And you know how many go there now. Nothing's changed except they added all those seats. They still have the same number of guys competing. It was a lot easier back then to keep everybody satisfied and happy. You could put your arms around it. But it blew out and it grew so quickly."

Much like Bristol, the sport was increasing its appeal, building upon its core in once-inconceivable ways. NASCAR always attempts to further clean and polish its image. And just when it seems ready to invite individuality and rebellion, it punishes it. You can push the throttle, but not too far.

Bristol, however, is that nagging reminder of a time when beating and banging, and pointing fingers and giving the finger, were routine. The track had long been old school; in 1999, Dale Earnhardt ensured it would always be thought of that way. And the loud crowd will continue to show up, especially in August, to see what happens when each lowered degree in temperature raises the heat of frustration, and the added seats make the place maddening and louder.

"People always ask me, 'Why don't they build another Bristol?' You *can't* build another Bristol," Larry McReynolds says. "If you picked that whole venue up and you moved it to *wherever*, if you moved it to Madison, Illinois, it wouldn't be Bristol. Because there's something about that place, that Colosseum atmosphere, sitting up there in the mountains of Tennessee, that makes the place special.

"It's easy to put 160,000 seats around even a mile or a mile and a half track," he continues. "But around a half-mile racetrack that's barely just a little bigger than the size of a football field?"

McReynolds's voice trails off, finding it difficult to consider such a plan.

It's understandable. Bristol will do this to you.

Father and son celebrate as Dale Earnhardt Jr. captures his first-ever Winston Cup win in only his 12th start.

Chapter Seven
Man to Man

"You don't know how it's gonna make you feel until you get out there and then you're just overcome with some sense of acceptance and accomplishment because he's the ultimate. What's he doing and what you've seen him doing for years is your ultimate goal. It's something that you get right away as a kid, to do what he's doing and be him and be like him."

—DALE EARNHARDT JR. in 1999, talking about the first time he'd been on a racetrack alongside his father

SITTING HIGH ABOVE THE TWO-MILE TRACK AT MICHIGAN INTERnational Raceway, Darrell Waltrip shifted energetically and leaned on the counter in the announcing booth, his eyes locked in. Glancing sidelong, he watched the disbelieving smile on Benny Parsons's face.

"Benny, I'll tell you," Waltrip said, "I've been in races where I thought Earnhardt was running first and second and there was only one. Today I can see it."

With nineteen laps to go, Dale Earnhardt Jr. had calculated right. Sitting in third place, he flew up the high lane on the curve between turns three and four. Pivoting hard on the gas, reading the lane's momentum, he glanced quickly as he passed Mark Martin to take second place. Now he was tucked in, right behind Dad.

This was race three in IROC XXIII, the four-race International Race of Champions series, pitting top drivers from different series against one another in evenly matched Pontiac Firebirds with thirty-three-gallon fuel tanks and no pit stops. IROC was a fun stunt, a chance for NASCAR guys to take on some open-wheel racers, a tradition more attuned to an era when guys like Mario Andretti and A. J. Foyt might actually run at Daytona or Charlotte.

Dale Earnhardt had won both IROC races earlier that year, first at Daytona and then Talladega. Otherwise, for the seven-time Winston Cup champion, 1999 was passable at best. He hadn't won a title since 1994, falling steadily down the rankings in the years since. He'd captured the 1998 Daytona 500, finally taking the big race on his twentieth try, but it turned out to be his only 1998 victory that year. Beginning the '99 season at age forty-eight, the murmuring about whether time had passed him by grew louder. The lingering ache in his neck, earned from a 1996 crash, grew more acute. The younger guys, ushered in six years earlier by Jeff Gordon, were the story more and more now. And the latest of those turks was Earnhardt's own youngest son, the defending champion in NASCAR's second-tier Busch Series. Maybe Senior would retire, people said, as if doing so would make way symbolically for Dale Jr.

All that talk of him retiring dogged Earnhardt, and that was good; that was healthy. He wanted only to make everybody who no longer believed in his skills to shut the hell up.

On the racetrack, Dale Jr. hung up close to his dad with some ease, stretching toward him and then back with accordion-like swings, depending on the corner or the straightaway.

Waltrip's excitement grew with each lap; you could hear it in his pitch.

"That little scoundrel's pretty good," he said.

Jerry Punch, in the pits, reported that he'd spoken to some Cup drivers watching the race, one of whom said, "It's been overcast all morning but in these last fifteen laps we'll see a son begin to shine."

"Yeah." Waltrip chuckled. "We might see some lightning, too."

Winning at something like this, besting his dad, would take more psychology than horsepower. The cars were set up to be equal, but in terms of mind, behavior, temperament, here on the racetrack, Dale Jr. felt the deficit keenly. To his dad, having Dale Jr. behind him was a *comfort*, not a threat. At least not now. Not with a whole mess of laps to go. Dale Jr. was much too smart to make a real play for the lead yet.

This was a game of bob and weave, and one of poise. Champ Car driver Greg Moore tried and made it past Dale Jr. into second, but Junior snatched it right back with twelve laps to go. Then Jeff Gordon creeped up into third, in the lime green car. That was IROC: The cars were differentiated by their colors. Dale Jarrett's was purple; Indy 500 winner Kenny Brack's was, of all things, rose; Rusty Wallace rode in cream; and Bobby Labonte's was powder blue. Dale Jr.'s car was orange but looked more like a kick-ass red. Dad's Firebird was medium blue, and Dale Jr. was focused on it. But Dale Sr. shifted slightly each lap, changing grooves, playing everyone behind him.

"IROC officials say the track is seventy-three feet wide," Punch announced. "And in the closing laps, Earnhardt makes his car 72½ feet wide."

It's not all Dale Sr., though. It's the two of them working together, the high side, the low side.

Dale Jr. had waited for this moment: the chance to try to beat his dad, yes, but really, he'd waited for all this, for this camaraderie in front of thousands of fans.

Two years earlier, he was twenty-three, running poorly in a handful of Busch races, hoping his dad would give him that full-time Busch shot, and much better equipment, the following season. He was sharing a double-wide trailer on his dad's farm, and he sat on the front porch one afternoon, drinking beer with two of his buddies, when the unmistakable groan of an engine and the thumping of tires on gravel produced his father, slamming the door of his truck, his eyes squinty and mean.

"Why don't you go out and do something productive?" he yelled. No doubt, his old man had been up at the crack of dawn, working. But Dale Jr. felt embarrassment more than bile redden his face.

"What are you doing around here, fuckin' off?" Earnhardt continued.

"He got mad and said that I needed to straighten up, that I was going nowhere," Junior said years later, smiling at the memory. "Just because I was sittin' there."

* * *

He had grown up with this, a slew of expectations, just like any kid, except he didn't always get to hear the list of those standards primarily from the source, firsthand. For years, Junior watched his father from distances, some geographic, some more complicated.

At age five, he'd seen Dale Earnhardt loom large on television, leading the 1979 Daytona 500, the first one ever seen flag-to-flag on television, and he swelled with pride. They'd even referred to the rookie Earnhardt as "that young lion."

"You look at that now and you think, those guys had no clue who they were watching," Junior said years later.

By then, his parents had separated and he and his older sister Kelley were living with their mom, Brenda. When their house burned down a couple of years later, the children moved into their dad's house, watched over by a succession of nannies while Dale and his third wife, Teresa, spent much of their time on the road, through the grueling NASCAR Winston Cup seasons, as he built his reputation and entered his prime. It wasn't a terrible way to be raised but it wasn't consistent.

Through everything, Junior's one steadying influence was Kelley. She was his alarm clock, moral compass, and protector. Early on, he got used to relying on her. When their dad and Teresa wondered what would instill a sense of purpose in Junior, who acted out as a teenager, the scrawny thirteen-year-old was sent to Oak Ridge Military Academy. Kelley, worried about the move, asked to go along with him and watched over him.

Junior wasn't happy, but he later admitted the place made him smarter and stronger and "less likely to get my ass kicked." In the years that followed, while in high school, he started working in one of his dad's auto dealerships, and began to race on local short tracks. He learned the same lessons again and again: No one—especially his dad—was going to give him an easy route, and he was happiest and safest hanging with the people who knew him best. He learned it was very cool to be Dale Earnhardt, and not very cool to be his son, at least in the eyes of some of the people he raced against early on.

He was running Street Stocks in 1992, he drove car No. 8, the number that his grandfather Ralph raced, and the car was beautiful. "I did all the work on it and I was really proud of it," Dale Jr. later remembered, his eyes narrowing. "And this guy said, 'Man, that car looks too good to be out on the race track.' And I thought he was giving me a compliment, and then later on I found out that he'd told a lot of other drivers that he was gonna be the first one to run over it because it was so good lookin' and he was jealous because here was an Earnhardt coming in with a brand-new racecar and he had to drive around in some ragged old heap." The car lasted till the first corner of the first lap before it was wrecked. "I'll never forget it," he said seven years later. "If I ever see that guy again, he's gonna get it."

But by then, Junior had had the last laugh, in a sense. Wins in Street Stock, wins in Late Model—and with Kelley and their brother Kerry on the track as well, family and friends recognizing that there was something raw and wild and different about his style behind the wheel. Waltrip had approached Dale Sr. at one point, asking if he could hire the kid. Rick Hendrick even signed a "contract" with him on a napkin. But Junior started doing this chiefly because of his dad: the gruff man who'd made him go to military academy and tried to get him to make something of his life; the face on television on Sundays, hoisting trophies and earning the love and respect of fans as the Intimidator; the man in black; the NASCAR icon.

"When I first started, it was all for that, no other reason, because I didn't have a lot of confidence in myself to be able to become anything important, and he was huge, you know?" Junior recalled years later. "He had gone to certain lengths to give me good schooling and make sure I had a good upbringing and things like that, so I wanted to become an asset to him one day where he could somehow break even on that deal."

Earnhardt, tentatively, gave his son the ride in the Busch series in 1998, and when Junior won in his seventh race, in Texas, his father greeted him with a wondrous bear hug, a beer shower, and a grin. The scene would be reprised through the season. Junior won seven times that year and hoisted the championship trophy at year's end.

He was headed for another title in 1999. A week before father and son found themselves running one-two at the Michigan IROC race with a few laps to go, Junior had taken over the Busch series lead from his friend Matt Kenseth after a win at Dover.

But the Busch racing was one thing; the pressing question now was, Would he be able to take care of family business in Michigan?

With three laps to go, Waltrip was already calling this, "The best IROC race I've ever seen."

Junior remained in second, keeping all other competitors behind him in some prevent defense, looking for an opening up high. He faked a move with two laps to go, a row of cars trying to tag along behind him.

The white flag flew: one lap to go, with Dale Earnhardt two miles from his third-straight IROC win. Junior was smart enough to know the time had to be now. His dad came off the corner in the exact middle of the racetrack before heading low, with Junior going even lower, and Mark Martin still lower. Junior turned the wheel and climbed high: no chance. Back down on the bottom of the racetrack with half a lap to go, Junior played to his strength one last time, racing high into turn three, his comfort zone, and for the first time, he was moving around his old man, just a tick in front, when they touched, zigzagging together, their Firebirds smacking, the noise rattling with a jolt. Then one more bump, and as if on cue, Dale Sr. veered on down the track, inheriting the momentum off that bump and the angle, with the checkered flag in sight and now *barely* in the lead again, and finding the finish line just in front. His youngest son followed, .007 seconds behind.

"Man oh *man*, Benny!" Waltrip shouted in the booth.

"Wow, what a *finish*," Parsons growled, his voice rough with glee.

It was close but Dale Jr. knew he'd lost, and something static and exhausting filled his chest. On the cool down lap, he came up beside his dad's car, looking into the cab through the passenger door, watching the man ride at 130 miles per hour while calmly taking off his racing gloves and putting them in his helmet before adjusting his goggles. Seeing his son, Earnhardt gave him a rousing thumbs up. Junior smiled back with his own thumb up.

As he was being interviewed in victory lane, Earnhardt motioned Junior over and the two hugged and stood side by side.

"I was hoping he'd stay in line there until at least the last lap," Earnhardt said. "The car was a little tight all day. . . . Dale Jr. was helping all he could, and then he got there and he wanted to race and here he comes and I knew he was working the high line in three and four and figured if he got on the outside of me we could drag race and we did and got a little fender bumping going on and it got exciting," he said, recapping the race just as he'd wanted to see it, the elation clear in his voice.

Then it was Junior's turn. "He knows how to use that air," he said, admiring his dad's ability to work the draft and the wind. "He's pretty good at it. He sucked it off the side of the car and got right back by me."

Junior said he figured his dad would win; he just wanted to make it close. But didn't he think he had a shot?

"No, I was gonna just hang right there with Dad. Once the tires get old you got to draft and help people; I tried to help him, some guy tried to pass me. But we just hung in there."

Junior saw his dad's hand raised high and slapped a high-five. He'd hung in there *this* time. They'd been a team, working well together.

But with one hundred yards to go, Junior had moved ahead by three feet, and that meant something. He could give himself some credit.

"I thought at one time, and this wasn't long ago, that it was gonna take a lot of practice to be able to do this as well as he does but it's not necessarily that way anymore," Junior said a few months after the race.

"If I'm in a competitive car, I can do what I wanna do with it. That's a lot of confidence and that's where most of it is, in confidence. I still hold him at the highest standards that I did before, but now I feel like I'm closer to reaching that goal."

His dad sensed it, even if he wouldn't have put it quite that way. These were, finally, among the better times.

"I'm proud of him, you know?" Earnhardt said of Junior. "Proud of what he can do; I'm just proud of him as a dad. Of course I'm awful proud of him when he wins, but I'm more proud of him being able to take the defeat, because he handles himself well.

"It's hard to top that, I think, in father-son relationships," he added, talking about the IROC race. "To be racing your son on a race-track at the speeds that we were, that's a pretty awesome feeling. I don't think you could top it. . . . I'm proud of all my children and what they've done in life. They're good kids, they work hard. I mean, they're not perfect, they make mistakes, but when they make mistakes they stand in there."

On and off the track, Junior was very much on his father's radar.

"In the past when I spent time with him, there's was rarely a lot of conversation," Junior recalled. "I didn't know what to say to him and I didn't know whether what I had to say was worth a dime to him because I was just a child. But now that I'm more accomplished as a person and a driver, I'm getting all sorts of attention in all areas that I'll say he respects me a lot more, he takes what I have to say into consideration more often and we can relate more than we did in the past. In the past, we had difficult times relating, just like any father and son would."

*   *   *

The expectations were reasonable for 2000, Dale Jr.'s first full-time season in Winston Cup: run consistently; run up front; some wins if possible, of course; Rookie of the Year, naturally; learn a lot about the cars and the tracks; and do your best.

The wins came with startling speed: victory in the year's seventh race, at Texas, and another in the eleventh race, at Richmond. And two weeks later, Junior became the first rookie ever to win the Winston, the annual all-star race, at the circuit's home track in Charlotte. It was at that race, thirteen years earlier, that his father made his famed "pass in the grass" to keep the lead over Bill Elliott before going on to gain the win. And it was where Dale Sr., who'd finished third, now came to pour a Bud over his son's head and celebrate an extraordinary win.

"Winning that Winston was the most fun single moment in my entire life and I've never been prouder of me and my dad for what he did putting this thing together," Junior recalled a few months later.

It would, however, prove to be the last highlight of the year. Two weeks later, Junior finished tenth at the early June race in Dover.

For the rest of the season—twenty-one races—he didn't score a single top-ten finish. He finished the year with only five of them in thirty-four races, and was runner-up to Kenseth for the series's top-rookie honors.

They were, as he put it, "shitty days." They were days that worked his mind much longer than any win ever did. "One day you're, like, 'Man, I'm good, I got this, I can drive, I can take anybody here.' And then the next day you're, like, 'Shit, man, I'm at the bottom—we've got a long way to go to get to where we need to be.'"

It was easy to get enveloped by a season like this, and overfocus on it. There were the attendant pressures on the two-time Busch Series champion and the son of the man that many believed to be the sport's greatest pure racer. It could be maddening, especially when he did not live up to his own expectations.

And it was already hard enough to be a rookie in 2000, a new kid in a year so beaten by tragedy. Adam Petty, son of Kyle and grandson of King Richard, had been killed in a Busch series practice crash at Loudon on May 12, eight days before Junior's win at the Winston. Less than two months later, Cup driver Kenny Irwin—the 1998 Cup Rookie of the Year—was also killed at Loudon.

Junior hadn't really known Irwin well; Adam Petty had been a friend. To know Adam was to understand how good-hearted a person could be. And Adam's extremely close friendship with Kyle—it had to be, if they were traveling this NASCAR road together, instead of Kyle being the team owner and Dad—was hardly lost on Junior.

"Every time I think about it I just go back to, man, it really sucks that a person—Adam personally, yes—but a person like Adam, as good as Adam, is gone," Junior said. "It makes everybody think. I mean they're going through all these ideas with safety changes and I applaud NASCAR. . . . They were going to be crucified if they didn't do anything, so obviously they had to try something.

"It's a turning point. They're at a time now where they can make the decisions that are gonna continue to make the sport better and allow it to continue to grow in popularity, or they're gonna make the decisions that will be the downfall of the sport. It's a very interesting time. I'm glad I'm getting to see it."

In 2000, especially given the season, it became harder for Junior to navigate through changes and pressures. As much as he may have learned from watching his dad on the track, it was Earnhardt Sr.'s ability to balance responsibilities that Junior envied. He didn't need to be more like his dad on the track; he was always going to be his own man that way. But he wanted to be more like Dale Earnhardt, the man who could be stern and unflappable with everything, especially a long set of bad Sundays. Earnhardt had struggled a lot until 1986 or '87, he'd told his son. "Every bad run would really fuck him over and disappoint him," Junior said. But then he had a realization, and it bore out: He was going to win again, and it'd feel like just as good as the first one. It required the same kind of patience as following a guy into a turn, waiting for a route to a pass.

So Junior kept watching this guy, who had once come over to yell at him for drinking and wasting his time. Now instead, he'd roll up with his truck, see his young son drinking with friends, and join them for a beer.

"I had gotten closer to his level, to where it was almost more enjoyable for him to spend time with me, because I had gotten out of that age where I wasn't badgering him with questions and aggravating him every second of the day I was around him," Junior said. "I would just sit there and we would heckle somebody on television or he would joke with one of my buddies about something."

There weren't enough of those times, however; not enough for either of their liking. That's how the season went, from commitment to practice to race.

"The best advice I could give my dad would be, 'You only have so many years of your life where you have your health and you have all the ability to do what you want to do and how you want to do it,'" Junior said late in the 2000 season. "My advice to him would be not to piss that away covered up in business ventures. My advice to him would be to let him be in control of his life instead of life being in control of him. You've gotta try to make the money and not let the money make you."

It didn't erase the fact that there was too much for both of them to do. Now that they wanted to hang together, it was harder to find the time, which was as good an indication as any to Junior that he and his dad had become great friends.

Junior had started doing a column for NASCAR Winston Cup *Scene*, the sport's premier weekly. It was fun, writing a bunch of stuff down and then having Jade Gurss, his main PR guy, smooth out the grammar a bit, a process that was going nicely as the two of them also continued working on a book about the rookie Cup season. Junior had written about his friend Hank Parker Jr. getting married (and himself remaining happily single), military school, even, infamously, his rules for the perfect party.

In October, the season almost over, Dale Jr. sat down one afternoon across from his dad, holding the piece that had come out of him the quickest—537 words, and it had taken him about ten minutes to get it down.

He told his dad he wanted to read the piece to him. Dale Sr. was a private person; anything that would eventually be called "Dale Earnhardt

Through the Eyes of His Son" would require his approval if Junior was going to submit it to *Scene*.

People had always tried to define Earnhardt, and define the steps his relationship with his son had taken. But his dad was greater than everybody made him out to be.

"He'd done so many things that were so awesome and really cool and I couldn't understand where he got his willpower and determination to do right and be right," Junior said months later. Dale Earnhardt was a great driver, but there was so much more: "He was almost like a Caesar, if you will."

So Junior stood up and began reading, describing this man who was stoic in the face of adversity, loyal to his friends, powerful, a fearless man of insight and vision, a general—and now also a teammate. He kept reading, the words poetic and evocative, even as he heard the shifting of his father's chair as he rose up and walked toward him. By the time Junior finished, his father was right in front of his face.

"You know, I know we've told each other we love each other," Dale Sr. said. "And I know you do, but that really, really tells me how you feel about me."

Junior smiled till he chuckled. "I'm *glad* that that really tells you because I've always *wanted* to tell you."

He'd gotten it out but it hadn't been easy for Dale Earnhardt Jr. "I mean you don't want to sit down and get all mushy with your old man," he said.

* * *

The garage had been his dad's idea.

It was in the back, behind Dale Earnhardt Jr.'s house. He hung out there a lot, whenever time allowed, playing around with his buddies.

There was one night, a few of his friends were over, and they were trying to put together shelves for a storage room upstairs. For whatever reason, all they could find were plastic hammers—clearly subpar for the job but good fun nonetheless.

"Three or four of us are trying to hammer this stuff together and it was a mess," Junior said. "And I know that if my dad had walked in, he'd have laughed his ass off."

Junior tried to picture that scene. He'd been doing that a lot: stopping, imagining what Dale Earnhardt would think or say about what he was doing.

All of 2001 had been like that so far, a study in snapshots and blinding flashbulbs, like something otherworldly, and so loud and endless that all you could do was try to set it aside in your head and be quiet with it. Otherwise, you'd go crazy.

The garage behind the house helped. His dad had thought it out with him, figuring out how big it was going to be. He'd had all the plans drawn up. As the time got closer to building it, Junior got more involved in the little decisions. When it was all done, he began filling it up, collecting favorite cars, along with an area to work, lots of tools. And upstairs there was a storage room and an attic: a place for his stuff.

"It's cool to have something fun like that because I feel that's how he started; he started with a shop," Junior said about his dad. "He just kept stuff in it. Then he ran a race team out of it and then he built another shop." Junior paused a moment. "That's the beginning of whatever empire I might have."

* * *

There were other memories, the haunting ones; those were set aside and frozen.

He could picture the puff of smoke in his rearview mirror, the scene of his dad hitting the wall, growing farther away as he kept his line behind Michael Waltrip in the last turn of the last lap of the Daytona 500. And what were they doing, he and his dad . . . they were being teammates, just like that moment in the IROC race two years before in Michigan, only reversed. His dad was keeping everybody else at bay, perhaps getting ready for his own late run at his son, and at Waltrip, the man he'd hired to race for him.

Junior knew his dad's crash was bad. He got to the hospital as fast as he could, not ready to believe what they were going to tell him. And then they did tell him, and he cried, and he thought he would never stop crying, and stopping was the last thing he ever wanted to do.

It would have been one thing if he'd just kept doing that. If he'd been able to stay right there, stuck in that moment, letting it all out. But all too quickly, there was too much to be done.

There was a funeral, and speeches and tributes, all of which exhausted him. People lined up outside Dale Earnhardt, Inc., the company office and shop right near Junior's home, and they stayed and cried and brought flowers and wanted some closure.

Everybody wanted to pay tribute. Dale Earnhardt was on the cover of *Sports Illustrated*, but he also smiled optimistically from newsstands on the cover of *Time* and other magazines.

Honoring gestures continued in the days and weeks after his death. Humpy Wheeler, then the general manager of Lowe's Motor Speedway, and a good friend of Earnhardt's, went to Las Vegas two weeks after Daytona to see Evander Holyfield fight John Ruiz. "And they did a ten-count for Earnhardt," he said. "It's boxing tradition: You ring the bell ten times in silence before the main event starts. It is done very rarely and I've never seen it done before for anyone not associated with boxing. I'd never heard it for another athlete."

Before a room full of reporters, downhill ski champion Picabo Street talked about how she'd named her skis her "Earnies," channeling the strength of Earnhardt, and then she burst into tears.

There were so many things people could say about him; they hurled absolutes. He was an icon; an Everyman. He *was* NASCAR. Wheeler thought of the shrimp boat captains on the Carolina coast. Very few of them, he said, didn't have the "3" decal on their boats. "They identify with him. It's hard work. There's little money. Dale Earnhardt had a difficult time making it and this is one of the greatest identity points with him." He was America's great working-class hero.

Junior couldn't deal in the absolutes. There was controversy, the questions about how his father had died, which would remain unconfirmed for days as doctors were brought in to study speed, trajectory, and angles of the crash. Death threats were delivered to Sterling Marlin, who'd bumped Earnhardt on the last lap; it became Junior's angry responsibility to remind people that such irrational blame "would not be tolerated." And Bill Simpson, whose company had built the seat belt in Earnhardt's car that had ultimately ripped, also got threats—Simpson, Earnhardt's friend, who'd spent his entire career in the pursuit of safety.

There were accusations that the sport hadn't done enough to protect its valued stars, that it had dragged its feet in the months after the deaths of a driver in each of its premier racing series: Kenny Irwin in Cup, Adam Petty in Busch, and Tony Roper in the Truck series.

People were practically lining up, ready to ask Junior questions about all that and more. It was too much, too quick, and impossible to process. Stars had died in the sport but the 2001 Daytona 500 was the first race of NASCAR's brand-new six-year $2.4 billion TV contract, and 32 million people had watched Dale Earnhardt die.

* * *

Fans took the loss as deeply as if he were a cherished member of the family, someone who stopped by for a barbecue every Sunday.

Parting would require a farewell tour, only without the guest of honor.

For Junior, it was a terribly odd paradox. There was no escaping the reminders of his father's life and death. But grieving for him had to be a private matter, and there was no privacy.

A week after Daytona, the Cup tour went to Rockingham, North Carolina. Ordinarily it wouldn't have been a desired stop for Junior anyway; he made no bones about his distaste for the place. "It's undriveable and unmanageable and it eats the tires up like a cheese grater," he said a few months before, toward the end of his rookie season. "It's like, man, what the hell happened to the asphalt that went there? You're damn near running on rocks and shit."

And yet, like everyone else, he'd have to strap in and drive. Going back to racing would be therapy for everyone.

"People didn't understand why I could go back immediately and race," he said. "If I had sat home, there's no telling where I'd be today. I don't think I would have ever gotten back in the car and I probably would have ended up a total failure at anything I tried to do, so I had to get back in the car."

The challenge of getting past the distractions would be great. Almost every driver and crewman wore a cap with a large swirling "3" on it. All sixty thousand fans in the stands had been given a Dale Earnhardt tribute flag, emblazoned with the number 3, and Earnhardt's bold, loping signature. The prerace rain delay was extensive, postponing Junior's inevitable climb into the Bud Chevy. But once he strapped into his car, trying to keep his eyes focused on the road ahead, he caught sight of the prominent Bud decal on his dashboard, which now had a large "3" next to it.

All the reminders were making Junior feel impatient with his own grief. He missed his father; he cried for him. But those were selfish tears, he said. There was work to be done.

At Rockingham, Kevin Harvick was making his first start as Earnhardt's replacement in Richard Childress's driving stable. There would be no No. 3 car; Harvick drove the No. 29 Goodwrench Chevy, but with Earnhardt's crew.

Junior had been one of the first Cup drivers to seek Harvick out, to tell him he appreciated what he was doing, and that he approved of the situation.

"Just go out there and do the best you can," he said, a sentiment that meant the world to Harvick.

* * *

The green flag flew and the cars groaned into quick action, patiently falling into line. The track surface was adequately dried, but in the early going it would be hard to gain a grip on the asphalt.

Half a lap into the race, some cars shook and shuffled a moment, an action that sent a wave on back. Some drivers checked up; others didn't.

Junior did; behind him, Ron Hornaday had no time to react and plowed into the back of the Bud Chevy.

Junior's car jumped forward, making contact with Kenny Wallace to his right. He spun the steering wheel left but the car, unresponsive, slung fast up the track and moved full-tilt into the wall. The impact jackknifed the hood and the Chevy shuffled forward, sluggishly waddling against the wall. The angle of the crash, it would be pointed out again and again, looked eerily similar to that of his dad's the week before.

"Oh no," Darrell Waltrip said from the announcing booth. "This can't be happening to this young man."

Cameras trained on the car and Junior emerged to wild cheers, limping down the high banking, his arm supported by a safety worker who would not let him go.

"Everybody at home, I'm doing all right; no big deal," he said on camera in front of the infield care center. "It's tough; I wanted to do good here, get the year started off right. We'll take it to the garage, see if we can get it back out there."

Rockingham was the first of five races where Junior didn't lead a lap and posted an average finish of twenty-ninth.

The tributes to his dad and questions about his life, legacy, and death continued. Junior's DEI teammate Steve Park won the race at Rockingham, scoring an emotional victory. Two weeks later, Harvick eked out a win by .006 seconds over Jeff Gordon in Atlanta in his third-ever Cup start, and it was hard for anyone to not think Dale Earnhardt wasn't looking down on all the proceedings, week in and week out, with a smile. All that did was make everyone wonder when Dale Jr.'s cleansing score would come.

Fox chairman David Hill had come up with the idea of his announcing crew remaining silent through the third lap of every race that Fox broadcast through the season. The fans did more than that by standing and silently raising three fingers in salute as the Chevys, Pontiacs, Fords, and Dodges made their way around the racetracks.

"I think early on it was obvious that all those tributes and continuing week-in, week-out saga of his father's death were affecting his performance dramatically," said Darrell Waltrip. "Even though he had a smile on his face and a cavalier attitude it was definitely taking its toll and there was no closure and he couldn't get past it. I know that was having an incredible effect on his performance as well as on his own feelings."

"I'm totally worn down now," Junior admitted as the year went on.

He would go without a top-ten finish until the April race at Texas, but that's where he began to put together a nice string, with five top tens in seven races. But just as quickly, engine trouble at Michigan ruined a good day, and that led to subpar results at Pocono and Sonoma. He was tumbling now, better than five hundred points behind Gordon, the series leader.

There'd be a two-week break now, followed by a return to Daytona for the July 7 night race. Junior had always loved Daytona. He wanted very much to be able to love it again.

* * *

The garage behind the house was really where the plan all came together. He was going to take five of his friends with him and get to Daytona a week early. They talked about it, hanging out and figuring it out.

"I wouldn't have done it by myself," Junior said afterward.

It would just be him and his friends, driving all night and getting there days before the race. They'd sneak into town, like they were on some scud mission, driving down 95, then over to Speedway Boulevard, past Ridgewood Avenue, and onto the beach. That way, he could greet the place again on his own terms.

"I thought, we're gonna rent a house; we're gonna party and raise hell," he said.

Junior had been to the Bahamas, he'd been to Jamaica, but the personality of Daytona Beach suited him. Daytona, he told his friends, had a roughness to it; you could fit in there easily. There were no pretensions to it, no judgment—something any number of NASCAR drivers had discovered going back to the days on the beach course. Everybody there was so "whatever the hell."

It didn't take much convincing. To go to Daytona early, hang out, drink, party, that couldn't be too bad a time. Yet nobody kidded themselves, thinking it would be a laugh-a-minute trip.

Maybe the first indication of that came the morning before they were set to leave. Junior called the local Chevy dealer, wanting to get something new for the drive down. They were going five hundred miles, and he hoped to inaugurate a Suburban for the trip. He was impatient from the moment he got on the phone, and the back and forth with personnel didn't help.

"I want a Suburban here by eleven tomorrow morning," he finally said sternly to a manager on the line after identifying himself yet again. "I want twenty-inch rims on it and it better fuckin' be here."

He hung up the phone and looked out at his friends sitting across the room.

"Damn," one of them said. "You just ordered that like a pizza."

"Yeah," Junior said. "You've gotta do business like that every once in awhile."

It would be an emotional day from start to finish. The Suburban showed up and the six of them piled into it and headed over to a local church, where Junior's sister Kelley was marrying NASCAR crew chief Jimmy Elledge. It was odd: He was Kelley's younger brother and she'd always been there to take care of him when they were kids. Now he walked her down the aisle, thinking his dad would be doing this if he could.

"If I ever win a championship; if I do things, I will wish that he could see it," he said later on.

The wedding over, Dale Jr., Kelley, and the family took a bunch of pictures and celebrated. Then Junior and his friends jumped out of their suits in the middle of the parking lot, threw on shorts and T-shirts, and climbed back into the Suburban, which was filled with all their gear, about 450 CDs, and enough food and drink to get things started well.

"I pointed it right at the damn exit of the road, said, 'We're going straight out of here,'" Junior said.

They drove through the night, making their way through the CDs, laughing, singing, carrying on, raising hell.

Dale Jr. would be behind the wheel, watching mile markers fly by. The song shuffling continued; Snoop Dogg was in the changer now, singing one of Junior's favorites, "Lay Low" from *The Last Meal*. Snoop Dogg was like an adrenaline shot. These are songs that you can climb inside of for a few minutes, like the anger of Korn and "Falling Away from Me." Plenty of Korn, and Snoop Dogg, and Matthew Good Band. Then 3 Doors Down and "Be Like That," and some Third Eye Blind singing "Jumper," about a boy dealing with his pain, facing his demons.

The cars on 95 all moved with a quiet, controlled rhythm. The Speedway could be like that: Everybody on the road, trying to stay out of trouble—but then you had to add in the draft, the current of air that carried cars along, one after another, until you broke free of one draft and tried to catch a different one. Junior was good at reading the draft; his dad had been the master. It was always said that Senior could see the air.

* * *

They hung out at the house in Daytona Beach for two days. On Tuesday afternoon they were back in the Suburban, and Junior asked if maybe they'd all like to go and see the Speedway.

There was practically nobody at the Speedway but a few workers and they let him in. His friends were in awe: Nobody could believe how big the place looked, and it seemed all the more huge without cars anywhere.

"It was really open and pretty," Junior said later on. "I showed them where everything happens."

They all stood around, having a great time, joking about getting the Suburban onto the track and seeing how fast they could get it to go if they really opened it up.

"Okay, I'll take you for a lap around the track, but they'll probably run us off," Junior said. "We'll leave as soon as we get back around."

They excitedly piled in and Junior slowly guided them up onto the high banking of the track, taking to the straightaway, up and around, picking up a bit of speed. Then they pulled down to that corner and stopped.

"Man," Junior said. "This is where my dad was killed."

He looked out through the windshield at the scene, pointing at spots to get it clearer in his head. "There's his tire marks, there's where he went up into the wall. He slid down this way; this is where it all happened."

They got out and silently walked up the banking, incredulous at how steep the climb was. Junior kept his eyes locked.

"Standing there just felt like being at his grave site almost," he said afterward. "It was really therapeutic.

"I felt like I was just going to see him, just to say hey, like I would if he were alive. And I was really happy I did that."

His friends had moved off and Junior knelt down and sat on the banking, feeling calmer and more comfortable than he had for a long while.

He looked over at his friends for a second. This wouldn't have been the same without them; it was now enjoyable, and a lot easier.

It was the right thing to do. To come back for the first time later in the week would have sucked, running into the onslaught of media and people. This was a lot better, to be here on an afternoon with clear skies, just like that one five months earlier.

He could have sat there all damn day. He didn't say anything; there was nothing to say, really. He'd said it all that day with his dad, reading him that essay.

After a while he rose up and they slowly piled into the Suburban, and Junior turned down the banking and onto the straightaway, heading back out the entrance to the Speedway, toward the beach house.

Days later, he came to Daytona, this time the most sought-after racecar driver among the throng, with everybody prepared to ask him how it felt to be there.

"I was so ready and so comfortable," he said.

* * *

There came a point, midway through the Pepsi 400 on that July night, when Junior sensed some next gear kick in. He was no longer just confident; he was holding onto the wheel, taking a ride and having fun.

The beach town's smooth night air ran off the nose of his Chevy, with the red and white Major League Baseball All-Star Game paint scheme gleaming under the Speedway lights. He'd had a great car all day: There are those rare days where you can feel your own invincibility.

Dale Jr. had the lead, growing more confident with each lap, and with every attempt that somebody made to pass him. And when he did lose the lead, the speed at which he could regain it eventually stopped surprising him. There was something extraordinary and magnetic about the run. He was exhausting the 165,000 fans that rose and stood and whooped for him resolutely. And in his own mind, with thirty laps to go in the race, the rest of the field might as well have been David to his Goliath.

A place like Daytona, however, has a mind of its own. Restrictor plate races have their back and forth, in the unpredictable draft. And just like that, he'd been shuffled back to seventh place. And after a quick caution, he came out in sixth place with six laps to go.

At Daytona and Talladega, anything was possible, good or bad. You could fall from first to tenth within a single straightaway, just by taking a chance and stepping out of the draft. But Junior's confidence still wouldn't wane.

Over the radio, Junior tried to make a believer out of his crew chief, Tony Eury Sr. "I really think I can pass them," he said, the excitement coming through clearly in the scratchy transmission. Eury, Earnhardt Sr.'s onetime brother-in-law, had circled this July date on the calendar in the days after Earnhardt's funeral, and had watched Junior do all that was needed to win, only to see the timing make that seem less likely now.

"I'm sorry, guys," he added, addressing the whole crew. "If we don't win this race—we should have."

"Just do what you need to do," Eury Sr. told him.

Junior wove back and forth during the caution, staring at the back bumper of Tony Stewart, one of his favorite drafting partners, and then looking beyond at the 31-degree banking. Getting a good run at Daytona on a restart, Junior knew well, was about reflexes, efficiency, and reading the field. And speed helped a lot.

The field was lined up behind leader Johnny Benson, followed by Dave Blaney, two drivers who'd never won a Cup race and could sense their best shot for one right ahead.

"Bottom line," race anchor Allen Bestwick asked over the air, "can Dale Jr. win this race?"

"Yes," announcer Benny Parsons answered before the question was fully out.

Bestwick paused. "You're thinking about it too long," he said.

The pace car swerved off the track and as the green flag waved, Junior kept up with Stewart. In half a lap, he turned high up the track and cranked swiftly past, finding a slot behind Jeremy Mayfield. The cars moved into sleek bullet paths now, wind-aided lines three- or four-wide, everybody searching for an advantage in the tumultuous bumping and banging at 185 miles per hour.

Junior tried to keep on the high side as much as possible, where his Chevy rode best. As it had been all through the night, the car remained fast off the corners, picking up momentum into the straightaways. Within a lap, he'd already wound his way into fourth. In seconds, as head of his pack of cars, he'd inched closer to Blaney, and he quickly passed him on the outside.

Only Benson remained ahead of him now. Junior swung the car like a dart, coursing through the curve into turn four, the spot where he'd sat days before, commiserating with the memories. He tooled his Chevy high around Benson. And when he crossed the start-finish line, there were four laps to go, and Dale Jr. was in front, with the field of cars reeling and scrambling behind him.

Bobby Labonte's frustration flowed; he also had a good enough car to win. He was now on Junior's bumper in the straightaways, but losing ground in the turns.

With two laps left, Labonte still held ground without making a definitive run. Junior would have to prepare for the inevitable slingshot move in the last lap.

Michael Waltrip, however, had other plans.

Moving swiftly and efficiently in his DEI car, he appeared out of nowhere, racing up from fourteenth to third in three laps, and settling in, poised behind Labonte and growing impatient with the passing games.

He dove below Labonte's Pontiac around the fourth turn, and as the cars passed the stand once again, with the white flag waving, it was Junior in front, with Waltrip now second, and Tony Stewart up to third and ready to join the battle.

It was the opposite of the Daytona 500, with Waltrip now drafting in second, keeping all comers off Junior's back bumper. There was nothing to do now but watch.

"Dale Jr., using lessons learned from his father, goes from sixth to first to get the win in the Pepsi 400!" Bestwick called, and Junior's car missiled past the start-finish line, the checkered flag a joyous blur.

"Yes!" Parsons called with unashamed glee. "Yes!"

* * *

His whoop, a "Yeeeaaaaaohww!" reverberated through Junior's cab, and then he was quiet. They shouted at him over the radio, Eury and the crew, but for a moment, he wouldn't say a thing. Then Waltrip's Napa Chevy moved alongside, and Junior pumped his fist at him again and again, the huge smile visible under his open-face helmet. For the moment, everything bad had been wiped away, and he was alone, in the place he loved best.

He slid onto the grass, cutting through the Winston logo as his father had done after winning the 1998 Daytona 500.

Junior climbed out and stood atop his driver's door, his arms raised high, soaking in the cheers of the crowd.

"I don't think there's anybody here who didn't want to see this," Wally Dallenbach said over the air.

Waltrip drove to a spot near Junior and he, too, got up, standing on the hood of his Chevy. It had been nearly five months since he'd won at this place while losing his friend and car owner. He wanted the release of celebration, too.

Junior saw him and rushed over, leaping atop the Napa car, and the drivers embraced, Junior grabbing Waltrip around the head. "This is what it's all about!" they shouted at each other and hugged again. It was the kind of embrace usually reserved for people returning from war.

Junior leapt from the roof into the arms of his crew, mosh pit-style, and then ran back toward his car to drive to victory lane. "Just like your daddy, Dale," someone called as he turned to drive off.

In victory lane, Junior stood atop his car; he cracked open a Budweiser, saluted and toasted the cheering crowd, and drank, before getting handed another can and spraying his Chevy with it. He could now bask in the only thing that mattered in a race: the win, and the sense of his own accomplishment.

But then he jumped off the car and came down to earth. No sooner did his feet touch the ground than he was pulled back into the drama of the moment. Race reporter Bill Weber stood by, waiting with questions.

"I don't know what to say," Junior began, the beer glistening on his chin. "I'm wore out, I can't think." Asked how he got to the front so fast, Junior gleefully said, "I had a great car. It was all car—100 percent. I was just holding on."

"You've learned a few things though, through the years, from certain people," Weber said, the wink playing in his voice.

Junior grew suddenly serious, the weight of the moment finally rising. "Yeah. Yeah. He was with me tonight," he said. "I don't know how I did it. But he was there—and Michael helped me," he added, pumping his fist as if trying to change the subject back to his own glee. "I guess we're even now."

But Weber wasn't done mining the melodrama. "You told Marty Snider, Dale, that you felt lonely on Father's Day," he began, "and that there were times you wanted to cry, but you couldn't. Did you cry tonight?"

Junior breathed heavily at the question, looking suddenly tired. "I'll be crying sooner or later," he said, lightly tapping Weber on the chest. "I don't know; I feel so good right now," he said, his voice pleading. "I'm wore out, too."

"You know when your dad got his first win at Daytona?" asked Weber, who loves few things more than playing with numbers. Junior looked at him: "Nah," he said.

"His first Winston Cup points win came eleven years ago today, July 7, 1990."

"It's special," Junior said. "I dedicate this win to him; I mean there ain't nobody else I could dedicate it to that would mean more to me. And I just wanna say hi to Teresa back home," he added, looking directly at the camera. "I hope she's lovin' this 'cause we sure are."

No one would have expected Teresa to be there at the track. As much as people respected her privacy, there were now too many bad memories. And Junior had nothing but admiration for her.

"She just seems so in control and so focused and she so knows where she wants to go and what she wants to do," he said a month after the race. "She's running the company, no ifs, ands, or buts. A couple of people have stepped up that have really made a difference, without that man around to really make the calls and saying, 'This is how it's done, no questions asked.' People have stepped up and been more affirmative. I'm still just a driver, twenty-six years old, really don't have a lot of business sense, I really don't want to get in there and make any mistakes and no decisions at this time. But she's solid as a rock."

So Junior, the driver, waltzed around victory lane, receiving more hugs and trying to refocus on the glee.

"I'm not ashamed to say I shed a tear," said Benny Parsons after the race was over.

In the corner of victory lane, Junior found the buddies he'd traveled to Daytona with. They joined in one big group clinch, and more beer was poured on Junior's head.

"Maybe," said Allen Bestwick, "this can give fans some closure."

* * *

"What do you think about people saying the race in Daytona was fixed?"

Dale Jr. blinked; for a second, the question didn't even register. When it did, he stared at the sportswriter who'd asked, and everything that had just been fun and light in the conversation got strangely quiet.

"What are you saying?"

And the sportswriter kept talking, saying all these things that were making the heat come into Junior's face. He just wouldn't shut up, and Junior couldn't remember ever getting that angry that fast, until he finally drew his arm back, his fist tight. It took real effort to keep himself from slamming his fist through the guy's face.

It had, until then, been a load of fun: He was in Seattle the Monday after the race, talking to a group of baseball writers before the Major League Baseball All-Star Game. It was less than forty-eight hours since the only moments of pure bliss he'd had in five months. And now someone was trying to ruin it.

Junior hadn't heard anything about the rumors. But the more he listened, and then the more he read about it afterward, the angrier he got.

Jimmy Spencer was the first to say something out loud, standing at the airport after finishing a disappointing nineteenth at Daytona, fanning the fire of what soon became an ugly controversy.

"If anybody didn't see this coming . . ." he began, shaking his head, when asked about the Earnhardt victory. "I knew going in that the No. 8 car was going to win this race. I mean, you know, it's not ironic the No. 8 car would win at all."

Johnny Benson, who fell from first to fourteenth in those last few laps, appeared to concur. "You don't go by yourself on the outside and make that kind of time up," he reportedly told the press, referring to Dale Jr.'s swift passage at the race's end. "But it's okay. It was good that Junior won."

An Associated Press writer offered speculation that NASCAR might have pulled a fast one with the rules in order to engineer the feel-good story of the season. *The New York Times* also suggested this, with a little nudge and a wink. And at least half a dozen columnists entertained the notion, with fan comments flying all over the Web.

Junior was apoplectic. What did he have to do to prove that he had the best car on the track? Who would write or ask such things?

On Thursday afternoon, he sat at a table in the media center at the brand-new Chicagoland Speedway in Joliet, Illinois, which was about to host its first Cup race. His hands were crossed on the table, his body thrust forward.

"Why would NASCAR do that?" he argued, looking at the stoic faces in the packed media center, with all eyes on him. "They have so much to lose and so little to gain by doing that. They're now just getting into the markets and areas they want to, so why take a chance and risk it all? Why would they want to do that?"

He could hardly contain his bile. He'd spent the season being respectful and what had that gotten him?

"I feel like everybody that I talk to about the race, that I've got to prove to them it's real," he said. "That's just a shame. I shouldn't have to do that. It was a great moment in NASCAR history, and it's been kicked in the balls, pretty much.

"Aside from the wins I had when my father was there, that's the day that I'll always remember and for someone to question its credibility, to question my credibility, I think that's a slap in my face, a slap in my father's face, a slap in Tony Eury's face," he said. "Those guys busted their ass to build a great racecar. . . . I've never driven any harder in my life.

"I learned a lot from my dad," he said a few minutes later about racing at Daytona and Talladega. "Learning how to run up front, learning how to read the air on the cars and get by people by yourself without help. In those races with him I'd always kinda get toward the front and it was always him that was pulling a trick on me that made me fall back. I felt confident because I saw him do things and knew why he did them. I could understand it easily. . . . Without him in that fray this past weekend, I felt invincible, unbeatable. I had everything that he had, knowledge, determination, confidence. I had it all, I felt like I couldn't be touched."

"I haven't even talked to Teresa yet," he said, referring to the win at Daytona, now almost five days past. "Haven't had the chance to get her feelings on it. And now this shit is what we're probably gonna end up talking about."

At the track, during practice sessions, Benson sought out Junior and swiftly apologized, saying his comments had been taken out of context. That seemed reasonable enough. Spencer apologized as well, but there hadn't been much context to take his comments out of.

"Johnny Benson came up to me, and he was really upset," Earnhardt said. "Spencer pretty much blatantly said what he said."

NASCAR issued a statement condemning the comments. And Junior was buoyed by a lot of his fellow drivers. But he'd already spent the season needing to get used to a lot of crazy questions. The notion of a fix was an insult added to the injury.

"For two weeks after the race, I was ashamed of everybody," he said later. "As bad as things can get sometimes, when something good happens, you can't let it be what it is. You've got to pick it apart. I was ashamed of everybody, felt bad for them.

"You have things that happen over centuries, good and bad, people are assassinated, then somebody comes along and prevails, an unlikely hero. I couldn't believe it—that might be the greatest I will ever be, so let it be what it is," he said. "That might be my moment. And it's a great thing."

The season continued on respectfully, with bursts of greatness. The first Cup event after the tragedy of September 11 was the September 23 race at Dover, and it was Dale Jr. who, before heading to victory lane, was handed an American flag, which he carried out his driver's window, slowly heading counter-clockwise on the track, mimicking champion racer Alan Kulwicki's famed Polish Victory Lap. A month later, he won again, taking the checkered flag at Talladega.

Slowly, he began to come around; at least that's the way it looked. "I've seen him come back and turn back into the cute little personality he has and [he's] got a little pep in his step. He's running better and I see him on the road to recovery," Darrell Waltrip said as the season wore on.

Junior couldn't be too sure of anything, other than the quiet refuge of the racecar. It was hardest sometimes when fans sought him out. One fan at an event told Junior about losing his father ten years earlier; he was shocked and frightened to see the man begin to cry while relating the story.

"I thought that maybe a year or two from now, that I would be totally all right, but ten years from now, will there be a moment where I go, man, I can't handle it, and then have a ten-minute fit and then be fine?" Junior said afterward. "I don't want to be like that but I'm afraid that that's what's happening because I've dealt with it but *not* dealt with it. It's almost like, to get over it, I don't know what you have to do. I don't know what you have to do to get over something like that. Whatever it is, I'm not doing it."

Jeff Gordon won his fourth championship in 2001. Junior finished the season in eighth place. He couldn't wait to put the season away. Just getting through it had been his most impressive triumph.

"I feel like I'm doing good by my dad," Junior said toward the end of the season. "It's like a father would send his son off to school and let it be his decision to either fuck off and party and not do anything, or maybe do a little bit of partying but make good grades and succeed and bring home the degree or whatever it may be, and I felt like if I got back in that car he'd be proud of that. And winning that [Daytona] race, I know that he would have been proud of that.

"There are all kinds of things we've done where I knew he would smile. That's been behind the direction of everything we've done. It is kinda cool to hear people's opinions on it. When somebody says, 'Man, what you're doing's great,' it's just as if my dad said that to me."

In 2004, Dale Earnhardt Jr. was on top of the world; he earned a career-best six series wins, including the Daytona 500 and the night race at Bristol.

Chapter Eight
Father's Day

June 15, 2008

"[My dad] lost his dad when he was twenty-two or so, and he adapted to being his own man and he went out and did things for himself. It took him quite a while really to get going, but he did. That's been a thing to me to say, it's okay, you're gonna be fine."

—DALE EARNHARDT JR.

DALE EARNHARDT JR. PULLED OFF HIS HELMET AND HUNG HIS HEAD loosely down, carrying, it seemed, a large weight on his shoulders, and he painfully tried to take deep gulps of breath that weren't entirely there. Everything moved slowly, as if he were in some dream, though nothing blocked out the pain. Coming upon his car, you'd think he had been fitfully dozing.

After contact with Kevin Harvick, coming off the turn on a brilliantly sunny late-April day at Fontana's California Speedway, Junior had smacked the wall with a severe diagonal, backward impact on the driver's side. Even though he was wearing a HANS device, the wreck sent the force of a pile driver against his chest and his head. Safety workers got there quickly, and Junior snapped up his head and rubbed his face exhaustedly. They reached in and pulled him out, and as he stood on solid ground, he grimaced and bent at the waist. But the safety workers pulled him toward the ambulance, and he almost trotted, trying to get away from them. After he bent over again, they pushed him through the open ambulance door.

"That doesn't look too good," said a worried Darrell Waltrip, eyeing the wreck from the Fox booth.

It wasn't. NASCAR was two months into the 2002 season. Everything seemed cleared for a good, solid championship run, but the vicious hit at Fontana had given Junior a concussion. For a couple of weeks, the symptoms were unstoppable. "You just felt like the room was spinning, like you couldn't keep your eyes focused because everything was moving," he said. "Your equilibrium was a bit off so when you lay down, you'd get lightheaded when you sat back up."

The problems, he said, never occurred in the car, so he got back in it; but he lost some of his ferocity, and it showed. The season to that point had been going very well. He arrived at Fontana in fifth place in the standings, but his average finish for the four weeks that followed was thirty-fourth, and it effectively ended his chance to be a late-season threat.

"I'm sure I couldn't drive as hard and as fast as I wanted to," he said afterward. "But even at 80 percent I still felt like I was as good as half the field."

Being better than half the field wasn't going to win him championships, and he knew that. Driving hurt had been a function of Junior seeing the need—both for Dale Earnhardt, Inc. and in himself—to take more things on. He would have to be the torchbearer for DEI.

"The year wasn't so much a crossroads as a good lesson in how serious you've got to be about this deal," he said as he sat at home after the season, where he'd finished a disappointing eleventh in the standings, not long after his twenty-eighth birthday. "We can race and do everything in kind of a nonchalant manner like we have in the past and have ups and downs, or we can buckle down and really try to get what we want to get."

He'd always felt tremendous respect walking into the DEI complex in Mooresville, North Carolina. Dale Earnhardt had proudly called the place the "Garage Mahal." But without his dad there—and with Teresa Earnhardt seemingly devoting a great deal more time and effort into protecting the legacy of her husband's name than supporting the current race teams—DEI was anchored in the past.

It was hard for Junior to look around DEI and not see every little thing that Dale Earnhardt would have done to make things better. And it was hard not to be frustrated by that. As good as management was at DEI, without Dale Earnhardt's insistence and vision the view wasn't going to change significantly.

He'd respected Teresa's public reserve, but he had already begun to question her lack of desire to shore up whatever support was necessary to win races and titles. And worse, he continued to get a whiff of a lack of respect on her part. Judging his immaturity when he was a twelve-year-old was one thing. But Junior now bristled at his stepmother's frequent unresponsiveness.

Dealing with contracts had never been part of Junior's DNA. His agreement with DEI was always good on a handshake, but the handshake had been with his dad. It was time to renew it at the end of the 2002 season and he wanted things in writing.

Kelley Earnhardt inherited her father's business acumen and had gotten her business degree at University of North Carolina at Charlotte. She wasn't prepared now to let her brother sign anything without her help, especially at the company that bore their father's name. It's what their dad would have expected.

Negotiations should not have been difficult but they turned out to be that. "We were basically in two separate offices, sending carriers back and forth, passing revised copies over and over," Junior said of his "discussions" with Teresa. "Eventually it was a stalemate."

To Dale Jr. it was more than that. "In my opinion," he said, "the importance [of my contract] was lost over at DEI compared to some other things."

Junior, who'd always had a good relationship with the press, decided to bring up how much he enjoyed racing Busch cars the season before for his father's close friend and longtime car owner Richard Childress. Suddenly, contract negotiations with DEI moved to the front burner, even though they made things frostier in the boardroom.

His father had built DEI thinking that someday Junior would have a larger stake in the place. But the idea that he might one day drive for another team, once considered unthinkable, had been forced into Junior's head.

"I will always wonder what that would be like, the responsibilities and drawbacks to that, and if I can give another team the results they need," he said with a smile, after signing his five-year deal with DEI at the end of 2002. "When things get low, you question if you're where you need to be. But the wins and the championships are sweeter where I'm at, with the people I grew up with."

*   *   *

With fourteen laps to go in the 2004 Daytona 500, Dale Jr. was out in front, having taken the lead from Tony Stewart four laps earlier. Several lapped cars were in front of him, and getting around them could be dicey, unless they gave up the bottom lane that Junior thrived on.

"Keep talkin'," Junior called on his radio to Stevie Reeves, his new spotter; Junior needed the constant chatter, the updates, the countdown of laps. It made him more attuned. At Daytona, the cars were packed incredibly tight, as if running together on a string at close to two hundred miles per hour. It had taken his dad twenty years to win his only Daytona 500, which he'd done exactly six years earlier. Junior was trying to do it on his fifth attempt.

Dale Jr.'s car to seemed to be the class of the field for most of the day; passing Stewart appeared so simple that, as Stewart later put it, Junior could have done it anytime he'd wanted to.

Junior kept watching Stewart and Kurt Busch, seeing their movements and mirroring them from in front, and the throng of 176,000 remained on their feet as the laps counted down. After an extraordinary, satisfying run, Junior crossed the start-finish line in front, steered back to it, and jumped off the door of his car and into the arms of his jubilant crew.

In victory lane, Junior received a happy, respectful hug from Teresa as the beer flowed.

Bill Weber was there to interview him, waiting to once again play "this date in NASCAR history." "Your dad won this race six years ago . . . today," he said, pausing dramatically.

Junior smiled broadly. "He was over in the passenger side with me," he said. "I'm sure he was havin' a blast."

This win in the sport's first race of the 2004 season felt like a continuation of a solid 2003, the first year of his renewed contract with DEI. Junior had won twice and ended up third in the standings in '03, his highest-ever Cup finish. Further into 2004, wins came at Atlanta in March and Richmond in May, along with twelve top tens in the first half of the season.

In 2004, the sport had changed in incredible ways. Nextel had replaced Winston as title sponsor of the Cup series, and NASCAR, in order to better compete with the NFL for ratings, inaugurated the ten-race Chase for the Championship playoff-type format: Only the top ten drivers after the twenty-sixth race could qualify to win the Nextel Cup title.

That added to the typically outsized expectations at DEI. Dale Earnhardt had been, in his son's words, "a tough-love kinda guy," and Junior's crew chief, his uncle Tony Eury Sr., was "the same way, demanding you to be on top of your game all the time." Junior had blossomed under Eury Sr.'s tutelage, and Eury's son Tony Jr.—Dale Jr.'s cousin—was the team's car chief, and all but ready to one day step into his father's role.

But along with victories in 2004, any gaffes in the No. 8 became harder to shake off. Disappointments worked their way deeper into the team fabric than the wins. The closeness of working with family, while a comfort, also had its challenges. Frustrations were too easily magnified.

"It's like a virus; when one guy's in a bad mood it can really dampen the whole spirit of the team," Junior said. "Me and my crew chief have the biggest effect on that. When things are bad you have to keep your attitude good and not dwell on the bad. There's already so much pressure on everybody to begin with."

The fissures ran deepest between Junior and his cousin Tony Eury Jr. They had played together as kids, with both of them chasing racing dreams. They were tight but they were also competitive.

"Tony Jr., in his life, no matter what he gets himself involved in, he always comes out on the good end of the stick," Dale Jr. said. "A lot of times, even as kids, we'd wheel and deal with each other over a couple of RC cars, by the end of the deal I'd look over and say, damn, he got all the good shit out of the deal. In the end, he was always able to have the last laugh. If you go fishing with him, you might catch more fish but he's gonna catch the real big motherfucker at the end of the day, always."

Tony Jr. eventually traded driving for the life that would lead him to the top of the pit box. The two cousins now both wanted to make the No. 8 car faster. When that didn't happen, Junior could be vastly, unapologetically bitter, especially during a race. By his own admission, that attitude could be destructive. Every criticism stung his cousin and kept them mired in a vicious circle. It would continue to be a challenge throughout 2004, with the Chase coming, and team exhaustion a real factor.

"I had no regard for how he felt about what I had to say," Junior said of Tony Jr. "And if he didn't like what I had to say, he could shove it up his ass. If I didn't like the car, if I thought the car was shitty, I'd say the car is shitty, and I was just really childish. And I think the way I acted rubbed off on him, made him childish. I think I set a bad example for him. And a lot of times, in your tone, if you get bent out of shape and cuss the car and get down, people wonder if your head's in the game."

* * *

Seeking some relaxation during a July 2004 off-weekend, Junior went to Sonoma to race his favorite car, a Corvette, in an American Le Mans Series Grand Prix race. He could enjoy doing what he loved without the klieg lights of NASCAR fully aimed at him. Plus, he'd be on a team with Boris Said, the renowned road-racing specialist whom Dale Earnhardt had once brought in, years before, to teach Junior the ins and outs of road courses.

A practice session had just begun and Junior was weaving around on the track, picking up speed, when he accidentally spun out and slammed the back of his C5-R into a concrete barrier with such force that it left him momentarily dazed. The wreck ruptured the fuel line leading to the nearly full tank, and fuel poured out the rear of the car. It quickly vaporized and, shockingly, ignited.

Junior sat in his car, trying to regain himself when the explosion in the tank rocked him. He looked around, startled: The cab of his Corvette was filled with fire, the flames everywhere, all around his helmet, his arms, playing against his shoulders. Even with all his protective gear on, he felt an achy twist in one of his knees and an angry, slicing pain against his neck.

Before the crash, sensors showed the heat inside the car registered at 115 degrees. In a second and a half, that number rocketed to 750 degrees. Then the sensors burned out completely.

Junior, already dazed, looked around him, left and right, instinctively falling into whatever process might get him out of the car. He was in shock, and yet as he unbuckled his seat belt and pulled himself out the driver's side window, he sensed he was being compelled toward safety, and he made it through the window and tumbled to the ground in a heap.

Medics carted him to the infield care center, preparing to airlift him by helicopter to a local hospital. Junior called out to one of his PR directors, grabbing him by the collar, feverishly asking to find the guy who had pulled him to safety from the car.

"Nobody helped you out," he said.

Junior sustained second-degree burns on his neck, chin, and legs. He would start the next two Cup races, but he was replaced in each, first by DEI Busch driver Martin Truex Jr. and the next week by John Andretti. They scored finishes of thirty-first and twenty-fifth, respectively.

On a *60 Minutes* profile, Mike Wallace later asked Junior if he'd felt his dad was watching over him the day he got his burns.

"He would have to be," Junior said, with a slightly spooked smile. "I don't want to put some weird psycho twist on it, like he was pulling me out or anything, but he had a lot to do with me getting out of that car. From the movement I made to unbuckle my belt, to laying on the stretcher, I have no idea how I got out."

Two months after his fiery wreck, the Cup field was reset for the Chase, with Junior in third place, ten points behind series leader Jeff

Gordon. After finishing third the following week at Loudon, he and Kurt Busch—who'd vaulted up from seventh place after winning the race—shared the series lead.

Junior held it outright three weeks later after gaining his fifth Cup win at Talladega. But when asked in victory lane about his historic success at the track, Junior without thinking replied, on national television, "It don't mean shit right now; Daddy's won here ten times."

NASCAR fined Junior $10,000—and, more important, docked him twenty-five precious championship points. Instead of being ahead of Busch by thirteen points after Talladega, he now trailed him by twelve.

Busch would continue to be just slightly better than Junior and Gordon, holding a small edge as the races wound down. And then Jimmie Johnson, who appeared to be out of the running for the title after poor finishes at Talladega and the next week at Kansas, went on a tear, beginning with a win at Charlotte. There were now five races to go.

Junior never found the handle the following Sunday at Martinsville, dealing with a too-tight car, bumping into competitors, and spinning out Carl Edwards and Dale Jarrett on separate occasions. He finally took his beaten-up Chevrolet back to the garage with fifty-one laps to go, and would post a thirty-third-place finish. Jimmie Johnson came home in front.

But Johnson and the rest of the field would find out after the race was over that a small plane chartered by Hendrick Motorsports—team owner for both Johnson and Gordon—had crashed that morning in the Blue Ridge Mountains near Martinsville. All ten passengers aboard had died. They included Rick Hendrick's son Ricky, Rick's brother John, and John's twin daughters Kimberly and Jennifer.

Ricky and Junior had long been friends. Ricky had tried his hand at racing but had always seemed destined to follow his adoring dad into the business side of Hendrick Motorsports. And Junior had always been aware of how much respect his own father had had for Rick Hendrick personally and professionally. Junior's grandfather Robert Gee had helped Hendrick get into racing in the first place, and Dale Earnhardt had driven Hendrick's first-ever Busch car. And perhaps most poignantly,

Hendrick had gotten Junior to "sign a contract" to drive racecars for him when the boy was fifteen. The contract was symbolic, written on a napkin, and Junior wasn't even a driver yet, but the gesture always stuck with both men, and their families.

After his poor showing at Martinsville, Junior now stood in third place, 124 points behind Kurt Busch with four races to run. Two weeks later, he came to Atlanta with a chance to make up some ground. But he got too eager late in the race and, while running a solid fourth, he wrecked in an attempt to pass Carl Edwards. Inconsistent finishes the rest of the way dropped Junior to fifth in the season's final standings. Busch eked out a title, beating the surging Johnson by only eight points. Junior, despite a series-high six victories, ended up 138 points behind.

As good as the No. 8 team was, its members couldn't fight the sense that they had let a great opportunity slide by. By now, Junior and his cousin Tony Jr. were openly hostile, and while the divisiveness sometimes pumped both men up, it more often had the opposite effect. If the wins would be "sweeter with the people I grew up with," as Junior once said, the losses could be twice as devastating.

* * *

The two cousins stood on opposite sides of the DEI auditorium, separated by the swarm of reporters, each among the members of his own new team. It still seemed unreal to the hundreds of people in the room: Tony Eury Sr. had been promoted to a car team management position within the company, and his son Tony Jr. was now set to be crew chief for Michael Waltrip's No. 15 car. Waltrip's crew chief at the end of the year before, Pete Rondeau, would take over Junior's No. 8. For the first time since he'd been in NASCAR, Dale Earnhardt Jr. would be working without the voice of a family member in his ears on race days.

The cousins had long been heading to this split; when Tony Jr. wouldn't even speak to Junior during practice sessions for the 2004 season finale in Homestead, matters had gone past the point of logic.

"This wasn't about trying to be more successful or winning more races or being a champion. I didn't want to get to the point to where I couldn't stand my cousin anymore," Junior explained months after the switch.

But the move was an indication of a still greater internal struggle at DEI. Junior's relationship with Teresa continued to atrophy, each believing that the other was somehow responsible for a lack of fresh championship hardware at DEI.

"Teresa is the final decision on everything that goes on here," Junior said of DEI management. "I fill the role as it becomes available. Some of it has fallen to me. In the situation with me and Tony Jr. it was hard for both of us to grow up so now we're in a situation where I've got to be my own man. I don't have a cousin to bark at. I think we all kinda held each other back."

The line on Junior's first eleven races of 2005 was certainly passable: five top-ten finishes, and eleventh place in the Cup standings. But for a team that had topped the standings for several weeks the season before, talk of underperformance became commonplace, especially given that in those eleven races, Junior led all of five laps.

What was worse, Junior was not gelling with Rondeau. As fiery as Tony Jr. could be, at least there was constant chatter and decisive action. Junior wasn't getting enough of that with his new crew chief.

At Lowe's Motor Speedway in the days before the May Charlotte race, Junior announced that Rondeau would be replaced as crew chief by Steve Hmiel. A DEI stalwart, Hmiel had been crew chief for Richard Petty and Mark Martin during his career.

It was with Hmiel that Junior won his only race of 2005, the July 10 USG Sheetrock 400 in Chicago. The team's results were hardly stellar, however, and Junior failed to qualify for the Chase. But Hmiel had made him more comfortable instantly.

"It was a huge learning experience for me because he gave me a lot of 'Atta boy' and 'You did good,' 'Good job,' when I did not hear that in the past," Junior said. "That sort of reinspired me as a driver."

For Tony Jr., success on the track—with Waltrip—had also been elusive. Nothing seemed to be feeling entirely right, and the separation through the season made both cousins reassess. Late in the 2005 season, they met to talk it all out. With Junior out of the Chase field, his hope was to use the last ten races of the year to get his team better set up for 2006. Junior asked Tony Jr. if he would want to work with him ever again—not just in 2006 perhaps, but anytime at all.

"Yep," his cousin said.

"When would you want to do that?" Junior asked. "We could do it next year if you want to."

And Tony Jr. smiled. "Sounds good to me."

The main stumbling block between them had been one of respect: With all the tirades back and forth, neither man really understood how he stood in the other's estimation. But that meeting—"a defining moment if there was one," Junior later said—helped a great deal.

"We both realized that each one is equally talented," Junior said. "I think we both had a more mature respect for each other's abilities."

Yet another switch was made, and Tony Jr., it was announced, became Dale Jr.'s crew chief for the 2005 season's final races, and presumably beyond.

"When I came back to [Tony] Junior, I was *confident*," he said.

Given the tumult, it was no wonder that Junior finished the 2005 season dismally, in nineteenth place, but he still earned his third-straight Most Popular Driver award. Most important, the air had been cleared.

"We really get along great and really care about each other away from the race track," Junior said of Tony Jr. before the start of the 2006 season. "You know, it's just family."

* * *

It was going to be fun in 2006. They had earned that at DEI, Dale Jr., Tony Jr. and the No. 8 crew. There were still going to be shouting sessions in the garage and over the radio, but they'd have more humor, and more respect.

Things were working out well, as if moving according to divine plan. Junior had, after all, made a deal.

"Every once in awhile, if I really get in a *bind*, I'll say a prayer or something like that," he said not long into the season. "And I told the Lord that I would trade in all my plate success for consistency everywhere else. I was, like, I don't care about plate races no fuckin' *more*, if I can just be consistent everywhere else, I'll give it away. And we did." He laughed a moment. "That's what it's gonna take to win a championship. If I got nowhere else to turn, I'll ask God to help me out. He's sorta like the last resort."

Whatever the formula, it was working in 2006. There were ups and downs but Junior was solid enough going into the deciding race at Richmond, and qualified sixth for the Chase.

Junior was anything but intimidated, but it was hard not to be realistic. The championship favorites were drivers on more powerhouse teams. DEI had been regarded as very much a player on the circuit, but they could not be called top-tier, and Junior knew it. In 2006, going into the Chase, the series' top-five was dominated by three organizations—Hendrick Motorsports, Roush Racing, and Joe Gibbs Racing. Together, those three groups had produced nine of the previous ten Cup title winners.

Part of what felt so good about winning Cup races with the No. 8 team was that they were doing things their way. His father had built DEI to be a player, but with his death, the company had fallen further behind the sports' true powerhouse teams.

"Our best shot at a championship obviously was '04. We were *right there*," he recalled before the 2006 Chase began. "We know we're capable. I have a way better team today than we did then, my cars are better, what Tony Jr. knows about how to set my car up is better. But we're not as strong as the 48 [of Jimmie Johnson]. We're not as consistent as a lot of the Roush cars; we're not. That's obvious to me; I'm not a fool. But you know, we're right on the verge of being there and who knows, what we're doing now, winning a race here and there, sorta periodically, but being consistent all the time, maybe that'll be enough. Maybe those guys'll get in those ten races and start running into each other."

His run in the 2006 Chase was solid but unspectacular, and it included five top-ten finishes. But his highest race finish among those ten contests was a third at Atlanta. Johnson went on to win his first Cup title—another for Hendrick Motorsports. Junior finished the season in fifth place, nearly 150 points behind.

It was this annual reality—being good but coming up short—that Kelley Earnhardt Elledge brought to the conference table at DEI. She and Junior had begun negotiations for a new contract several months earlier. As distracting as it may have been to become involved with terms during a competitive season, 2006 turned out to be the perfect year to showcase Junior and Kelley's point.

"My cars are good, my people are good, all that shit's all there, we're great here, we've got the unit, but that don't mean they're always going in the right direction," he said toward the end of 2006.

The right direction, the siblings, decided, involved the two of them having more say, especially in terms of the competition aspects of DEI. Kelley was thirty-four years old; her brother turned thirty-two at the end of the 2006 season. They were ready to do what they felt was best for themselves and their father's legacy: gain a controlling interest in Dale Earnhardt, Inc.

The outside racing organization that Junior had started, JR Motorsports, was young and thriving; he'd seen good results with his teams in the USAR Hooters ProCup Series, and regarded any failures and lack of sufficient effort from his Busch series drivers with a degree of intolerant anger that would have made his father proud. Junior and Kelley's mother, Brenda, now also worked for JR Motorsports, where his one-time crew chief Tony Eury Sr. had moved over to become car chief.

Beyond key personnel, JR Motorsports had some of the more modern equipment that DEI teams lacked, to the point where JR provided some of those resources. It seemed counterproductive.

"I want consistency and stability, and every time we fix one problem we uncover another one," he said of the company. "DEI is like this big-ass dam and there's all these guys standing there with their fingers in these holes and every time you plug one, you're taking your finger out of another one; it's frustrating. Dad's death brought a lot of spirit and emotion, and it made us all wanna work really hard and that got us so far. The funny thing about DEI is when they get it all figured out, it's un-fuckin'-beatable. When every cylinder is firing, they're bad-ass. I know; I've won races with them. It's just hard to get all those cylinders firing sometimes."

Teresa grew indignant with her stepson's implied criticisms. During the off-season, she wondered aloud if perhaps Junior might have better success if he'd spent less time enjoying the limelight of his popularity. An angry Junior said of his relationship with Teresa, "It ain't no bed of roses." And while Kelley continued to discuss terms, the relationship between driver and car owner remained a stumbling block.

The 2007 season hadn't even begun and the distractions were already piled high. Junior went public with his and Kelley's desire for majority interest in early February, and the war of words got even more complicated. When Childress racer Kevin Harvick was asked whether he'd like Junior for a teammate, he replied, "I'd jump up and down. I think it's hard when you have a deadbeat owner that doesn't come to the racetrack. You always see Rick Hendrick, you always see Richard Childress, all these other guys, they all come to the racetrack. It's not just a money pit that somebody says, 'Well, I can make money off Dale Jr., I can make money off Dale Earnhardt.' You have to play the politics of the sport and you have to be part of your team and understand what's going on."

Such comments put Junior in the strange position of having to defend his stepmother. But Harvick and fellow drivers such as Jeff Gordon were, in their own way, trying to have his back. The struggle for DEI would require a lot of fortitude.

In January, Junior and Kelley were in Max Siegel's DEI office, going over the terms of one contract proposal of many. Siegel had been brought into the company to head up DEI's global operations; having him there improved the conduit of negotiations, and Siegel considered signing Junior to be his most important task.

Teresa was also in the room, and the four of them talked through numbers and negotiating points. But nothing about the way Teresa spoke to Junior made him feel anything significant would be changing. He left the table that day, once again, with nothing resolved, except perhaps having reached the conclusion that it didn't make much sense for him to be speaking to his stepmother anymore.

* * *

Negotiations continued in 2007, into yet another distracting season. Siegel helped, but the gulf between the two sides was too broad. For Junior, a decision to leave DEI—once considered unthinkable—would be incredibly sad. And yet he appeared to be heading incontrovertibly in that direction, as much as everyone who knew him in the sport hoped it wouldn't be the case.

"To say he's beleaguered would be an understatement," said Humpy Wheeler, then the general manager of Lowe's Motor Speedway. "When you get right down to it, it really hasn't been that long since his father died and then after his father died, I know he wanted to stay there because that place was his dad's dream."

By May 10, 2007, Junior had been living with the idea of departure hanging over him for a year. The stalemate had affected two seasons and it was time for it all to end. There was only one way for him to take control of his own racing destiny and that was to force the issue.

"After a year of intense negotiations and intense effort on behalf of Dale Earnhardt, Inc., and JR Motorsports, we've decided it is time for us to move on and seek other opportunities to drive for a new team in 2008," he told the assembled media and members of his family. "We've both worked extremely hard to find a common ground, but as the negotiations continued, one thing became evident: We both want to get to the same place, but we both simply have different visions on how to get there. . . . At thirty-two years of age, the same age as my father was when he made his final and most important career decision, it is time for me to compete on a consistent basis. . . . It is time for me to continue [my father's] legacy the only way I know I can—by taking the life lessons he taught me, be a man, race hard, and contend for championships. Since that is what I plan to do, I feel strongly that I would have my father's blessing."

Part of that sense of having his father's approval came, Junior believed, from the symbolic link in their ages: His dad signed up with his good friend Richard Childress in 1984, and for the rest of his life, driver and owner enjoyed incredible success. It was now his time.

"Dale loved Dale Jr. and he built that company for him and Dale Jr. to enjoy together," said Darrell Waltrip after the announcement. "But knowing Dale the way I did, if that company was in the same condition today—if Dale were there and that company didn't have all the things Dale Jr. thought it oughta have in place to be a winner—Dale Sr. would tell Junior, 'You've got to go find another ride. If we can't provide you with what it takes to build championships and races, if you don't have the confidence in us to do that, than you've got to go find another ride.'"

He and Kelley would now spend time talking to all interested parties. But there were three organizations chiefly in the running: the formidable Chevy teams of Hendrick Motorsports, Richard Childress Racing, and Joe Gibbs Racing.

There were advantages to each of the three. Psychologically, the connection was strong at Childress, where Dale Sr. had achieved so much success, and where Richard would no doubt be willing to resurrect the No. 3 car if Junior wished him to.

But in many ways, the connection was strongest at Hendrick. In a sense, Junior had already "signed a contract" with Rick Hendrick on a napkin while still a teenager. His maternal grandfather, Robert Gee, had been instrumental in helping Hendrick get into the sport in the first place; and Dale Sr. had driven Busch races for him.

Even before Junior announced he was leaving DEI, he sought advice from Hendrick, who eagerly and objectively guided both Junior and Kelley whenever possible. The talk had brought Hendrick some hope that perhaps one day they would work together.

And then there were the memories of Ricky Hendrick who, with a perennial smile, always told his dad that Junior would one day end up at the company.

The move wasn't going to be about money; Junior was going to get similar, significant deals wherever he went, deals that paid him respect. The important questions were: Which place would give him the best stop to contend for championships, and which place would make him feel most comfortable?

He was, in a sense, looking for someone to do all the things that his dad would have done had he still been there.

"I think Dale Jr. misses his dad and he misses him not just as a father figure but as someone who would keep him on track," said Waltrip at the time. "I think Dale Jr. would really thrive under the leadership of someone who would put their arm around him and say, 'Dale Jr., you're the best, you're the man, I'm proud you're driving my car, I'm glad you're here.' Dale Jr. wants to be wanted and he wants to be respected and those are things he misses personally. I think a lot of times, drivers don't realize that their personal life affects their professional life. I think it's really critical that Junior gets someone to guide him and direct him."

Among racers on the circuit, Junior always had a lot of respect for Jeff Gordon. That view grew stronger in 2007. In the weeks before Junior's announcement about leaving DEI, Gordon had ended a twenty-five-race winless streak with a victory at Phoenix. It was his seventy-sixth career Cup win, tying him with Dale Earnhardt for sixth on the all-time wins list. As part of his postrace celebration, Gordon drove around the track hoisting a "3" flag out the window.

While the move angered the Earnhardt faithful at the track—many of whom regarded the gesture to be Gordon's attempt to rub their noses in his achievement—Junior was touched by the move. Gordon and his father had been business partners on several ventures, not hated rivals. His dad had been excessively helpful to Gordon when he'd first come into the sport, and had always maintained a friendship with the younger champion.

"Jeff can't win for losing," Junior told the press.

Gordon appreciated the support. He had been surprised and saddened by Junior's departure from DEI. As with Junior, the move reminded him of all the things left unaccomplished by Dale Sr.

Gordon also saw the emotion that Rick Hendrick was now investing in his own hopes to sign Junior. And he saw the pain of his boss's loss of Ricky all over again. Even before Junior had announced his departure from DEI, Gordon felt the need to make sure that Junior wasn't stringing his boss along with all the counsel he'd been seeking.

"Jeff said, 'Rick told me you were talking to him about driving for him,'" Junior later recalled. "I said, 'Yeah, we're talking a little bit.' And he said, 'Don't fuck with that guy. If you're fucking with him, I'll kill you.' He said, 'You're putting hopes in that man's head. If you're playing around, that's bullshit.'

"That told me right there that Jeff was real, because I'd always wondered where Jeff was, where his dedication lay, but that showed me right there how much he cared for Rick. It meant a lot to me, even though he was sort of saying, 'Look, you'd better be serious, because you can't fool around. . . . Don't be talking to Rick and getting him all excited because you're just gonna bum him out and that's gonna piss me off.' It made me feel good, knowing that."

* * *

On June 13, Junior sat at a table alongside his next team owner, Rick Hendrick, and it was hard to keep a grin of excitement and relief off his face.

"It became apparent to me the man I wanted to drive for," he announced. "I've known him since childhood, he competes with integrity, and most of all, he wins races."

The relationship he had with Hendrick, he went on to say, "Had a huge impact on my decision. . . . He was really genuine to me. Even when I was thinking about my decision to leave DEI, his main concern was my well-being. He had no motives other than to help me be as happy as I could. That was one of the things I never forgot."

For Hendrick, hiring Junior meant cutting ties with one of his drivers; the odd man out, as had been rumored, was Kyle Busch. Negotiations with the young, brash, and talented Busch had been incomplete, and both sides agreed to a parting. The split was an unceremonious one. Lost to many at the time, in the sweeping publicity, was Busch's raw talent, and the idea that he might instantly improve whatever team he decided to sign with. Much was made of the Texas race, two months before, when Junior had substituted for Busch toward the end of the day. After wrecking with Busch during the race, Junior's engine had blown and his car was finished. Busch, thinking his Chevy was unfixable, bitterly left the track. But Busch's crew had been able to repair the No. 5, and Junior asked if he could take it to the track for a few laps. The move—typical of the early days of NASCAR—allowed Junior to see what he was missing in the Hendrick equipment. And Busch's early departure didn't exactly help his relationship with ownership.

The whole switch seemed to leave Busch bitter, and he would channel that after agreeing to drive for Joe Gibbs Racing starting in 2008.

For Junior, signing with Hendrick carried its own public-relations hurdles. A good number of his fans may have felt he was disloyally going over to "the enemy," the organization where Gordon and champion Jimmie Johnson toiled. But to Junior, the move was about getting "my fans on their feet more often than I do; I feel that they'll find a lot of things to get excited about in the future."

The future, however, was months away; the rest of the season would be filled with still more distractions. Budweiser would not be coming with Junior as his chief sponsor, and Teresa Earnhardt would not be permitting him to use the number 8 for his car. Hendrick ultimately was able to secure the 88 from Yates Racing, a car number that had, until then, been most often associated with Dale Jarrett and the UPS Ford.

The loss of his car number hit Junior particularly hard. Negotiations had broken down when Teresa insisted on retaining a share of the licensing revenue, along with a promise to get the number back from Junior upon his retirement. They were, one could argue, requests that seemed centered on protecting the Dale Earnhardt legacy.

"I don't have the rights to my name," Junior told *Charlotte Observer* writer Scott Fowler at one point. "I'm tryin' to get 'em. [Teresa] don't want to come off it too easy, because she wants to make sure my dad's name is always thought of as the way it is. If I didn't have the same name—and I kind of wish I didn't sometimes—I wouldn't have to be worrying about it."

Tony Eury Jr. had opted to follow him to Hendrick Motorsports, which would be one more degree of comfort for them both. Questioning the move and analyzing it became a new and constant topic among writers and fans. Another disappointing season came and went—Junior finished 2007 in sixteenth place, with no victories for the first time ever in Cup—and missed the Chase again. It had become an unfortunate pattern for him: So much of what he'd been judged upon was happening off the track instead of on it. It wasn't shocking, given that he was, by far, the sport's most popular figure.

But popularity notwithstanding, he'd be headed for a fresh start. He'd have to earn wins and good finishes under a different kind of spotlight at Hendrick. But he'd at least have a built-in kinship with the boss.

"Every time I talk to Rick," Junior said, "he makes me feel good about what I'm doing."

Hendrick understood that the bond with his new racer would be different; they were able to speak in a subtext that few others, thankfully, had to understand.

"I love being around [him]," Hendrick said. "Because I don't have Ricky, it kinda rejuvenated me."

* * *

"I just hope I get to keep my job," Junior said to his boss one afternoon at the racetrack. Rick Hendrick stared at his thirty-three-year-old driver with a frozen, confused smile.

The 2008 season began with incredible promise. Junior had won the Budweiser Shootout at Daytona; though it was a non-points event, it was a victory essentially in his first race as a Hendrick driver. As the season progressed into the spring, he was running best among the owner's vaunted slate of Chevy racers, with seven top tens in the first nine races. He stood third in the standings, behind only Jeff Burton and, of all people, Gibbs racer Kyle Busch, who'd already won twice.

Surely, thought Hendrick, Junior was playing him.

"Are you serious?" he asked.

"Yeah, I'm serious," Junior said.

Hendrick chuckled. "Yeah," he said, "I think you're in good shape."

Junior had entered Hendrick Motorsports feeling, for the first time in Cup, like he didn't own the place.

"I know the job security thing is more of a metaphor," he said. "But for me to be able to get out from under my [dad's company]—not having that security is good for me."

If he was tested anywhere in 2008, it was on the track. Through the season, constant chatter arose comparing Junior to Kyle Busch. As Busch's success reminded everybody of the breadth of his raw talent, couch racers wondered who got the better of the swap.

The May 3 race at Richmond was turning into a fan's dream. Busch had the lead with Junior running second. Both men had top cars and had each led at various points in the race. Busch was trying to make it two wins in a row after a victory at Talladega; Junior hadn't won in well over a year.

There were two laps to go as the pair weaved and rolled, side by side, each getting a nose in front depending on the curve or straightaway, Busch down low, Junior up high. Coming out of turn two, Junior was making a good run; passing Busch, putting him cleanly behind could mean all the difference.

The racers shot into the straightaway with Junior inching farther in front.

"They're side by side down the back straightaway," shouted Larry McReynolds on the TV broadcast.

Midway through turn three, Busch's Toyota seemed to jerk ever so slightly, right into the No. 88 car. It was just a touch, but enough to send Earnhardt's car on an immediate spin and slide, smacking backward into the wall twice.

"Oh he turned him!" shrieked Darrell Waltrip, also from the booth. "No! No!"

Busch ended up finishing second to Denny Hamlin, who had snuck in front while contact was being made. Junior finished a dismal fifteenth.

The question of whether Busch intentionally turned Junior hung in the air, addressed by a massive chorus of boos from the Junior Nation faithful, all showering down on Busch. While some joked that the young driving star would need security to make it out of Richmond, Busch refused to be overly repentant.

"That was just a product of good, hard racing," he said after the race. "I apologize that that happened, and I hated that it did. Fortunately he didn't get hurt, so he was able to continue. He'll see another day of racing." Later on, he added, "If I apologize up and down, even though it may or may not be my fault—it would not make a difference. Dale got wrecked; he should have had a win tonight—quote, unquote."

If Junior's immediate reaction was subdued and somewhat stoic ("I haven't seen the replay. Tony Jr. said it looked like Kyle got loose underneath me. That happens."), his later reaction in an ESPN2 report stoked the rivalry.

"I was really mad and I really wanted to kill him," he said with the trace of a smile days after the race. "As I was spinning out after he hit me, for some reason I knew it was coming. Just knowing the type of person Kyle is and the way he reacts to things, I didn't expect anything different than what happened right there. I would have actually been surprised had he raced me clean. . . . I don't have an urge to go out and wreck Kyle or wreck his racecar or ruin his day. Some of my fans don't like you to race like that even though some of them would rather have me do that. There are some that do appreciate you taking the high road and being the better man about it."

The pair had tangled a number of times previously, and this latest bitterness fueled all kinds of talk. In fact, Busch would end up having a blazingly great regular NASCAR season, collecting a parcel of race-winning hardware in all three major series and competing for multiple titles. Though he'd end up tenth in the Cup series and sixth in the second-tier Nationwide (having run thirty of thirty-five races), Busch was clearly the driving star of 2008. One could argue that his dogged determination to shut up all naysayers was crystallized that day in Richmond.

Junior also made the 2008 Chase, but two DNFs and some less-than-stellar performances mired him in twelfth at season's end, last among the Chase competitors. In the days before the Homestead finale, where he'd finish the race in forty-first after wheel-bearing problems, circumstances nudged him to comment about one of the more bittersweet entries in the trend of NASCAR team mergers, this time between Dale Earnhardt, Inc. and Chip Ganassi Racing. Watching the ignominious end of DEI as a fully accredited racing organization—especially after he'd once hoped to gain majority ownership—couldn't have been easy for Dale Jr. But facing the question of how his father might have reacted to the merger left him momentarily riled up.

"I don't know. Your guess is as good as mine," he said testily, and paused a moment. Later, he added, "When my Daddy died . . . everything about everything changed. If he was here, he would be sad, but he is not and everybody has to go do their own thing and make their own way. Everybody has got to take care of themselves. He ain't here to take care of everybody, so you have to do your own thing, and I ain't got nothin' to do with it and I don't really have an opinion about it.

"I want them to succeed, I want them to be happy. I want it to work. But I can't exhaust any of my emotion over it because of what I got going on myself. I have to get my own thing going, I got to do better. I got things I could do better."

The season had ended up being, at times, a struggle. But it could not have gotten any better than in the middle of the year, on June 15—Father's Day—at Michigan International Speedway. As that race wound down, with Junior racing well but short on fuel, Tony Jr. suggested that if he could conserve some gas during cautions and ride low on the track when possible, he'd have a shot to stay out and win.

With twenty laps remaining, the cousins cemented their gamble: Junior would either make it or sputter to the finish.

"Look, worst-case scenario, we finish twenty-fifth, so who cares?"

Eury said. "You're going to wind up twenty-fifth or win, if things roll right. So go for it. Just save gas."

But the gamble paid off—even though a late caution led to a green-white-checker run for the win. With half a lap to go in the race, Michael Waltrip's car spun and set the caution out yet again, with Junior still in front. All he'd need to do was return to the start-finish line at proper caution speed and the win would be his.

Kasey Kahne crept up right behind Junior, prepared to push him across the finish line if necessary, but with a few yards to go, Junior already had his fist out the window, pumping for the crowd, as he took the win.

He got as far as turn one of the next lap before running out of gas. His crew came down and joyously pushed their driver to victory lane.

Team owner Rick Hendrick was waiting for him, and after Junior emerged, and was soaked by celebratory suds as he stood on the door with his arms raised in triumph, he climbed down, looking spent.

Twice during the postrace TV interview he made sure to say, "Happy Father's Day." After the second time, which he declared loudly into the camera, he turned to be embraced by his crew.

"It's special," he said afterward in the media center. "You know, my daddy, he meant a lot to me. There's a lot of people that I look up to that just happen to be great fathers themselves, role models for their sons. It's a special day for my family, special for my sister. She's very, very happy at home and in tears on the telephone so it means a lot to her. I'm glad she's as happy as she could possibly be today under the circumstances.

"And it makes me feel good. I know I can't tell my father happy Father's Day but I get the opportunity to wish it upon all of the other fathers out there, and I genuinely mean that when I say it, because that's what today is all about," Junior said. "It's for all of the fathers out there."

* * *

Earnhardt and Tony Eury Jr. now had a season under their belts with a new team, as part of the successful Hendrick Motorsports system.

There was renewed optimism—as there seems to be at the start of every season—along with talk that *this* would finally be the year the driver might shine.

And Junior was running comfortably, in third place, some sixty laps into the Daytona 500 when he came in for a pit stop . . . and overshot his pit stall. And he did so poorly enough that he had to run another lap under caution and pit again, and ended up losing a lap. It was a move that may have shocked his millions of fans, though no one more so than the driver himself. "Nothing's easy, but coming down pit road into your stall is like breathing, it's like shifting," he said months afterward. "You try to relax and let things come naturally to you because it should come natural to you, but at the same time, you try too hard sometimes, but when you fuck up like that, you miss your pit stall or slide through or something, it makes you totally aware. I usually don't have to worry about that and I fucked it up. Why did I fuck it up? What's wrong with me? And so you definitely start to dwell on those issues more than you should and it takes the focus away from the racetrack."

He had pit stall troubles for several races, and even had his 88 team construct a garishly large pit board sign so he wouldn't miss it. "I said, why don't we just make it a ridiculous one since everybody's giving us shit about it. Let's just give 'em more ammunition."

Earnhardt had already given fans and non-fans plenty of ammunition to question where his head was as the season wore on. He'd caused a wreck in Daytona that ended the day for, among others, a dominant Kyle Busch. By the season's eighth race, in Phoenix, where he needed to answer questions about the loss of sponsorship for the No. 8 car he'd once made so famous, he'd already logged four finishes of twentieth place or worse. A month later, a fortieth-place finish at Charlotte sent the burners spiking high on the rumors that the poor performances would cost Eury his position as crew chief. Though Hendrick had grown used to hushing such a move, one week later, longtime Hendrick fixture Lance McGrew was brought over from the Research and Development department to sit on the box, starting with the race at Dover. Once again, Earnhardt and his cousin, who'd worked through so much, were separated, with Eury now taking a post in the company's R&D unit.

The move turned what many thought to be an already lost season into a rebuilding one, and the results showed. Earnhardt suffered through his worst-ever full season in 2009, finishing in twenty-fifth place, with a dismal five top-tens. The sight of him resting his chin on one hand as he sat in the garage, late in the second-to-last race at Phoenix, while his crew feverishly tried to repair his wrecked auto, summed up the season better than any result. Meanwhile, teammates Jimmie Johnson, Mark Martin, and Jeff Gordon filled the top-three spots in the Cup standings by season's end. In a sense, Junior's spot in the limelight had never seemed quite so dimmed.

And that kind of break may have been the thing he ultimately needed most. Junior led something of a Spartan existence in the off-season before 2010, hoping to simply regroup. "You hope it allows you to totally disconnect from where your psyche got screwed up," he said, "so you can start the year almost like it didn't happen, and maybe that is not the best way to go about it because it did happen and you should be trying to dissect the issues. But the psyche has to be rebuilt."

Things got better in 2010, or at least they were not quite so dire. It was another Chase-less season, but the year lacked the desperation and clueless pursuit of consistency that had marred 2009.

However, once again, the stirring emotional highlights occurred in the shadow of his father. On May 23, the inaugural class of the NASCAR Hall of Fame was inducted, a class that included Dale Earnhardt. Dale Jr. wiped away tears after watching a video of his father's career, and his dad's car owner, Richard Childress, broke up the crowd with stories of his best friend. Childress recounted Earnhardt's comments to fellow drivers who claimed to be worried about excessive speeds before a race at Talladega. "He said, 'If you're afraid to go fast, stay the hell home. Don't come here and grumble about going too fast. Tie kerosene rags around your ankles so the ants won't climb up and bite your candy ass.'"

The evening was a reunion, of sorts, for Dale Jr. and Teresa, who stood onstage together, along with Dale Jr.'s siblings Kelley, Kerry, and Taylor. "He carried the same grit and competitive spirit in his racing and [in] everything else in life, too," Dale Jr. said, honoring his dad.

By then, he, Teresa, Kelley, and Childress had agreed that Dale Jr. would drive the favorite of his father's paint schemes—the classic blue-and-yellow Wrangler Jeans design from the mid-1980s—during the early-July Nationwide series race at Daytona. For one last time, Dale Jr. would field the No. 3. The car would have a Hendrick Motorsports engine, with bolts turned in pit stops by the driver's No. 88 Cup series pit team. Sitting in as crew chief: Tony Eury Jr.

Earnhardt clearly had a dominant car that evening, but the dice roll that is an evening at Daytona meant that nothing would be certain. One by one, however, it was Earnhardt's main competitors who became victims of poor luck. Kyle Busch, Justin Allgaier, and Brad Keselowski found themselves chasing the 3 car from farther back as the laps passed. With one final green-white-checker start, Earnhardt received a mighty bump from Joey Logano, setting the pair ahead of the tightly packed group of frontrunners. As much as Logano hoped to have some extra speed in reserve, Earnhardt ran away from him and, to the extreme delight of the thousands of Junior Nation faithful in the stands—and those who loved his father—took the checkered flag.

The emotions were too much for Tony Jr. "I appreciate your work, man," Dale Jr. called to his cousin over the radio from the No. 3 cockpit. "I love when I'm racing with you, buddy." Tony Jr. shook his head and broke down. A moment later, cornered by a reporter, he could only think of what had just happened, and what once might have been.

"Man, you know we lost everything here," he said, his voice breaking. "And to come back with that number and do this, that means everything."

In the booth, Dale Jarrett—a close friend of Earnhardt Sr. and Dale Jr.'s longtime go-to advisor—was also caught up in the moment. "His father would be extremely proud," he said, his voice trailing off.

In victory lane, Dale Jr. looked up as the shower of cheers rained down on him. "I feel real lucky," he told ESPN reporter Dave Burns. "I was so worried we weren't gonna win because if you didn't win, what a waste of time. Why'd you do it? So I worked hard to try to win it. Not only for Daddy," he said, pointing upward. "I'm proud of him going into the Hall of Fame, and he would be proud of this, I'm sure. He has so many great fans, not just mine; this is for his fans, I hope they enjoyed this. This is it. No more 3 for me."

Beer flowed between crewmembers and sponsors with Earnhardt, pressing down his red mustache and beard, beaming at it all.

"I feel lucky to have won the race and it's real emotional," he added. "Hell, I want everybody just to be happy."

* * *

Dale Earnhardt Jr. is already one of the most recognized athletes on the planet. And, after a full season with crew chief Steve Letarte, operating fully inside the successful Hendrick Motorsports system, he made the 2011 Chase, finishing seventh on the year. He's experienced heaping personal and professional changes throughout his career. And yet, despite the spotlight, the challenges, and the adoration, he keeps his honesty, his perspective, and his code. Few things better explain his nine-straight NASCAR Most Popular Driver wins than that.

"He's a very influential figure in the sport whether he wants to be or not," says NASCAR TNT commentator Andy Petree, who was crew chief on Dale Earnhardt Sr.'s 1993–94 championship seasons. "I admire a lot of things about him because he's been through a lot. It's been tough to lose your dad, and especially the kind of person that he was, and it was a time when he probably needed him the most, and he's really done a lot with his life and made a lot of good decisions. He's a great talent and there's a reason he's the most popular. The name definitely helps but they love him; they really do."

Personal matters aside, it would be hard, professionally speaking, to imagine a worse time for Dale Jr. to have lost his father than when he did. After winning two-straight Busch series titles, he'd come into Cup with great expectations, enjoying the highs of early-season success, and enduring a late freshman-year fall. His second season was going to be different. He'd come in with a nice head of steam, a new commitment to gaining the consistency he'd found in Busch, and a chance to ride the circuit with his father. And then, 199 laps into the season, Dale Earnhardt was gone, and Junior was forced to mourn in silence while NASCAR Nation paid endless tribute.

In the decade since, Dale Jr. has stumbled and, at times, stunned with extraordinary wins. He's made moves once thought unthinkable—as unthinkable as the loss he's had to come to terms with.

But if there's a consistent guiding presence in his life—along with the expert, caring counsel of his sister—it remains his dad. Dale Jr. has always needed to, bittersweetly, learn from Dale Earnhardt. He watched his father on the track and on TV, saw him vanquishing fellow racers with brains and brawn. Even under his father's roof, when his dad was away much of the time, Junior, the adoring son, learned all he could about his dad, absorbing the cool history of stock car racing the way some kids soak up stories of military might.

The moves he's made since February 2001 have been perfectly intuitive, with his own and his family's best interests in mind and at heart. Winning races would be great; winning championships even better. But there's no doubt that his actions would have long earned him something he'd have coveted more: his dad's respect.

"It's not something I think about a lot, but it is oddly similar," Junior said, referring to his own and his father's paths in the sport, a few months after Dale Earnhardt's death. "He lost *his* dad when he was twenty-two or so, and he adapted to being his own man and he went out and did things for himself. It took him quite awhile really to get going, but he did. That's been a thing to me to say, it's okay, you're gonna be fine. Whatever decisions you make or however many may be wrong, there'll be several that are right that take you where you need to go. That's been a reassurance."

In 2005, starting here at the road course in Sonoma, Tony Stewart won five races in a stretch of seven, including his first-ever victory at his beloved Indianapolis Motor Speedway.

Chapter Nine
His Greatest Move

"If I wanted to remind myself, all I had to do was go down a flight of steps and stare at that trophy, and I could stare at it and it wasn't gonna do anything. It was still gonna be there."

—TONY STEWART in 2005, after winning the
Brickyard 400 Indianapolis Motor Speedway

A T THREE O'CLOCK IN THE MORNING ON A WARM LATE-MAY NIGHT in 2001, Tony Stewart climbed down the steps of his motor home and went walking. He took slow, careful steps, listening to his shoes shuffling against the grass, and the few cars in the distance on nearby Georgetown Road. He was alone, standing in the infield of his favorite place on earth, the Indianapolis Motor Speedway, in the dead of night. All should have been perfectly quiet, but he'd felt the urge to come outside because he'd heard something mysterious in the dark.

But he was going to be doing double duty soon. In the space of a single day, he would run the Indy 500, on the afternoon of May 27, and then immediately helicopter out to Charlotte, North Carolina, to run the Coca-Cola 600, the longest race on the NASCAR Winston Cup schedule. All told it would be 1,100 miles of racing in one day, and he had every intention of running them all, and finishing very well in both.

It would be exhausting, and Stewart's priority had to be NASCAR and his Joe Gibbs Racing team. But Stewart revered Indy, the majestic, historic track that stood some fifty-one miles north of his childhood home in Columbus, Indiana. He'd dreamed of winning here since he was seven years old, when his father, Nelson, first put him into a go-kart in West-port, Indiana. Gibbs, who admired his determination, reluctantly gave permission for the double.

And then Tony George, CEO of the track at Indianapolis, gave him permission to park in the infield and make this beautiful place his home for a single night. That was a gift. Since Stewart had joined NASCAR full time in 1999, all the pressures of racing in Cup caused him tremendous stress. He'd had two years of personal struggles, competing with few choice successes. He hadn't been sleeping much; fueled by anxiety, the five-foot-nine racer was now down to 160 pounds, his lowest weight since high school. There was never any free time. Coming to Indianapolis each August for the Brickyard 400, NASCAR's race at the track, was a constant rush, with no time to enjoy the place he loved best. Home didn't feel much like home anymore.

But this night was different, quiet and serene, and Stewart had gone out and come back late, and as he drove up to the track, he was sure he heard something a little otherworldly. Standing now in the infield, being so tied into this place, Stewart could only think it was the ghosts of Indy's past.

"You could hear people and you could hear cars," he recalled of the night a few years afterward. "And maybe I was just crazy or caught up in the moment but to me, that place is a living, breathing organism.

"There's been so much tragedy, so much joy and accomplishment, it's its own thing. And to go there in the middle of the night—I stood out there for a half hour and I didn't feel I was by myself," he said. "You felt like you were eavesdropping on someone else's conversations."

Those "conversations" relaxed him. And he could recall the times he'd sat in the stands watching his idol A. J. Foyt battle Mario Andretti and the Unsers on his way to winning four times at Indy. And then he recalled too many near-victories of his own in his years driving in the Indy Racing League.

And in a few hours, he'd get another shot. To Stewart, winning anywhere was a thrill. But winning at Indy, etching his name on a trophy at this hometown place where he'd never won, would be something indescribable. Kind of like trying to wrap one's mind around these ghosts talking in the middle of the night.

*   *   *

Two years earlier, in 1999, Stewart had reset the definition for rookie season triumphs in NASCAR Winston Cup. He became the first rookie in series history to win three points races in his first year, finishing fourth in the standings.

Whatever satisfaction that seemed to promise, it eluded Stewart. Feeling ill-prepared for the fame that followed his performance, and the responsibilities of racing and representing a grateful but demanding sponsor in Home Depot, Stewart became more petulant as the season wore on. In July, before he'd won his first race, he led a race-high 118 laps at Loudon. And then, with three laps to go, his racecar ran out of gas.

Enraged and disappointed, he walked past the media directly into his motor home. From outside, reporters could hear the muffled, angry yelling. "I needed some place I could go scream and not have a bunch of people hear me," he later explained.

As much as he felt compelled to excuse himself afterward for not giving an immediate comment, his heart wasn't into it. "I apologize to everybody for the inconvenience," he said two days later. "Unless you're a racecar driver and you are put in these positions it's hard for you to understand how much emotion is involved in a big race like that." Then he added, with a brilliant flourish of ambiguity, "I guarantee you it probably isn't going to happen again, that's for sure."

With a week off following Loudon, Stewart spent three nights racing at local tracks and another night as a crew chief for a Sprint car race. These were labors of love. "I'm going to have some fun driving a racecar and that will give me a chance to forget about the disappointments we had," he said.

The joys were always temporary. Back in NASCAR, he felt too often like he was under a microscope, his frustrations or grudges magnified.

Martinsville, Virginia's famed paperclip-shaped half-mile track, was a NASCAR stop that Stewart always disliked making; passing was often an issue, and he felt the place would serve much better as a parking lot. Or, as he liked to say, "I wish they'd just fill the place up with water and put bass in there."

At the October Martinsville race, Stewart found himself tangling all afternoon with a familiar target, Kenny Irwin. Irwin, also a native of Indiana, and driver of the No. 28 Texaco Havoline Ford, had won Winston Cup Rookie of the Year in 1998; Stewart, in 1999, was well on his way toward succeeding him. But much earlier in their careers, both had spent a decade on the competitive local sprint car circuit. They'd been fierce competitors then and the dark feelings had carried over.

Early in the race, Stewart spun Irwin just as his rival was passing him. Though he immediately apologized and asked his spotter to explain that he'd accidentally climbed too high up on the track, the pair squared off twice more through the race until, with Stewart readying for Irwin to pass, Irwin first punted him into a wall.

Stewart exited his car and stood on the track as the caution flag flew. He waited, his hard shoe-protection heat shields in his grip. When Irwin's car approached, Stewart clapped his hands sarcastically then reeled back and tossed the heat shields at Irwin's car, before jumping over to the passenger side, lunging in, and grabbing Irwin by the fire suit. Irwin gave the car some gas and Stewart jumped out quickly, his furor still rising. A NASCAR reprimand soon followed.

"Tony's the kinda guy, when he's away from the race track, he's very relaxed, but when he's at the track, he wears his emotions on his sleeve," explained team owner Gibbs. "NASCAR is one of the few sports, he's driving that racecar, it's his life, everything's riding on it, if something bad happens, in many cases he's confronted within thirty seconds with people. . . . It's his life spinning on top of something getting ready to explode and he's extremely ticked off and you put those two together and sometimes bad things happen."

Stewart's list of bad things began piling up. He won six races in 2000, finishing sixth in the standings, but he'd also logged six did-not-finish races (DNFs). Then the pressures seemed to build that much more in 2001. The season began at Daytona, where Stewart was caught up in a vicious somersaulting crash. He'd escaped with only bruises, but then Dale Earnhardt, a mentor and a kindred spirit, was killed on the last lap of the race. Everybody was on edge after that, and at the April race at Bristol, Stewart and Jeff Gordon renewed a feud that had cropped up the year before. For angrily spinning Gordon out after the race, Stewart was slapped with a $10,000 fine and a five-month suspension. After he ignored a black flag call during the July night race at Daytona—and quarreled with a newspaper reporter when the race was done—NASCAR docked him sixty-five championship points and extended his suspension.

The 2001 season ended with Stewart finishing a distant second to champion Jeff Gordon, and yet still complaining about everything from some new stringent safety policies to a few competition moves the sport had made after NASCAR had signed its huge TV package before the start of the season. The sport, he said, was now less about who drives the best car than about how to put on the best show for fans.

"No, I'm not happy," he said a few weeks before season's end. "I've been unhappy for over a year now. But I'm not quitting. I'm just unhappy with NASCAR."

For all of Stewart's complaints, the sport clearly needed someone like him. Earnhardt's death had brought a seismic shift to NASCAR, and it needed its old-school heroes more than ever.

"Behind closed doors, I think NASCAR has to like a guy like Tony," said series-champion-turned-commentator Benny Parsons. "In the end, you can't have a rubber stamp kind of guy and still grow your sport."

* * *

It was looking as if things couldn't get much better on August 4, 2002. Stewart had won the pole for the Brickyard 400, and had led forty-three laps during the day. Inside the No. 20 Home Depot Pontiac, he tried to keep both his concentration and his racing line. Stewart sat in fourth place with four laps to go and a bona fide chance to win at Indianapolis. It was all good.

And then a restart came, and just as quickly, it was all bad. The No. 20 Home Depot Pontiac suddenly, mysteriously faded, losing whatever racing edge it had previously held for most of the day. NASCAR veteran Bill Elliot, with whom Stewart had been competing for much of the afternoon, took off. Several more cars passed him, as if he were practically standing still. Stewart brooded silently on his end of the radio as Joe Gibbs and Stewart's crew chief Greg Zipadelli asked questions and tried to keep him calm.

In the last four laps, Stewart lost eight spots and ended the day in twelfth place.

Zipadelli, sitting on top of the pit box, struggled with what to say over the two-way radio to his driver. Every week was important, but Zipadelli understood quite well that Indy week was always going to be different.

Zipadelli had been Stewart's crew chief beginning with his 1999 rookie campaign. Both men were passionate, with fiery tempers and a predilection for having things done their way. While Zipadelli was taller than the five-foot-nine Stewart, both men had dark hair and dark eyes and frequently furrowed brows. From early on, it was clear they were not going to be your typical driver/crew chief combination. There was something welcome and aggressive about them both.

But both Zipadelli and Joe Gibbs knew their driver would have to be finessed, if possible, after a loss like this.

Stewart parked his racecar in Indianapolis's Gasoline Alley and began charging off toward his hauler. Gary Mook, freelance photographer for the *Indianapolis Star*, moved in front of him, trying to get a good shot. He took one before Stewart punched him in the chest and pushed him aside. Stewart got to his hauler, dressed quickly, and was gone without a word.

His actions, however, spoke loudly enough to inspire everybody's displeasure. Gibbs immediately met with Mook, NASCAR fined Stewart $10,000 and placed him on probation for the second consecutive season, and chief sponsor Home Depot, in an unprecedented move, also fined Stewart $50,000 and put him on its own probationary short leash.

By now even Stewart was ready to acknowledge the problem went beyond reasonable explanation. He accepted all penalties, met and apologized to Mook, and even signed up to take anger management classes. Still, the pressures continued. Through August and September, two more alleged shoving incidents arose at separate tracks; in both cases the charges were dismissed. And Stewart began keeping more to himself.

Zipadelli faced all the commotion with mixed emotions. He had been making apologies and excuses for his friend for close to four seasons now, deflecting pressures as much as possible. Stewart had a great capacity for warmth, humor, generosity, and friendship, but these matters tested his crew chief's patience.

"Greg is probably the one person that has been the driving force behind us being where we are right now," Stewart said. "He's been a much larger leader in our race team than I have. Greg cares more about me as a person than as a driver. And Joe [Gibbs]'s always had the same approach and that's not the kind of attitude you see with a lot of car owners or crews. You're a piece of property at this level to a lot of people."

The remarkable thing, for Stewart and Zipadelli, is that as much as the 2002 season spiraled away from the racer emotionally, it was coming to him in a big way in the points, much as had been the case the season before.

On October 6, Stewart finished second to Dale Earnhardt Jr. at Talladega and, thanks to bad days for Jimmie Johnson and Mark Martin, Stewart vaulted into the lead in the Winston Cup standings. For the last six races of the year, he posted two top fives and didn't finish worse than fourteenth until the final race at Miami-Homestead, where he posted an eighteenth-place finish. It was enough to keep him ahead of perennial Cup bridesmaid Martin by thirty-eight points. Tony Stewart, most improbably, had won his first NASCAR championship—while on probation with both the sport and his main sponsor.

In what should have been one of the highest points in his career, Stewart found himself, at season's end, exhausted and completely on edge. And as much as Zipadelli had also fulfilled a dream, he'd been put through the ringer. It was strange accepting congratulations all around while watching his driver constantly invite trouble into his life.

Stewart knew how much his crew chief loved Corvettes; as a gift for all Zipadelli had done, Stewart handed him the keys to a brand-new one.

Zipadelli was humbled by the generous gesture, and he offered one of his own. He told Stewart that if he could, he'd gladly exchange his crew chief title to see his friend get to a more contented place in his life.

Stewart was bowled over by the sentiment, and he wished for the same thing, but at the moment it didn't seem very likely. As much as Stewart loved the triumphs, the claustrophobic pressures still offered him very little relief. There was no guarantee that even a championship would help. In fact, if anything, so great a win would only invite more attention and scrutiny.

* * *

You never know what to expect when, having won a championship, you're given the honor of meeting the president of the United States. For Tony Stewart, chances are he wouldn't have guessed George W. Bush's first words when the two shook hands. "So, he's a tough guy, huh?" the president said, turning to Home Depot's then-CEO Bob Nardelli. "The guy beats up photographers."

The season over, the championship won, time had created enough distance to joke a bit about the odd rollercoaster that had been the end of the 2002 season. Even Stewart got in on the self-deprecating act. When a reporter pressed a question about his short fuse at the annual pre-season Media Tour in January 2003, Stewart cautioned him with a smile, saying, "Obviously I'm not scared to hit people so don't make me have to do what I do."

For all the smiles, a wary undercurrent of criticism could be felt for the extremely talented racer who'd won a title despite bringing some unwelcome attention to a sport obsessed with maintaining its mainstream reputation.

"Tony and I handle ourselves very differently, and one of the reasons I handle myself the way I do is because when I was Tony's age, coming in, I wouldn't have had a job very long," said Mark Martin at the time. "You had to say the right things, you had to kiss up, or else you wouldn't have a job. Times are not the same. So it's okay for Tony to be who he is and what he is and I'm a big supporter of Tony Stewart being a racer, a guy who'd much rather go to a dirt track than a cocktail party. I'm the first guy standing back there going 'Yeah yeah.' But I had to go to those cocktail parties fifteen years ago or I wouldn't have had a job."

"The self-imposed pressure is part of what made Tony explode all the time," added Darrell Waltrip. "But now that he's the champion, he can be a little more relaxed. Tony's a perfectionist; most drivers are. And sometimes when that's your expectation, you can get disappointed and down. You've got to be able to take the highs and lows."

The lows, however, would continue to be problematic. Stewart won two races in 2003 and finished the year in seventh place, far off the pace set by champion Matt Kenseth. The 2004 season began with a different level of pre-season pressure, thanks to the new Chase for the Championship format. Stewart would eventually qualify for the Chase and finish the year in sixth, with two wins, but that was, once again, hardly the headline for another season that appeared to unravel at times, especially in the early going. In various races, he collected Gordon, Kasey Kahne, and Scott Wimmer in wrecks. Angered by a poor showing at Talladega, Stewart vented after the race by driving up pit road the wrong way, sending a would-be TV interview crew scurrying for safety. And a week later, at California Speedway, Rusty Wallace became so angered by a tangle with Stewart that he yelled, "The guy needs some help. He's in a ditch right now. He's really screwing up a lot lately."

And yet this was all a prelude to the June road course race at Sonoma. With rookie Brian Vickers not giving him the proper leeway at one point in the race, Stewart bumped him hard and ultimately made the pass. The incident seemed innocuous enough but it stuck in Stewart's craw.

After the race, Stewart stuck his head in Vickers's car to argue his point. Vickers, amused by the one-sided discussion, began to laugh, trying to calm his competitor down. Stewart, enraged by the laughter, slammed his open palm into Vickers's chest and then tried to yank the still-belted racer out of his car. Vickers's crew, having seen enough, ran over and dragged Stewart away.

NASCAR put Stewart back on probation for the fourth time in his career, fined him $50,000, docked him twenty-five championship points, and nearly made him sit out the next race, at Daytona. A week later, at Chicagoland, Stewart got a little too close to leader Kasey Kahne and spun him hard into the wall, despite having, what Kahne later called, "the car to beat all day. All he had to do was go through a couple more turns and he probably would have passed us."

The incident sent Stewart and Kahne's crews into a shoving match. Kahne's car owner, Ray Evernham, had lost all patience. "He should have his ass beat," Evernham said, shaking his head. "That's the problem with him. Nobody has ever really grabbed him and given him a good beating. If he doesn't get suspended, maybe I'll do that."

But the only one really getting hurt was Stewart, and he knew it.

"The last three years of my life have been unhappy and you finally get to the point where you say, 'What do I have to do to make myself happy?'" he said when asked about his stress and behavior. Stewart clearly welcomed any kind of positive diversion.

Two weeks before the Sonoma race, he'd gone to the opening ceremony at the Victory Junction Gang Camp in Randleman, North Carolina. The new summer camp for chronically ill children, built by Kyle and Pattie Petty, was meant to honor their son Adam, who'd been killed on May 12, 2000, in a practice crash at Loudon. Stewart hadn't known Adam well, but Kyle was among the Cup drivers who'd welcomed him most warmly when he'd come over from Indy cars.

After Adam's death, Kyle switched teams, putting a temporary hold on his long career in Cup to begin driving his son's No. 45 Petty Enterprises car in the Busch series, trying to prepare what would have been Adam's team for Cup competition. Stewart saw this tremendous loss in one of the people who'd always been able to maintain his bear-

ings and sense of humor in Cup, a quality that he'd found very difficult to keep.

Less than two months after Adam Petty's death, Stewart's longtime
rival Kenny Irwin had been killed in a crash as well, also at Loudon. And
then Earnhardt had died at Daytona.

Stewart had begun to contribute more to charity, helping support
Kyle and Pattie as they built the camp Adam had asked them to. It opened
officially in 2004, on Father's Day. The first time Stewart went to visit
during a campers' week, he'd been running late due to a sponsor commitment. Kids with spina bifida were attending that week, and one of the
campers wanted only to see Stewart; he built a No. 20 car in shop class,
wore orange to match the Home Depot colors, and repeatedly asked Kyle
Petty when his hero was going to get there.

Stewart arrived and the only thing the camper could muster was a
small "Hi."

"Wait a minute," Kyle said with a coaxing smile. "I've heard everything about Tony Stewart from you all day long, heard his life story, and
all you're gonna say is, 'Hi?' Tell him about the car you made."

For the rest of the day, Stewart trailed the camper, sharing the
experience of the place. There were the bright, celebratory colors of
the bunks, the dock and gazebo by the fishing pond, and the two-story
garage facility, housed inside a building shaped like Adam's No. 45 car.

"I got to see kids who probably never had the opportunity to go
anywhere but their house and the hospital for treatment," Stewart said.
"Being able to see them having the most fun they've had, knowing they've
never been around that many kids before, going to a dance for the first
time, being able to do things they've never been able to do, that was really
gratifying."

It was hard for Stewart to tear himself away from the place.

"He went from cabin to cabin, visiting the kids into the evening,"
recalled Mary Barr, then the director of development at Victory Junction.
We literally had to tell him he had to go because the kids had to go to bed
and he had to go back home.

"He's made comments abut this: the two sides of the Tony Stewart coin. He's sort of got this bad boy image. But you'd never know that if you saw him at Victory Junction."

* * *

During a few days' break in the 2004 Cup schedule, Stewart decided the sanest thing he could possibly do was to go home, since he'd been living in Charlotte, in the center of NASCAR action. So he grabbed a Charlotte friend of his and, without a race coming or any interviews scheduled, headed to Indiana.

Home was Columbus, about an hour south of the Speedway. Seven years earlier, he'd bought the house he grew up in, a simple three-bedroom home on a middle-class street where the neighbors—who embraced their boy who made good—still remembered with a shake of the head the kid who made more noise than anyone, smacking around a soccer ball, catching bouncing fly balls off their roofs, or tooling around in a small go-kart.

He spent the time reveling in the nonstop sarcasm he enjoyed with his good friends. And there were trips to the local Dairy Queen for chili and chocolate shakes.

Home was where he and his dad, Nelson, had dug a small go-kart track. Later, Nelson and Stewart's mom, Pam Boas, mortgaged the house so Stewart could keep go-kart racing. That had been Nelson's dream; Tony was his project, reminding him that not winning races was unacceptable.

Nelson had first taken him to the Speedway to see the 500 when he was five years old. They'd gotten up when it was still dark to catch the bus on race day. The bus had a luggage rack, and Nelson placed his boy up there. Someone had a pillow for him and everyone threw their jackets on the boy to keep him warm and let him sleep. The race was a magical blur as they sat in turns three and four, right in the middle of the short chute. He could hardly see a thing as the action whizzed past. But under caution, the cars were sleek and beautiful, and the pungent methanol fumes rose into the air, and then the flag waved once again and the classic drivers, Mario Andretti, Gordon Johncock, Johnny Rutherford, Bobby and Al Unser, and A. J. Foyt, who'd one day be Stewart's hero, went back to work.

The house was a warehouse of memories, some good, some bad. In 1990, when Stewart was in high school, Nelson and Pam divorced and sold the house, and Stewart went to live with friends of the family in Rushville, Indiana, a little more than an hour to the northeast, where he could more easily continue racing. He worked part-time for a friend with a tow truck company, and every once in a while there was a run by the Speedway, and Stewart would look out his window and see the grandstand and pit lane.

Seven years later, the house was back on the market, and Stewart, by then the Indy Racing League champion, bought it. Being there those few days in 2004 helped the better memories come back.

"When we got back to Charlotte, I was a totally different person when I got on that plane from when I got off that plane," he said afterward. The visit back home had rejuvenated him; the return to Charlotte brought the anxiety rushing right back.

By season's end, Zipadelli and Stewart's team had had enough of the great pressures of wondering when their driver might next blow a gasket. A team meeting was called and driver and crew were able to air out their grievances. "The guys basically explained to Tony how some of the things he did affected their lives," Zipadelli said later. "We're a family, and I think that kind of opened his eyes to what they go through when he has a bad day."

Stewart returned home to Columbus after collecting sixth-place money at the 2004 year-end Cup banquet, along with two awards for his philanthropy work on behalf of Victory Junction. There were the same great sarcastic friends he'd long bantered with, the ones who'd known him since before anything huge had encumbered him. He hung around his friend Steve Chrisman's fishing spot on the Flat Rock River, warming his hands on the bonfire. There were more shakes to drink at the Dairy Queen, Christmas presents to buy and deliver, and the comfort of helping to fix up a friend's three-quarter midget. "You've got to stop and hit the reset button once in awhile," he later said.

When it came to the point where he'd normally pack up and head to his place in Charlotte, he instead chose to move back home to stay. Charlotte was the center of the stock car universe, but it was too far away from Indy. Stewart decided that for his team, for Zippy and the crew, for himself and his peace of mind, it might be good to stick around awhile.

*   *   *

Throughout his NASCAR career, Stewart has always done best when things grew hotter. In six seasons on the circuit, he'd won exactly one race before the start of May, a March race at Atlanta during his 2002 championship season.

"When the tracks are starting to get warmer and slicker, it's getting harder to get grip on the race track, that's where we really start gaining momentum," he has long maintained. "So I always look forward to the month of May coming around."

Early-season racing frustrations were compounded during 2005: Beyond the typical bad spell, the team didn't seem to have the right handle on the car. And a fire after a crash during a Busch series race at Texas in April left him with first- and second-degree burns on his elbow and thigh.

For all the adversity, including his seesawing spot in the standings, Stewart was able to set bitterness aside. It was easier to shake off the madness with a glance out his living room window in Columbus. Here at home, he could walk the walk of anger management.

And there was another reason now for Stewart to look forward to the month of May. In Indianapolis, May meant the Indy 500, and Stewart was able to fly home between races, steal away for a bit of time, and walk through the paddock area, cutting up with old friends and one-time competitors. The desire to win at this place in an IndyCar was never going to leave him, but in May, some of that pressure was off. It was another feeling of return.

Months before, during the off-season, Stewart had also purchased Eldora Speedway, a premier sprint car dirt track in Rossburg, Ohio. Longtime owners Earl and Berniece Baltes had come to him with the idea, hoping to entice Stewart to take over the place. He regarded the offer as a privilege.

"Earl and Berniece worked so hard to build that facility to what it was the first fifty years and all we've tried to do was what we thought Earl and Berneice would be proud of, something they'd approve of," he said of owning the place. I'm very adamant about trying to preserve the history of that track. It's just a special place."

The 2004 late-season conversation with the No. 20 Home Depot team had cleared the air well enough to where Stewart embraced a new role and attitude as team leader. Down times at the track became a good excuse to pick one another up instead of fighting, accusing, and arguing. Driver and crew would play cards, go to movies, and cut up together.

"We find more things to do as a team now than we've ever done," Stewart said.

"Before this year, Tony kept his team in such a state of turmoil internally they were imploding," said Darrell Waltrip. "I give Greg Zipadelli credit: He's a calm, cool, confident guy. And if it hadn't been for him, Tony would have been driving for someone else. But he believed in Tony. Emotion is a great thing. Passion and emotion, but it has to be under control. And when you take passion and emotion and control it, it becomes a really valuable tool."

As it usually did, something eventually clicked for the team as the temperatures rose. As frustrating as it was to finish second at Michigan—his third runner-up finish of the season with a win—it indicated to the team that a corner had been turned.

He won the road race in Sonoma and then, a week later, won his first-ever points win at Daytona, taking the Saturday night race during the July 4 weekend. Afterward, caught up in the wonder of winning at the place, he stopped his car at the base of the fence under the flag stand, got out, and began climbing, taking a page from IndyRacing champion Helio Castroneves, who'd come to be nicknamed "Spiderman" for this stunt. Two weeks later, Stewart won again, this time at Loudon, New Hampshire in dominating fashion, leading 232 of 300 laps. It was his third win in four races. And up the fence he went again.

"I'm too damn fat to be climbing fences," he later joked. But it felt too good to be doing it.

"It's our way to really connect with the race fans," he said. "They expect that now. Until they decide that that doesn't mean anything to them anymore, I'm not gonna let those people down."

Stewart was clearly on a good roll. The Brickyard 400 at Indianapolis was coming in two weeks. No joy would match earning the opportunity to climb that fence.

* * *

The F-15s from the 122nd Fighter Wing out of Fort Wayne, Indiana, tore through the sky overhead, and the high-eighties temperature baked 250,000 fans jammed into their seats at Indianapolis Motor Speedway. Tony Stewart sat in his car, absently readjusting his equipment and breathing heavily, set to start twentieth at the Brickyard 400. The team had gone to Indy a month earlier to test their car. It had been a disappointing day—so much so that afterward, driver and crew chief agreed they needed to bring a completely different car come race day. They chose one that they hadn't yet run all year, and put a brand-new body on it. On Saturday, during a practice session, the thing had run smoothly enough to justify the decision, but still, to take an untested car to the one race he wanted to win above all others made Stewart antsy.

At the green flag, the field of cars began their circuits around the 2.5-mile speedway. There are suites at Indianapolis and Stewart owned one outside turn two. At every lap of the race, he passed the place and saw the cheering fists and arms. His father, Nelson, was there; even at speed, Stewart could see his dad and the fists.

Elliott Sadler was out front at first. In the clean air that was so important at this place, his car was practically on a train by itself. Indy could be very deceiving that way. Three laps in, Sadler was ahead by 1.5 seconds.

Watching the field splay, Stewart tried to remain patient. Talking to Zipadelli over the radio, there was no trace of anxiety; it was another day at the office. Both men were determined to keep it that way. After a caution in the early going, Stewart came in for tires, and major changes on the track bar, getting the car looser in the corners, just the way he liked it.

The tires were a problem for many of the drivers. Jeff Green and Bobby Hamilton Jr. each blew left front tires. After twelve or fifteen laps on new tires, you might be worn down to the cords.

With each pit stop, Stewart's Chevy responded better, and he began rising up the leaderboard. A cloud cover rolled in, and the temperature fell slightly, and the handling changed once again. After Joe Nemechek's left front tire burst, Stewart came out of the pits in seventh.

By the midway point in the race, the Home Depot crew had succeeded in making the car great. And coming out of the fourth turn, on lap 100, Stewart took his first lead of the day on the yard of bricks, and the fans—especially those in the Stewart suite—went into a standing frenzy.

"How about *that*, guys?" Stewart shouted over his radio.

"Yeah, you just take care of that right front tire," Zipadelli called back, warning about going too fast and getting too excited. "That's all you need to worry about."

Lap 101 out of 160 was the fastest lap he'd run all day, now out in the clean, steamy air. He quickly built a four-second lead. The last thing he'd wanted was a caution to eat that away, but his teammate Bobby Labonte lost a right front tire and headed straight into the wall. Zipadelli had been right about the tires, and now the field came back into the pits.

"I want no changes made to this car," Stewart said, his voice steady but shaky.

Zipadelli nodded. "You're the man driving it," he said.

With twenty-eight laps to go, Stewart knew his car was fast, but fellow Indiana native Kasey Kahne's was faster—by as much as four-tenths of a second per lap. And it was beginning to feel like a two-car race.

One could look at Stewart's and Kahne's cars and see that they weren't in the same league. Kahne used much less track; Stewart began to waver. There was a time when the two had not been good friends at all; Kahne had come up from the same ranks and Stewart felt the competition. But they'd since mended fences.

Kahne took the lead but it seemed he could not pull away, even in the clean air. Both men wanted nothing more in NASCAR than to win at that track. There were sixteen laps to go.

Jimmie Johnson, caught in a swerve with a tire now down, headed at a terrifying, diagonal angle into the wall. The SAFER barrier absorbed much of the blow, but the fuel pump had been knocked off his car and he drove with a cab full of smoke toward the pits. Johnson stopped in his stall but crew chief Chad Knaus climbed swiftly down from the pit box, making a wide-eyed, strained dash to the car. Johnson's crew looked too relaxed, until Knaus got there.

"Get out!" he shouted, pulling at the window netting. "Get him out of the car!"

A fire had worked its way underneath Johnson's Chevrolet. Knaus climbed inside: His friend was hardly moving, reaching up to his helmet at a snail's pace. Rear tire changer Tim Ladyga dove in through the passenger side and together with Knaus they undid Johnson's belts and pulled him to safety. His helmet off, Johnson looked frustrated and confused, then dry-mouthed and scared, like he could easily vomit. Knaus stood at his side, applying a bag of ice to the back of his head.

It was, Johnson said a moment later, the hardest hit he'd ever taken. Asked to describe what happened after the crash, he blinked and rubbed his blurry eyes, and said he had no recollection of coming off turn four and into the pits. "But it's all good," he said, squinting in the harsh sun.

Stewart thought pitting would be a good idea, but Zipadelli shouted, "Stay out!" Both he and Kahne did stay out, Kahne still in front. It would now be a question of fuel reserve, speed, and strategy. The two cars slalomed back and forth slowly, behind the pace car, and Stewart heard the click in his headset. "Be smart," Zipadelli told him. "Make me proud here."

The pace car veered off and the green flag came out, and Stewart held back just a bit, just enough for a bit of trickery. Kahne, eyes on his rearview for an instant, seemed to hesitate as Stewart pushed full bore in his direction, diving underneath.

Stewart passed Kahne, working his way into first, and he passed his suite at turn two. Kahne was angry, frustrated; he'd been suckered. Now he was right up to Stewart, who shuffled back and forth, making the track seem twice as wide, an impenetrable barrier, low then high on the long straightaway, keeping Kahne guessing which way he might run or dive. Six laps now remained and Stewart began to pull away slightly.

But there was great nervousness, especially passing turn two. Stewart could see his father, stretching farther and farther over the railing in the suite, ready to fall over in the excitement.

Kahne was gearing himself up for one last darting attempt to pass, but he didn't have the horsepower. With five to go, Stewart was ahead by half a second. And he raced past the ninety-six-foot scoring tower where the number "20" blazed on top as if in neon. With two laps to go, the lead was .8 seconds.

There'd be no way to lose now; no way, unless something happened. Stewart hugged the line, faster than he'd run all day, and then the white flag came out, and in a sense, everything seemed to shut off and get very quiet.

He thought about the fuel now, whether he'd have enough, his eyes on the pressure gauge. And then that last half-lap, he stopped looking. "I just drove my lap," he said. "I drove my race. And I was watching the crowd because you couldn't help but watch the crowd."

It was his time, and he soaked it in. He didn't think about Kahne or the lap time. He had to make two clean corners and the long straightaway, and then he was home.

The checkered flag flew and the volume of cheers was overpowering, tumultuous.

He shouted and whooped into the radio, pumping his left fist as if on a pivot.

On the pit box, Zipadelli shared the moment, and the camera crews came over to ask what a win like this means. "You have no idea," he answered, his voice cracking after keeping it all together throughout the day. "I've never prayed so hard in my life." And then, speaking of his driver, his friend, he added, "Just to see the look on his face when I get there will be worth everything."

But it would take some time. The No. 20 team rushed over to the flag stand and began climbing the fence. Stewart turned the car around, taking the route backward in a Polish Victory Lap. He headed slowly along the backstretch, his fist high out the window.

Who knew that all it took was to make that measured decision, and come back home? It amazed him that it could lead to all this.

"The racing fan can never understand how important the mental part is," Benny Parsons later said. "It's more important than horsepower, aerodynamics, chassis, springs, shocks, it's more important. All the cars have just about the same everything. So why does one team succeed? Communication, the teams are getting along."

Stewart circled the grand track, the breeze playing against his face. "Tony! Tony!" the fans began to call, and the tears streamed down his cheeks.

He was taking in this moment by himself, adding his voice to the ghosts he'd heard back in 2001. He pulled over and parked by the fence now, at turn two, by his suite. Climbing up, Stewart and his father locked eyes—they'd done this together.

"Can you imagine the thrill of his father, the thrill he felt?" Parsons said afterward. "There's absolutely nothing better than someone wanting something so badly and it coming true. It's like the kid wanting the pony at Christmas and getting up and there's the pony and you think *man*! It's an adult sport, a grown-man's sport, but he could've been five years old."

Stewart headed to the flag stand, where he gingerly made his way up a few steps on the fence as the fan tide raised to its loudest salute, and then down he climbed. The adrenaline that had buoyed him had seeped out, and with a grin, he lay on the concrete wall, laughing. In the championship standings, he was now the leader, by seventy-five points. Three months later, he'd hoist his second Cup trophy as series champion. It would mean just as much to him that Zipadelli, at the end of the season, bought the championship-winning car from Joe Gibbs Racing and gave it to Stewart for Christmas.

"Today's been my entire life," Stewart told NASCAR reporter Allen Bestwick. And Stewart closed his eyes and listened to the cheers, with Zipadelli and the whole team surrounding him.

The feeling wouldn't get old. "Just to be a part of history there," Stewart said a year later, sitting in his motor coach, his voice trailing off as he shook his head. "When I said it was the greatest day of my life, I meant it 100 percent. All I ever wanted to do was win a race at Indianapolis. We've got our place in the history of Indianapolis Motor Speedway.

"To not only have your family involved, but to be on the racetrack and physically see them once every lap, that just adds to that experience and excitement. And driving with tears in my eyes? No, it's not a bad feeling to have."

Years later, he'd have other astounding shifts and triumphs: His leaving Joe Gibbs Racing to co-form Stewart-Haas Racing starting with the 2009 season, his inspired mind-boggling run to his third Cup title in 2011, and his reunion with Zipadelli, who joined Stewart-Haas as Competition Director starting in the 2012 season. But nothing would ever dull the glory of that first win at Indy.

At his home in Columbus, the Brickyard 400 trophy sat on display, right downstairs from the bedroom. "If I wanted to remind myself, all I had to do was go down a flight of steps and stare at that trophy," Stewart said. "And I could stare at it and it wasn't gonna do anything. It was still gonna be there."

In 1998, 18-year-old Adam Petty continued family tradition, becoming the youngest-ever winner of an ARCA series event and topping the record set years earlier by his father, Kyle.

June 20, 2004

"Our family won so many races and did so much that it always meant just winning. And I kind of look at what we do here as, we're helping other people win now. For so long it was all about us, and now it's about other people. Hopefully that will be the legacy."

—KYLE PETTY, talking about the Victory Junction Gang Camp

N THE MIDDLE OF MAIN STREET, A SMALL THREE-BLOCK AVENUE A FEW turns off the interstate in downtown Lexington, Kentucky, the faithful waited patiently. The late-afternoon sun was baking the fans lined up in the parking lot of the Chik-fil-A, the well-known Southern family restaurant and longtime chief sponsor of the Kyle Petty Charity Ride Across America. The franchise was set to host about two hundred motorcyclists who'd spent the day riding in from Lombard, Illinois, and they'd be greeted properly after a hard, fun, successful day on the road.

There were lots of fan shirts among the several hundred who showed up. Many wore Tony Stewart, a bunch of Dale Jr. and Jeff Gordon, and, of course, a healthy supply of Kyle Petty. Despite split allegiances, they were each hoping for an autograph when the time came. The line snaked around a sleek, classic Petty Blue Plymouth Firebird in the front of the lot, which looked every bit the museum piece.

Kyle Petty was midway through his 2008 annual Charity Ride, a three-thousand-mile journey lasting several days from Traverse City, Michigan, to Savannah, Georgia, to raise money in support of Shriners Hospitals for Children, and the Victory Junction Gang Camp, a summer camp started by the Pettys to give respite to children with chronic illnesses and their families. The annual ride had begun in 1995. "We did it like a bike-a-thon," Kyle remembered. "It was just twenty-five, thirty of us and we asked people to pledge a penny or a nickel a mile. We got sixty people to do it the next year and we doubled the money. And then we realized you can't have ten million people doing it because you can't control them on the highway so we capped it off. Then we got sponsors like Chik-fil-A and Coca-Cola and Wells Fargo and people like that and it grew to what it is. Last year we raised a substantial amount. We were able to stop at a hospital and give, you know, twenty-five, thirty thousand dollars. Doesn't sound like a lot but it goes a long way."

The Ride has raised more than $12 million in its time. A lot of the money raised now goes toward supporting Victory Junction, which is located in Randleman, North Carolina. Kyle and his wife, Pattie, started the camp at the urging of their son Adam, who'd gotten the idea after coming with them to visit one of Paul Newman's Hole in the Wall Gang Cmps for kids. Adam knew the value of the family's visits to hospitals to raise the spirits of children, but he'd grown frustrated by the swoop-in, swoop-out nature of the exercise. He wanted to build something that would endure.

Adam's greatest passion, however, was racing, and he followed in the footsteps of the racers in his family. When Adam was killed in 2000 in a practice crash, the Petty family poured much energy and passion into Victory Junction. Adam was to be the future of Petty racing. As it turned out, he was destined to become the symbol of another legacy.

* * *

Richard Petty had been the sport's first true ambassador, flashing a friendly smile to welcome fans at races. Kyle could trace a line through the sport's history from his father's popularity to his own equally uniting successes in philanthropy. Somehow, it all came together when Adam died, inspiring a huge outpouring. It both shocked and humbled Kyle.

"I've always joked and said all we do is ride around in circles, but I don't think I even realized how many lives you touch," Kyle said in 2000, at his emotional first press conference after Adam's death. "What we do out here, it brings a lot of enjoyment, and they begin to feel a part of your family, and they begin to feel like you're a part of them, and that's been phenomenal for me. I should have realized that a long time ago."

In the middle of the Charity Ride pack, Kyle Petty rolled up on his Harley Davidson Electra Glide Classic, wearing a white shirt covered with sponsor logos. His helmet soon off, he put on the No. 45 cap—Adam's onetime car number—that has became as much a part of who he is as the ponytail extending past his shoulders, and the goatee now generously speckled with gray.

The silver console and fuel cap on his motorcycle has doubled as his high-speed memo pad; with an erasable marker at the ready, he scrawled notes and song lyrics while on the road every day. "My son-in-law's a songwriter and sometimes I'll write ideas down," he said. There was, in Lexington, a note to send someone old photos from a past ride, and the start of a song about a guy who drinks and lies, and then wonders how many times he'll have to say "I love you" to make up for it.

Football great Herschel Walker was along for the ride, as was model Niki Taylor, along with her husband, NASCAR driver Burney Lamar. Matt Kenseth counted among the part-timers cycling for a few days. The route had taken Kyle and company across the Mackinac Bridge in Michigan, where the temperature dropped to 35 degrees, a cold ride by the Great Lakes. Then down through Milwaukee and a visit to the Harley Davidson Museum. "We've had a blast," Kyle said.

The ride is also an annual trip down memory lane, and it clears Kyle's head, as he takes the open road with his wife, Pattie, and friends he's come to know well. Until the off-season merger of Petty Enterprises with Gillete Evernham Racing to form Richard Petty Motorsports, Kyle had remained a Cup driver, balancing part-time life behind the wheel with a gig as a racing commentator on TNT. But whatever he did then and continues to do now all feeds into raising money and awareness for Victory Junction.

"You use racing and your other businesses as a platform," he said, standing outside the Chick-fil-A, getting ready to sign autographs. "It's funny—ask me ten or fifteen years ago, my focus would have been all about winning a trophy; now it's all about getting a kid to camp and getting a sponsor for a week of camp."

There was a time when the trophies did come, first for his grandfather, then for his dad, and then for him. But those days, like the road he'd just come in on, were now memories, crowded images in the rearview mirror. The next day would soon come, and there would be more riding and more money raised for more kids.

*   *   *

The first time he drove in what later became know as the Sprint Cup Series, in a July 1958 race in Toronto, Richard Petty ended his day by being punted into a wall by his dad. Lee Petty had loomed behind Richard's car long enough. He'd been trying to stay in front of rival racer Cotton Owens, and his kid, already a lap down, was in the way.

Lee had won the first of his three NASCAR championships in 1954; he'd win titles again in 1958 and '59. Richard and his younger brother Maurice were there to help get the cars ready and learn from their father, a driver-owner who raced to put food on the table.

The wreck knocked Richard around inside the cab a bit and it smacked the bumper clean off the car. But his father won the race, salvaging the day. "It was all a part of the learning curve," Richard said. "You start out, you're going to wreck a bunch of cars. That's what rookies do. We put the bumper back on, got ready for the next race"—which was run the following afternoon in Buffalo.

At Petty Enterprises, Lee did most of the driving, Richard built the engines, and Maurice worked on the cars. And Lee's word was law. Asked to describe his working relationship with his father, Maurice Petty said, "He told me what to do and I done it."

In the mid-1950s, most races were held on short tracks in the south, classic half- or one-mile dirt tracks such as Asheville-Weaverville, Hickory, and Occoneechee, and long-forgotten racing outposts with names such as Hayloft Speedway, Chisolm Speedway, and Oglethorpe Speedway in Savannah, Georgia, where Lee Petty won an early-March 1955 race in a '54 Chrysler. It was not unusual to have several races run in a given week. Fifty-six races were run in 1956; fifty-three the following year.

Lee was a thin, robust man, whose short, dark hair, warm smile, and open face belied a laconic nature, immense determination, and the desire to have everything done just so. When Richard appeared to win his first race at Atlanta's Lakewood Speedway in June 1959, his father protested the result. Scorecards were checked with Lee declared the winner, and his son second. The following February, Richard finally earned his first win at the half-mile Charlotte Fairgrounds. His dad wasn't ashamed to admit he may have helped his boy; driving in relief of racer Doug Yates, Lee Petty smacked into Rex White, who was challenging the younger Petty for the lead in the late going.

"Lee Petty was kinda like I was," said two-time champion Buck Baker. "He was a guy who'd like to run over you and then say, 'Excuse me.'"

Lee and Richard Petty were among the fifty-nine racers on the track for the 1959 inaugural Daytona 500. Richard was wiped out by engine trouble after eight laps, but his father won the race by two feet in a photo finish over Johnny Beauchamp. The only problem was there were no track cameras to confirm that. Beauchamp was mistakenly tagged the victor and a frustrated Lee Petty waited in Daytona Beach for three days until Bill France had gotten absolute confirmation from a slew of photos and videos. Petty finally took his $19,000 earnings on Wednesday and left to get ready for the next race in Hilsborough, North Carolina.

Daytona had been Lee's greatest triumph, and two years later, it would be the scene of his undoing. On February 24, 1961, Lee and, ironically enough, Beauchamp came together toward the end of their Daytona 500 qualifying race, with both cars taking a sickening journey up the track and over the guardrail, plummeting past a tall track fence toward the parking lot below. Beauchamp came away with head injuries; Petty suffered a punctured lung, and multiple broken bones and internal injuries. There was no guarantee he'd live.

"Daddy was still the boss man, mother always signed all the checks but Daddy done all the business, and all of a sudden here I was, twenty-three years old, and my brother was a year younger than I was, and we'd always done what he said to," Richard said. "There was no sponsorship, so there was no money. And he's laying there in a bed and I talk to him and he says go on up to the dealership and get another car, start getting it ready. He said, 'Me and your mother'll be home by Friday.' Four months later he come home.

"And all of a sudden we were having to do the business part of it, the mechanical part, all the thinking, the strategy, whatever it was. You was running the family business, and there was no money. But, you know, the combination of my brother and myself working together, even though we had a lot of arguments over it, we worked our way through that. We were looking after a lot of people who had depended on Daddy to do it. I grew up real quick."

* * *

Richard Petty was not classically handsome and restless on the track like Curtis Turner; exciting and enigmatic the way Fireball Roberts was; or the matinee type that Yankee-born golden boy Fred Lorenzen was. But he understood the lesson of engaging the fans. The folks at Plymouth offered a generous supply of material and Petty shone, especially on the short tracks that dominated the circuit.

It also didn't hurt his popularity—and the growth of stock car racing in general—that one of Petty's favorite classes in school had been penmanship. It took Petty a good fifteen or twenty seconds to complete his loping, swirling autograph, a level of dedication the race fans appreciated. And Petty signed for as many folks as would ask.

"Daddy's big deal was, you got to sell yourself before you can sell your product," he said. "Even though mechanical ability and a bunch of this driving deal and stuff I learned from him, the biggest thing that's lasted throughout life probably is, you gotta get along with people. That makes everything else work."

For Petty, it all worked. Starting in 1966, he won six championships in fifteen seasons. But 1967 was his career year, when he won twenty-seven times in forty-eight starts, highlighted by an amazing run of ten straight victories.

"It got to be a pretty big deal over the whole country," he recalled of the streak. "Now, you couldn't even live if you won that much. There'd be so much hullabaloo."

The season earned Petty the nickname "King of Stock Car Racing," and his status among fans—he won the sport's Most Popular Driver award seven times between 1968 and 1978—only increased when Petty Enterprises signed with STP in 1972, trading additional support for the large STP logo on Richard's "Petty Blue" hood that boosted sales for Andy Granatelli's oil additive company.

But for the team, which included Petty family cousin Dale Inman as long-time crew chief, the most important logo on the car may have been the one on the left rear quarter panel reading "BY Petty," an indication of family handiwork and craftsmanship—and his and Maurice's ability to see past conflicts and build winners.

"I got scars here, I got scars right here, scars all over—we used to fight all the time about something," Richard said of himself and Maurice. "About '56, '57 was the last time I remember us having a fight. I think we finally decided we were big enough then to hurt each other. We had a lot of arguments, ain't no doubt about that. But we were after the same thing; we wanted to win. I had my way and he had his way, and we'd argue about that. We'd usually settle on somewhere between me and him, and we got pretty good at it. But he built more winning engines than any two or three of the best ones that's ever been. They ain't even close to him."

"We had a good driver, and luckily we were fortunate enough to keep all our pieces together," Maurice said of those top years. "A lot of credit goes to Richard and his driving style. Here again, we didn't know nothing else. It was our livelihood. We ran the business a lot like Lee ran it. It put bread on the table, and you had to do it. You *had* to do it."

* * *

Buddy Baker, who ran almost thirty races for Petty Enterprises in the early 1970s, remembered a day when Richard's son Kyle, who was then about ten, ran into the company's fab shop with the sneakers his dad had just bought him.

"Brand-new tennis shoes," Baker said, as if he could still see how gleaming white they were. "And Kyle'd take them over and paint them. Everybody would go, 'God, do you believe that?' He'd have big red stars and half moons on 'em. Kyle always did hear a different drummer."

But when Kyle started racing in 1979, the son of the king started out in a manner befitting his heritage: He became the youngest driver ever to win an Automobile Racing Club of America race, at eighteen. Kyle captured the Daytona ARCA event—in his first-ever professional attempt—on the same weekend that his father won the "500" after Cale Yarborough and Donnie Allison famously wrecked out on the last lap.

Kyle was the anointed one; granted, Richard Petty was still the king, but while he won his seventh championship in 1979, it would turn out to be his last. And with Kyle on board, Richard's hands became increasingly tied by the time-consuming economic realities of running a full-time two-driver team, something Petty Enterprises hadn't done in the twenty years since Lee and Richard Petty ran the whole schedule in 1960.

In five-plus Cup seasons driving for the family team, Kyle scored no victories in 140 races, with only four top fives. Much was made of his focusing on a number of outside passions—music perhaps being chief among them—and the negative publicity based on his performance dogged him.

"You gotta realize that whatever you do at work, you're gonna take it home, no matter what," he said. "That's a hard balancing act to work with."

After one more season of struggle in 1984, Kyle left Petty Enterprises, beginning a four-year driving stint with Wood Brothers Racing.

Kyle did his level best to live up to his promise but the arrangement still wasn't ideal. At the end of the 1988 season, he signed on for a part-time ride in 1989 with SABCO, the team begun by Felix Sabates. There, experiencing great chemistry with his hungry, first-time team owner, he blossomed into a solid, quality racecar driver. Kyle and Sabates saw the rebel spirit in each other; they were, in a sense, like long-lost brothers.

Kyle's eight victories came during these years; in two consecutive seasons, he finished fifth in the point standings, his highest ever. But he was plagued by factors that hurt his consistency, from a bit of a revolving door with main sponsors to crash injuries that sidelined him twice. But at his best, in the early 1990s, during years of intense, joyous rivalry in NASCAR, he was competitive with Davey Allison, Dale Earnhardt, Tim Richmond, Alan Kulwicki, and Bill Elliott. Some days Kyle was spectacular. But he was less so by the mid-1990s, and after two uninspired seasons, he and Sabates parted company.

Kyle's return to Petty Enterprises for the 1997 season may have been inevitable, but both father and son had long-lasting memories of what had once gone wrong. Kyle was going to do things his own way, not the way his father had; he opened PE2, an arm of Petty Enterprises, driving the No. 44 Hot Wheels Pontiac. That season, he earned five top fives and finished fifteenth in points.

But after slumping badly the following season, Kyle closed up PE2 and moved the operation back to Petty Enterprises, where he took over CEO duties from his dad. His underwhelming driving performances might have weighed on him but Kyle was perennially busy, trying to arrange for sponsors and keep other areas of the business running smoothly. Plus, he suddenly had a much more important task at hand. His own success was a footnote. He was still the present, but Adam was the future.

* * *

On June 27, 1998, Adam Petty stood with his crew, soaking in the pleasures of perhaps the proudest moment of his life. He'd just charged back from two laps down to capture his first American Speed Association win, on a half-mile track in Odessa, Missouri. Only one thing would have made the moment perfect.

"Get me a cell phone," he told a member of his crew.

Kyle Petty was in Sonoma, California, having finished practice runs for the next day's Winston Cup race at which he'd start eighth, his highest qualifying spot of the year so far. When the phone rang, he answered it and heard the shouts of the crowd through the receiver.

"Where are you?" Kyle asked, squinting.

"Victory lane," his son yelled.

It was only Adam's tenth-ever ASA start, and at two weeks shy of his eighteenth birthday, he'd become the youngest driver ever to post a victory in the series, besting Mark Martin's record from 1977.

Adam's love of racecars was unreserved and unrestrained. Except perhaps in his most dialed-in moments, Kyle knew that he could no longer boast of having his son's total commitment and lack of self-consciousness.

"When my dad came along, people expected him to live up to who my grandfather was," Adam recalled. "Halfway through his career, people realized that there was never gonna be another Richard Petty. And, at that time, it became easier on my dad. And then I came along and started racing. And that gave him something else to look forward to."

But with Adam, it was more than the racing, and Kyle knew it. The purpose that Adam really mastered was an understanding of what it meant to be a Petty, in and out of the sport, with a determination and a generosity of spirit.

Adam began racing go-karts at six but he was only somewhat inspired, until the chance to run stock cars passed from hobby to obsession. Suddenly motivated, he changed his diet and took on Kyle's personal trainer after starting to drive Late Models. He was an overweight teen until he lost seventy pounds. He was caught by his parents charging items for his racecars on their credit card; the punishment was a temporary suspension of his racing. Then Adam finished high school early so he could race sooner, and he moved to Grand Rapids, Michigan, and started on the ASA circuit. And after he'd won that first ASA race, he stood around, signing autographs for fans for two and a half hours, no doubt with the patented family smile on his face.

Like his dad and grandfather, he stood a bit over six feet, but while

Kyle was around 195 pounds and Richard closer to 180, Adam was only about 145, and even lankier than Grandpa Richard had been as a kid. He kept his dark hair short and was happiest when he was participating in a favorite family discussion: going faster. There was a refreshing innocence—and yet a seriousness—about him.

Two-and-a-half months after his first ASA win, Adam was running in the ASA Miller Lite 300 at the half-mile Minnesota State Fair Speedway on September 7. During a late-race caution, he drove his Pontiac Grand Prix in for a pit stop.

Adam's crew chief and close friend Chris Bradley had called for four tires and fuel, but Bradley also realized, in a split second, that the car needed a sway bar adjustment to improve handling, and without mentioning it to the crew, he reached under the car to do it. It was one little movement, but it was outside the structure of the carefully rehearsed pit-stop ballet, a change in a routine that Bradley himself had orchestrated. And he was underneath the car, still working, when the crew finished. The jack man dropped the car back onto the track, trapping Bradley there, and Adam, recognizing the signal, sped off, feeling at first like he must have rolled over an air wrench or another piece of equipment. He was out on the track for a few laps when the race was stopped, and Adam was told what had happened to Bradley.

Adam rushed to Regions Hospital in St. Paul, immensely distraught. An ASA chaplain was at Bradley's bedside. He sensed the mix of guilt and pain in Adam and offered comfort. But this was also a lesson, he told him, a test of his will. "This will either make you or break you," the chaplain said.

Bradley died a little more than two hours after the accident.

Adam's friend and crew chief was in his mind three weeks later, as he lined up for his first-ever Automobile Racing Club of America contest, at Charlotte Motor Speedway. It would be Adam's first speedway race. This time, his parents and grandparents were there, along with several Cup and Busch series team owners, who'd come to size up the field's talent.

Adam was strong for a good portion of the day, and as the laps were winding down, he inched closer to leader Bobby Hamilton Jr., finally catching him with fifteen laps remaining. His father and his grand-father had both given him enough advice to fill notebooks about this place. Among the bits of counsel: You don't pass a car on the outside on turn four at Charlotte.

Seemed like a smart plan, in theory. But Adam was especially good on the high side. And neither Kyle nor Richard was driving this racecar.

Adam made a swift, clean outside pass on Hamilton and began to open up a gap. With one lap to go, Mike Wallace, who'd passed Hamil-ton, was creeping up toward Petty's rear bumper. A little nudge made him wiggle but he held true to his line. And Wallace, coming into turn four, tried the same strategy on the young Petty: He raced him up high, pulling right alongside on the outside. As they entered the straightaway, Adam's car had the better angle. He moved down the track and Wallace's momentum could not carry him past, and Adam saw the car begin to fall back.

Adam took the checkered flag, and the applause was tumultuous for the hometown hero, the next generation of Petty. Adam had broken another record: He was now the youngest-ever ARCA race winner. And the former holder of that record, his father, Kyle, came running over to victory lane to greet his son.

As joyous as the moment seemed, Adam was subdued. This win was inspiring, but Adam knew Chris Bradley's death would redefine him.

"I had just turned eighteen and that was the turning point in my life," he said of the Bradley accident. "It made me realize: This is a man's sport. Stuff happens to you that sometimes shouldn't. You don't think it should happen to you. But losing Chris—not only did it make me closer to the Lord, and make me a better person, but it made me realize a whole lot of things. . . . You realize how precious life is, and how quick it can be taken away.

"Chris was a great friend of mine—he taught me a whole lot about racing. But after losing him and going on to win the ARCA race, it brought my confidence level back to where it was, and that was pretty special. I think the good Lord did that. You know, he works in mysterious ways sometimes."

* * *

Kyle had it all planned out: Adam would run two full seasons in the Busch series, 1999 and 2000; in 2000, he'd also run a few Cup races, getting prepared for a full-time Cup ride in 2001.

With most of the Busch schedule mirroring the Cup stops, father and son were able to travel many of the same roads together; they often drove to races in separate motor coaches but most of the time Adam ended up bunking with his dad.

It couldn't have been better for the Pettys: Adam's career had become something of a family gathering point. His mom, Pattie, and his sister Montgomery Lee and brother Austin, not to mention his grandfather, visited Kyle and Adam on the road several times. It was as if they were going through these building-block days all together.

"We go out to dinner together, we stay on the bus together, and we talk racing," Kyle said. "I watch his race on Saturdays, and he tells me what he thinks he did wrong, and I tell him what I think he did wrong. And then he watches me on Sunday and tells me what I do wrong. You know, we've always been father and son. But I think, at some point in time, it's evolved into a little bit deeper relationship between a father and son."

"It's a father-and-son relationship Monday to Wednesday, but I think Wednesday to Sunday, we're more brothers," Adam said. "We're more best friends than we are anything."

Watching Adam's resolve, and the way he carried himself on and off the track, it was easy for Kyle to acknowledge his own shortcomings, and even suggest that the Petty magic had passed over him.

"My son," he told reporters after Adam's big ARCA win, "can be what my father was."

With Sprint along as Adam's sponsor in the Busch series, Kyle made sure the resources were in place in a way they hadn't been for him at the start. The family line felt complete. Lee Petty had driven car number 42; Richard made the 43 famous; and when Kyle returned to Petty Enterprises, he began driving the 44 car. Adam, next in line, drove the 45.

The 1999 season was as up and down as one might expect from a rookie year on a major racing circuit. Adam finished sixth at Daytona; a week later, he failed to qualify for Rockingham. In late May, he posted his third top ten of the season at the race in Nazareth Pennsylvania; the next two weeks, he finished forty-third and fortieth.

And early in May, he'd accompanied his family as usual on the Kyle Petty Charity Ride.

The ride had become a much-anticipated family tradition, filled with visits to children's hospitals. It was hard for kids to stay shy or upset when the smiling Pettys entered the room.

Adam loved the Ride, but he couldn't stop thinking about what happened when the riders hopped back on their motorcycles and left for the next location. He'd spend at most a few minutes with a child, and then leave behind the same medical problems and family frustrations. A visit from some NASCAR drivers might be a nice lift but it would not sustain anyone.

A few years earlier, the Pettys had visited Florida's Camp Boggy Creek, one of Paul Newman's Hole in the Wall summer camps where children with chronic illnesses could spend a week safely playing and having fun in a medically supported environment, attending for free. While touring the grounds, Kyle and Pattie wondered if they could build the same kind of camp.

The idea lay dormant until Adam resurrected it. He became insistent that any camp the Pettys would build would have to mimick Boggy Creek.

"Adam went to [Boggy Creek] with us and said, 'Mom, this is what we need to do,'" Pattie remembered. " 'Our family needs to build something that's ours, and when Dad and I go out and make an appearance and we tell someone it costs ten thousand dollars, hey, five of it goes to the camp.' And he said, 'I don't want to give money to hospitals anymore; I want to grow our own.' He loved the camp and loved the idea that it was free.

"When we visited children's hospitals it was very devastating to him to see the families struggling. Families are ripped apart, marriages are ripped apart; 52 percent of families with a chronic illness end up in bankruptcy and divorce. Adam was very sensitive to that."

Kyle and Pattie moved forward with the early groundwork, contacting doctors, getting in touch with Paul Newman and Boggy Creek executives to plan things out. Adam began scouting locations, searching for a setting large enough for the camp. The seed had begun to sprout.

In 2000, Adam was set to run another full year in Busch and perhaps five or more races in Cup. The previous August, Kyle had run a paint scheme at the Brickyard 400 celebrating the fiftieth anniversary of Petty Enterprises. It was Kyle's twentieth year as a full-time driver in Cup. The company's Web site boasted, "50 Years, 10 Championships, Four Generations . . . and we're just getting started."

But past and future quickly collided. As Adam was working his way through early-season struggles, Lee Petty suffered postsurgical complications and, at eighty-six, feeling the effects of a stomach aneurysm, began to decline further. He was, however, able to watch as his great-grandson became the first fourth-generation driver to start a Winston Cup race when Adam qualified thirty-third for the April 2 contest at Texas Motor Speedway. But Lee and everyone else in the family would be robbed of a thrill: Kyle failed to qualify for the race, and the chance to run on the same track as his boy.

Three days after the race, Lee Petty, the family patriarch who had famously begun his journey in the sport working out of a 20-by-25-foot open-air reaper shed on the Petty farm, passed away.

The sixth annual Charity Ride came in early May 2000. Two weeks later, Adam was off to Loudon for the May 13 Busch race. Kyle, with a week to spare before the Winston All-Star race in Charlotte, decided to take Montgomery Lee on a father-daughter trip to Europe. Given all the weeks he'd spent with Adam, Kyle thought the one-on-one time would do both him and his daughter good.

Kyle was a little fidgety, though; he wasn't used to being away from it all: the racing with Adam, the enthusiasm, the learning. On the plane ride to London, fourteen-year-old Montgomery Lee was enamored with the air phone; she couldn't believe you could make calls while in the air. She and Kyle called Adam in New Hampshire three or four times during the flight so they could tell him they loved him. And soon enough, Kyle's phone was bound to ring, and he'd hear all about how it was going.

Meanwhile, Adam did his preparations and strapped himself in behind the wheel of the No. 45 Sprint Chevy, ready for Friday's practice. And when the signal came to go, he left pit road, taking to the track with the enthusiasm that only the fortunate among us can give to the things that we truly love.

* * *

Kyle's entire world seemed to stop when NASCAR President Mike Helton called him in London, telling him the news that was impossible to register. . . . The throttle had hung open on Adam's car during his practice run at Loudon and the 45 had gone into the wall. And then everything culminated with the irreversible truth: Adam Petty was gone.

Days later, a thousand people came to Adam's funeral, and Austin and Montgomery Lee spoke beautifully about their big brother, who loved and was good and kind and wanted only to race and help people. He was nineteen years old.

Kyle, Pattie, Austin, and Montgomery Lee were in their own world for two weeks. Letters came in from everywhere, support from friends and complete strangers. And then they had to go on.

"It was incredibly hard for Pattie and I, hard to go back to Adam's race shop," Kyle told reporters at his first news conference after the accident. "You'll never know how hard that was. To see those cars there with his name on it, to see his seats and uniforms and stuff like that. . ." Kyle trailed off a moment, overwhelmed. "But at the same time, there's nothing Adam loved more than racecars and being around his car and the race people."

Together, the family made a decision they believed Adam would have wanted, and perhaps the only one Kyle could have lived with: He would take over his son's ride, give up driving the No. 44 in the Cup series, and tread the path Adam would have.

Kyle could never be Adam; he knew that. And he could not give up racing. A part of him wanted to, but he was resolute: this is what he did, what the Pettys did. By taking over Adam's No. 45 Sprint Chevrolet, he could at least somehow share these moments with him.

After Sprint agreed to remain the sponsor of the No. 45 car, Kyle set about completing the season. He mandated that his name not be put above the driver's door of the car where it normally would; that spot remained blank. It would be Adam's car; Kyle was only the driver. He put a No. 45 cap on his head and it seemed to never come off. He'd wear one out, and switch right away to another one.

Kyle missed the two weeks of races in Charlotte, and he and Pattie rode their motorcycles from home to Dover, Delaware, for Kyle's first Busch race in Adam's car. Thursday night had always been his and Adam's night at the track; they'd size everything up, go out to dinner, and just be together. Getting there that first Thursday night with Pattie, it was hard for them to even put one foot in front of the other.

But when he did finally walk through the garage area, Kyle was overwhelmed by the show of support from drivers and crewmen. What had happened to Adam, to the last of the Petty family drivers, seemed to hit everybody personally. Kyle, picking himself up this way, displayed immense courage.

As he made his way through the 2000 Busch season, Kyle was energized by the focus: His only comfort was in keeping his gaze forward, in being inside that car.

In 2001, the team, as planned, moved up to race Winston Cup full time, under the glare of the sport's new TV contract, where Adam would have shone as a NASCAR prince. Before the season-opening Daytona 500, Kyle stood quietly in a daze, tears springing to his eyes. It was too much: This would have been Adam's moment.

And then Dale Earnhardt came over and put his arms around Kyle to comfort him. The two friends embraced for several minutes, and Kyle stood there, letting it all out, until he had a better grip on the moment.

The hug would stick with Kyle through the day, as generous a show of friendship as any he'd ever gotten.

But that made it even more devastating when, hours later, Earnhardt crashed the same way Adam had. After contact with the wall in the last lap of the 500, Earnhardt was dead.

The sport reeled from yet another towering tragedy. More talk arose of safety and what-ifs. And Kyle was plunged back into grief.

There were few comforts to take his mind away. But there was the car.

"I go out there because that's what I love to do," he said midway through the 2001 season. "But the wound never is able to heal. It almost gets to that point where you begin to feel comfortable and then something shakes your world again. But I don't want it to totally heal."

* * *

Kyle watched as the death of Dale Earnhardt led to an agreement among drivers and officials for more stringent safety measures in stock car racing. The reaction to Earnhardt's crash remade the sport, leading the way for soft walls at the tracks, the sport's new car, and the mandatory HANS devices to protect a driver's head and neck during a wreck.

Kyle knew many of those changes had already been discussed after Adam's crash. None of them would bring either Adam or Dale back, but they'd protect against the same thing happening again.

Keeping with the multi-car trend in the sport, Kyle and Petty Enterprises fielded three full-time teams in 2001—for himself, John Andretti, and Buckshot Jones—with Kyle struggling.

"Adam was always saying, 'Dad, you've got to fix this or that,'" recalled Andretti. "In a lot of ways, our motivation has to do with getting there in remembrance of what might have been."

"He's still the driving influence behind where we're at," Kyle said of Adam. "As we've made changes, I look at it and say, 'Would I do this for myself?' Hmmm, maybe not. But I would give Adam every opportunity to have the best stuff he could have. I want to make sure that [with] this team we put together for him and the changes we continue to make, I can look back at some point and say, 'Yeah, he would have been a winner.'"

Doing so got harder. In 2002, eight different drivers suited up at various times for the company in the Cup series, yielding very little success.

Kyle had been looking to Cup success as the best way to honor Adam, and it had brought only frustration.

Two years after the accident, the Pettys circled back around to the other project that Adam had wanted to create.

"It became evident to us that even though we didn't think we had the energy or the emotional stability to build the camp, we needed to do it in Adam's honor and to keep what he believed in alive," Pattie said.

Newman had given the Pettys the $500,000 seed money to get their project moving. Going forward with the necessary arrangements would be a different matter.

"It's not easy to raise $30 million and then another $2.5 million every year," Pattie said.

But if Earnhardt's passing had cemented one kind of unity in the sport, Adam's had led to another.

Kyle and Pattie's announcement that they were building the Victory Junction Gang Camp inspired an unprecedented show of support. Thousands of fans sent donations, many of them in amounts such as $4.50 or $4,500.

Richard and Lynda Petty donated eighty-four acres of land near their Randleman, North Carolina home for the project. Drivers organized and participated in fundraising efforts to add to the necessary capital.

"We all lost someone we really cared about when we lost Adam Petty," said Tony Stewart, who has raised several million dollars for the camp. "To have a kid who in his late teens had such a passion for children, to want to build a camp that takes care of those children—you don't see a lot of kids at his age wanting to become a part of that. There's thousands of charities out there but when it hits close to home like this, it's a very, very easy decision."

After two years of effort and focus, the place came together.

There was the big fishing pond, which would have a strict "Catch, Kiss, and Release" policy. A ring for horseback riding, which had become Montgomery Lee's great passion. All the bunks were done up in bright colors, bearing the names of NASCAR tracks, and the nightstands next to the beds were shaped like gas pumps. The mess hall was dubbed the Fuel Stop.

But best—and biggest—of all, as the place took shape, was the workshop, memorabilia center, and racing-simulation attraction known as Adam's Race Shop, a two-story building shaped like an enormous car parked on the side of the road, awash in green, purple, pink, and red, with the large, yellow "45" emblazoned on the door. "It is," said Pattie, "the coolest building ever built."

No matter how bad things might be going for Petty Enterprises on the racetrack, Kyle and Richard could walk through the camp and begin to see a different kind of legacy taking shape.

Victory Junction Gang Camp opened for its first week of campers on June 20, 2004—Father's Day—as buses filled with excited kids made the gentle left turn onto 4500 Adam's Way, and headed down the grass-lined road to a kind of paradise. And yet, with all the screaming and laughing, Kyle and Pattie felt a reserved joy.

Camp was open for a couple of days when word came to the front office that a little boy with hemophilia was refusing to come out of his cabin and participate in activities. Kyle walked over to the bunk to see if he could urge him to join in. When he got there, he found the boy bitter and upset.

"You lied to me," he said to Kyle.

"What are you talking about?"

"You said everybody here at this camp was sick like me; they're not sick," he said, the muted sounds of glee audible outside. "None of them are sick," he said.

Kyle called the boy over; together they stood, staring at their reflections in a mirror in the bunk.

"What do you see about you that's different from the other children here?" Kyle said to him. "Look; you've got a chin, a mouth, a nose, everything I've got, and you look healthy. You're just not, and neither are they."

"And the boy figured it out," Pattie said afterward. " 'I don't look different, I've just been treated different.' He perceived himself to be the only one with problems, the only kid who looked terrible, the one no one let on the teams at home. That was a huge thing for us."

Kyle got back to the office and told Pattie the story. "Now we know why we built this place," he said. "We thought we knew why, but now we do."

* * *

Touring around Victory Junction now is, in one sense, akin to walking past the haulers in a Sprint Cup garage. The Hendrick Motorsports Fuel Stop is walking distance from the Michael Waltrip Operation Marathon Sportscenter; keep walking and you'll get to the Kurt Busch Superdome, along with the Jimmie Johnson Victory Lanes Bowling Alley. The place is filled with memories of the drivers who've come to visit. There was the time when Kurt Busch came for a day and was asked by one of the campers if she could redo his hair. Busch quickly agreed. A little while later, he emerged from the Fab Shop with something resembling a pink-and-purple mohawk. Tony Stewart remembers his first visit to the camp; he spent a good portion of the day with one particular fan, and ended up leaving the camp past curfew, being unable to pull himself away.

"If you leave there and you haven't shed a tear, you'll surprise me as a person," he said. "I've not left there yet and not had tears in my eyes when I left, and you never want to leave."

That had come to be Kyle's feeling as well. He'd spent years wearing, and wearing out, the 45 cap in honor of Adam, and the cap had come to represent all his efforts across the board in all businesses.

"Everything falls under that umbrella," he said. "Everything we do, whether it's racing, the charity ride, Victory Junction Gang Camp, it all just intertwines and connects. There's a common thread running through it and that's just helping people."

Fortunes for the race team, however, declined. After the 2007 season, Richard Petty moved the company facility from his childhood home in Level Cross, North Carolina, to the building that had housed Robert Yates Racing, in Charlotte. The best way to attract the sport's top talent, he figured, was to be near all the action.

To Kyle, who'd grown up next to that shop, the move spelled the end of Petty Enterprises as he knew it. He couldn't hide his disdain. Six months later, Petty Enterprises merged with the investment firm Boston Ventures. But then the ensuing economic crisis forced still more changes. Before the start of the 2009 season, Petty Enterprises merged again, this time with Gillett Evernham Motorsports. The combined company was renamed Richard Petty Motorsports, RPM. Clever naming notwithstanding, it was clear that Petty Enterprises, author of the greatest success story in the history of stock car racing, no longer existed.

In the aftermath of the mergers, Kyle found himself without a Cup ride entirely. His plan was to run some Grand Am races and continue his time in the announcing booth for TNT.

Much was made of the dissolution of Petty Enterprises; that it spelled the end of an era only brought back thoughts of what might have been.

"Look at how many generations they've been here—nothing lasts forever," said two-time champion crew chief Andy Petree, now Kyle Petty's fellow commentator on TNT. "I think we ought to just celebrate the accomplishments. But I think they would still be here and be very vital if Adam hadn't been killed. Let's say he lived, and he fulfilled the potential that he was getting ready to have. He was looking to be another Richard, not another Kyle, and that would have just been incredible for the sport and Petty Enterprises but it just didn't happen. Fate didn't have it that way."

And then there is the camp. Kyle no doubt dreamed of one day lining his shelves with racing trophies. Instead humanitarian awards hang on the walls.

In May 2009, Kyle and Pattie led the two hundred plus motor-cyclists on the fifteenth annual Chick-fil-A Kyle Petty Charity Ride Across America. During the 3,500-mile trip, the group stopped at 8205 Riverview Road in Kansas City to lead the ground breaking for Victory Junction's Midwest camp. As with the first camp, all operations are paid for by donations from corporations and individuals.

When he's back home, Kyle continues with his businesses. He can no longer take the quick trip from his home to the Petty Enterprises race shop. But it's just a few miles down Randleman Road to the turn onto Adam's Way. The tree-lined route is beautiful, serene, and familiar; it's home. And once he makes the turn, he can hear the happy shouts of children.

"There are certain people who when I am around them, I feel like Adam's there," Kyle said. "When I come on this piece of property, that's how I feel. I pray that never goes away."

In 2007, Jimmie Johnson won a mind-boggling four straight Chase races, including a blazing victory in Texas.

Chapter Eleven
Pair of Aces

November 16, 2008

"Comparing Cale Yarborough to Jimmie Johnson is like comparing an apple to a green bean."

—NASCAR Fox Announcer and Former Crew Chief
LARRY McREYNOLDS

CALE YARBOROUGH STOOD ONSTAGE AT THE GRAND BALLROOM OF the Waldorf-Astoria, addressing the crowd, with Jimmie Johnson behind him. It was November 2008, at the NASCAR Sprint Cup championship banquet, and Johnson had just matched Yarborough's greatest accomplishment: winning three consecutive championships in the sport's premier racing series.

Despite Yarborough's tuxedo and his sixty-nine years, there was no masking his considerable old-school grit. He was there to help fete Johnson, but he couldn't resist one prideful dig.

"All records are gonna be broken," he said, resignedly, but quickly added, "and tied. *Tied* really is all he's done, so, boy, you've got some work to do."

Johnson and his crew chief Chad Knaus shared a victor's laugh. For Knaus, whose dogged work ethic has become the stuff of legend, picking up championship hardware was a rare break from the comfort and joys of toiling on the No. 48 Hendrick Motorsports Chevrolets that Johnson drives.

Johnson seemed extraordinarily touched by the presence of Yarborough, an early career hero of his. And Yarborough responded in kind.

"If anybody was to *tie* my record, I'm glad Jimmie did it," he said. "He's a great man, great racecar driver, and got a great future ahead of him—and I'm sure you're gonna win a lot more. Just skip one year and come back later," he joked.

When it was Johnson's turn to speak, he was equally effusive. "That's the *man*," he said, sounding more like the preteen he'd been when he first got involved in racing. "When my parents were dragging me across the country racing motorcycles, we were pulling up to this Hardee's," he said, singling out Yarborough's chief sponsor through much of the 1980s. "I was a huge Cale Yarborough fan, and I thought we were going to meet Cale; this is *fantastic*. We go in, I got a burger. That was it. There *is* no Cale."

It was an ironic hope of Johnson's that a Hardee's would turn out to be, as he also put it, Yarborough's "race shop." The racer was, in all probability, either at his real shop or on the track, steering car owner Harry Ranier's Hardee's Chevrolet to victory. Yarborough won two of his five Daytona 500s during those years.

Both Yarborough and Johnson achieved their distinctions during what NASCAR has always tagged its "modern era," but it would be hard to imagine much similarity in their tasks and circumstances. For Yarborough, who won his third consecutive Winston Cup championship in 1978, when Johnson was a three-year-old in El Cajon, California, stock car racing was a grueling mental and physical challenge. Cars had no power steering, racing suits were often made of wool, and the inside of a stock car, on a hot summer day, could easily push past 125 degrees.

In the current era, cars are four-wheel models of speed and safety, with much-improved ventilation systems. The competition is much stiffer now. Contending drivers ran thirty races during each of Yarborough's championship seasons, and the wins, on average, were spread among seven drivers. The current Cup schedule calls for thirty-six points races per season, but during Johnson's runs, there were an average of fourteen different winners per season.

Yarborough the racer was physically meaty, the perfect extension of his tough-as-nails team owner, the legendary Junior Johnson. Jimmie Johnson, on the other hand, is slender, all-American handsome, and a diligent spokesman for his sponsor, Lowe's Home Improvement Warehouse; he often credits the "thousands of Lowe's employee-owners" for their hard work and inspiration after races. By appearance and temperament, Johnson is built in the mold of his car's co-owner, Hendrick teammate Jeff Gordon.

But as Yarborough and Johnson stood together on the Grand Ballroom stage, the elder statesman no doubt had a gleam in his eye, looking at a younger version of himself. They are each the perfect drivers for their respective eras.

Both men can claim to be members of racing teams that found formulas for success so foolproof, they made their championship runs look easy: a lack of struggle that also somehow decreased their renown. Yet neither man particularly cares. The victories, the championships are all that matter. Everybody else on the track was trying their best to topple them, and nobody came especially close.

Johnson's run of consecutive titles—which ended, amazingly, at five—meant he has left Yarborough behind in comparisons. It would be understandable if more people now thought of him alongside Richard Petty and Dale Earnhardt—and perhaps they will one day, even though, generally speaking, he makes it all look so damn easy.

"As much as they might have enjoyed the accolades from outside, [both Yarborough and Johnson were] really doing it for themselves and their teams," says 1999 Winston Cup champion Dale Jarrett, whose father, Ned, competed for wins against Yarborough. "Did they both get the respect? I'm not sure when it happened with Cale that there was a huge amount of respect then.

"But you look at all the tremendous drivers throughout all these years, and these are the only two who did this. You had Richard Petty and Dale Earnhardt winning seven championships, you had Bobby Allison, David Pearson. As good as they were, they never did anything like this."

* * *

For Cale Yarborough, who grew up in Timmonsville, South Carolina, the world's greatest joys were to be found fourteen miles north of home, in Darlington. At age eleven, he managed to curl up a thick patch of fence bottom and sneak into the town's brand-new raceway. With the intoxicating gasoline filling his nose and the menacing growl of stock cars, the local boy watched Johnny Mantz outlast the field to win the first-ever Southern 500.

Bit hard by the bug, Yarborough had begun running in the soap-box derby league at ten, built his first short-track racecar at fifteen, ran the local circuit, and, three years later, qualified to run the Southern 500, his day ending early with wheel-hub issues.

The eighteen-year-old had lied about his age—you had to be twenty-one to race in NASCAR. But it was already folly to attempt to stop the formidable "pudgy farm boy" from competing. In a Limited Sportsman division race at South Carolina's Ashwood Speedway, he'd flipped his car off the track, landing in an adjoining lake. Once free of the wreck, he swam back to safety.

In 1965, already a regular on the Grand National circuit, he started the Southern 500 in a Banjo Matthews Ford. During the race, while battling for the lead with Sam McQuagg, Yarborough's car vaulted over the track's guardrail and fell one hundred feet to the parking lot below, ending up a crumpled heap on its side. Yarborough emerged with barely a scratch, his smile intact. "I sailed through the air like an astronaut," he said. By then, he had already played some semipro football, was a Golden Gloves boxer, had done more than two hundred skydiving jumps, had wrestled an alligator, and had been bitten by a rattlesnake. By his own count, he'd been struck by lightning twice.

"I looked up to Cale Yarborough as Hercules," says Mark Martin, the NASCAR stalwart who raced against Yarborough early in his own career.

At about the midway point of the 1968 Southern 500, Donnie Allison led the field to the green flag after a caution period. Yarborough, in third place in the Wood Brothers Ford, began an insistent charge toward the front. Banging first off one car, ricocheting off the outside wall, snaking swiftly to the inside of Allison, and landing a shot to Allison's driver's side for good measure, Yarborough took the lead in little more than one turn. He went on to win the race, calling it his single greatest victory in a career that includes four Daytona 500 wins.

"He was just a very hard-charging driver when he drove for us," says Leonard Wood. "I talked him into running slow one race, taking it easy; he was running back in about third place, and somebody wrecked, and throwed something out, it went up and cut his oil line off, put us out of the race. He says, 'Never again!' You couldn't make him pace himself."

That would change, somewhat, when he began driving six seasons later for Junior Johnson. By then Yarborough had made an ill-advised detour into Indy racing during NASCAR's manufacturer wars, and returned and earned a seat in what became a premier Chevrolet team.

Johnson had famously driven on his own terms, and had never won a title behind the wheel. He'd essentially brought Winston into the sport; the company's willingness to sponsor NASCAR's top series may be the sport's most transformative moment. And Johnson was determined to grow with racing and reap the benefits.

"Junior had a knack for picking the best talent, but also he could get the most out of them because he felt—up until the last day of his [driving] career—that he could just get in that car and go faster than any of them," says ESPN racing analyst Andy Petree, who won championships as Dale Earnhardt's crew chief in 1993 and 1994. "And so he wasn't intimidated by a racecar driver. It was just, 'Hey bud, you're not getting it done, or do you want to win this race? Show me.' And that's a different way of motivating a driver."

He found his match early, and he knew it, when he began working with Yarborough. Johnson had officially taken over ownership of the No. 11 Chevrolet in mid-1974, just in time for the July 4 Firecracker 400. The first three races of the partnership went supremely well:

Yarborough finished Daytona tied for third—the only tie in modern NASCAR history—and followed that up with a fender-banging win at Bristol and a victory at Nashville that, thanks to a scoring controversy, wasn't officially announced till several days after the race.

The next Sunday, the field started the Dixie 500 at Atlanta Motor Speedway on an exceedingly hot late-July day. Yarborough had won the pole, and was competing early on with Richard Petty, David Pearson, and Buddy Baker, the four trading the lead, with Yarborough arguably the class of the field.

But then Yarborough heard the metallic grumble under the hood and felt the jerks. He eased a bit off the throttle of his 1974 Chevy. The car—so wondrously reliable all day—suddenly had valve problems; transmission fluid leaked, and the cab soon filled with the smell of burnt oil. Without power steering, and the sweat on his neck and arms pouring and pressing against every fiber of his wool racing suit, Yarborough pressed on. The temperature inside the car pushed easily past 130 degrees. Even drinking from the icy water thermos wasn't helping to wash away the smell; in a way, that would only make things worse. As usual, he'd have to ride this thing out.

The great racers of Yarborough's time—Petty, Allison, Pearson, Baker, and Benny Parsons among them—were not above asking for relief on the worst of racing days. Substitute drivers—usually other veterans who'd been knocked out earlier by car trouble—would be inserted and often finished the race, earning points for their rivals in a kind of gentlemen's agreement.

Yarborough could have done so, to rest his lungs from the nauseating fumes. But he always looked at this as relinquishing the wheel, something he was particularly loath to do. People could shake their heads, smile, and joke about how tough a particular driver might be. But even the toughest racers would cede such a title to Yarborough. When asked which driver he most hated to see in his rearview mirror, Baker said, "I can answer that very quickly: Cale Yarborough. He was pretty tough."

"I remember a race at Bristol on a terribly hot summer afternoon—*terribly* hot," said Humpy Wheeler, longtime general manager of Charlotte Motor Speedway. "The temperature was at least 100—[it was] that valley of death that Bristol could be in the summertime. The cockpit temperature was probably in the 140-degree range. It was like running across the Sahara Desert. Drivers were dropping like flies 'cause it was just so hot. And Cale kept going. Even as tough as he was we knew it was just gonna be a matter of time when he'd bail out of that thing or he made a gesture going into the pits that he needed relief. He was drowning in sweat and there was no way that he could make up the body fluid loss that he had that day. And yet he won that race and he became the only driver, to my knowledge, that ran more than ten years when we did not have power steering, that never needed relief at Bristol. And that just says a tremendous amount about him."

At Atlanta, Yarborough finished twenty laps off the pace, in fourteenth place. Once the race was over, the fumes, the fiery heat and the effort caught up with him. "I threw up two quarts of Valvoline," he told *Sports Illustrated* reporter Kim Chapin.

By then, NASCAR was fully enjoying the financial support of large companies. It is funny to think that even recalling a moment of such distress, Yarborough was careful to name a sponsor.

* * *

Jimmie Johnson was eight years old when he hopped on his motocross bike, raced hard toward a six-foot platform, rolled up, and vaulted sixty-five feet through the air. He landed perfectly, but the jolt made him open his eyes—while jumping, he'd been "too frightened to look," he told *USA Today*'s Nate Ryan years later—and then he skidded across the ground, scraped but unbowed.

By then, he'd already been racing motorcycles for three years, and was on his way to a championship. It wasn't easy to stand out in El Cajon, the San Diego-area city that remains a motocross capital. But Johnson was willing to attempt pretty much anything. And he had a top mentor in Rick Johnson, the Motorcross and Supercross champion. Johnson—who was no relation—was friends with Jimmie's father, and saw big things in the kid.

After Jimmie hurt his knee in a racing accident, his father—who drove trucks and tested racing parts—arranged for a ride that would eventually find Jimmie racing off-road buggys, karts, and trucks—four-wheel autos instead of two-wheel. He was a determined, charming kid with Hollywood looks, who was as comfortable racing impetuously in off-road competition—and winning championships—as he was playing high school water polo.

Every risk and opportunity seemed to lead to something better. Johnson was methodical, winning races, meeting sponsors, handing out self-made business cards, and looking ahead. He was humble but confident, feeling at times unstoppable.

The famed Baja 1000 off-road endurance race on Mexico's Baja California Peninsula was going to be another challenge, a classic race stretching one thousand miles from Tijuana to California Sur, over paved roads, craggy mountain passes, and dry river beds. Johnson was keen to do it in 1994 when he was nineteen, and though he had a co-driver, his plan was to be behind the wheel the entire way.

He was racing along very well in the event, shifting from road to unpaved surfaces in the sweltering Mexican heat. The route would take him about a day, and he was still behind the wheel and determined, some twenty hours and 880 miles into the journey, when lack of energy slowly got the better of him. He nodded off for a moment, and when he woke up, he was already airborne. His truck had careened and swerved, and began an arching flip before slamming down into a sand-bank. His codriver had only minor injuries; the truck was mangled. Johnson's pride suffered most among his own hurts.

With no way to make contact in the desert, Johnson spent a good portion of his time stewing on a rock in the heat. For a day they waited, hoping to see a rescue car or competitor come by. A day stretched into two, and Johnson first felt fear and then anger, both of which slowly cooled to a kind of resignation. He and his partner slowly made their way through a sandwich and a few other rations, conserving as much as possible. If he could only get them out of there, he reasoned to himself, things would be different.

The pair was discovered after two days. Johnson has since come to look at those days as the bridge between a career marked by impetuousness and one thought out with more meticulousness. He began to concentrate his efforts on stock cars. In 1998, he turned an opportunity to run in the American Speed Association (ASA) short-track series into Rookie of the Year honors. In Charlotte, he sought out four-time NASCAR Winston Cup champion Jeff Gordon, to ask his opinion about various car owners. Gordon was impressed by Johnson's pursuit of knowledge and information, his determination to press him for opinions, and his on-track performance. When Gordon's team owner Rick Hendrick began looking to add a fourth car to his stable, it wasn't a stretch for Gordon to suggest Johnson. Gordon saw something of himself in him, a kid with great potential, a warehouse of confidence without hubris, and talent without flash.

Johnson had two seasons of steady improvement in the Busch series and, at age twenty-six, began the 2002 season with a full-time Cup ride and a major sponsor in Lowe's Home Improvement stores. Interest in young blood in the sport was particularly high. Tony Stewart, Matt Kenseth, Dale Earnhardt Jr., and Kevin Harvick had come in as prized rookies and had made an immediate impact. Nobody had any idea how well Johnson would do; he'd given no sign of finding his calling entirely in this series. But the first thing he did was win the pole for the Daytona 500. Gordon and Hendrick suddenly looked like psychics.

In his first full season, Johnson won three races, became the first rookie ever to lead the series in points, finished fifth in the standings, and was barely edged by Ryan Newman for Rookie of the Year.

More important than any statistics, Johnson had found common ground with Chad Knaus, who'd returned to Hendrick after a year as Stacy Compton's crew chief at Melling Racing. Knaus embraced the comfort and rigors of his new job, and the task of making Johnson go faster.

His driver finished the next season in second place behind Matt Kenseth, ending the year with six top threes, and fulfilling whatever promise he'd had. And if, thirty years earlier, Cale Yarborough was a master of physical strength, Jimmie Johnson had achieved a level of mental toughness, intelligence, and control that fueled talk of an eventual championship. The top hardware in the sport seemed inevitable, even ordained.

* * *

When Cale Yarborough began driving for Junior Johnson in 1975, NASCAR, which suffered through a wild state of transition due to auto manufacturing shifts and money, began to settle down. The sport hit a turning point. NASCAR introduced a new points system—one that would remain in place for nearly thirty years—rewarding consistency, honoring lap leaders with extra points, and encouraging all drivers to compete in the schedule's thirty races for the title. Wins were still huge, but the championship became a bigger thing to seek, with a larger payoff. More consistent television coverage was around the corner; exposure and even better money would follow.

Yarborough's Junior Johnson team had its difficulties in 1975. The team was between sponsors and suffered a series of engine troubles. Yarborough ended up finishing ninth in the standings. And this came after 1974, when he had finished second to Richard Petty, matching the King with ten victories in Yarborough's best season yet.

Whatever disappointments Yarborough had to work through, Johnson had continued confidence in his crew. The Ronda, North Carolina, native had assembled a perfect race team for the car, an especially loyal group of long-time friends and workers.

"Most of my guys that worked for me was local, and we grew up together," Johnson recalls. "They didn't have to go off and live somewhere else. All they had to do is just get up in the morning, go to work, and it's close by. I could keep 'em all together that way. We were sort of a family-like operation. A lot of teams, they work together but they don't get along. You ain't gonna [win] nothin' like that."

Johnson was as hands-on an owner as one could be. "He would sit in his passenger car, behind his pits, until it was time to make a pit stop—this is before radios," recalls Humpy Wheeler. "And [Yarborough crew chief] Herb Nab would run and slam on the window and tell Junior it was time for a pit stop, and Junior would jump out and grab his jack and become a superb jack man."

Johnson recognized Yarborough's toughness behind the wheel, bringing mediocre cars into the top five and winning with some less-than-perfect ones.

"I think Junior recognized that, I've got a guy that's a lot like me," says Hammond. "And if I give him something that he can't break, he will break the competition. And that is what they did."

The team started the year off in abysmal fashion, finishing dead last at Daytona after engine trouble knocked them out on lap one. But Yarborough scored seven top threes in the nine races following Daytona, including three victories, which put him in a standings lead that would continue more on than off through the season. David Pearson had won Daytona after he and Petty nearly knocked each other out of the race on the final lap, and he also captured the Southern 500, and the World 600 at Charlotte. But with the Wood Brothers team not competing in every race, the 1976 championship went to Yarborough easily.

In 1977, Yarborough dealt with a couple of vexing distractions, but they did not derail his team's resolute standing. The trouble seemed rooted in the tough new challenge Yarborough faced in dealing with brash, motormouthed racer Darrell Waltrip. Yarborough was thirty-eight, Waltrip was thirty, and the latter was boasting happily, pushing a generational war with the racers then comfortably on top of the standings.

The problem was, Waltrip was backing up all his talk with results, and Yarborough wasn't finding himself as formidable as he'd been the season before. On a steamy and frustrating August day at Talladega,

Yarborough fought engine trouble all day; as was his fashion, he kept driving through it all, finishing the day in second when a raft of regulars turned to relief drivers. Yarborough emerged from the car complaining of having "the sorriest Chevrolet" on the track, adding that if he'd won the race, "I'd be in court Monday for stealing."

Team owner Johnson, shocked by the comments—especially given that Yarborough still led the standings—replied to the press, "We're in the middle of some engine problems right now and we're also in the middle of the championship battle. If Cale starts running his mouth, he'll be looking for another car. We don't have to listen to a bunch of lip from him."

Anyone else on the circuit might have wished for Yarborough's "problems," and perhaps the stirring points battle was momentarily bringing out his worst. Weeks later, after a spirited battle with Waltrip at the Southern 500 ended with a wreck, Yarborough nicknamed his annoying rival "Jaws," after the shark tale that had then captured the nation. But when Yarborough complained about the heat at a Martinsville race—which several other regulars failed to endure for the entire race—Waltrip began describing a track's conditions based on a "Cale Scale" of difficulty, adding, "I think [Cale's] problems could be his years." It was an ironic choice to tab Yarborough, the toughest driver of his day, but the name stuck.

Not that it mattered; Yarborough eventually won the title again in 1977, becoming the first driver in seventeen years to be running at the end of every race.

A season later, as Waltrip battled with his team owners, Richard Petty struggled with his new Dodge, and Bobby Allison switched to a new team, Yarborough demolished the field for his third-straight title. Junior Johnson had switched from Chevrolet to Oldsmobile before the start of the season and it caused hardly a blink. The engine program was that good.

During those three championship seasons, in ninety total Grand National points races, Yarborough won twenty-eight times and filed an astronomical seventy top-five finishes. It may have been the most perfect melding of styles between team, owner, and driver ever.

"If you look at Junior's and Cale's records, it would almost be like you were looking at a mirror image of one and the other," says Hammond. "Junior was a no-nonsense type of man just like Cale was. They knew but one way to race, and that was as hard as they possibly could, and I think that what Junior was able to give Cale was a car that was basically bulletproof."

To Johnson, the key to the string of championships was doing one's best to reflect the points system at the time: It was the team's consistency, more than its speed, that brought the titles home.

"Cale, he's a determined driver. There's no question about him being a good driver," Johnson says. "But when you go into a championship race, if you're gonna win you've gotta have a good team on that car to keep it together all the time. The driver can't carry that car; the car's gotta carry him. If you get the right kind of people together and have good luck, it's more the team than it is the driver. Ninety-nine percent of the time, if a team wins two championships, people will start splitting up and going, with people hiring them away. But if you keep that team together, that's where it's at."

* * *

At the start of the 2004 season, NASCAR was once again going through a tidal shift centered on points and money. Jimmie Johnson and his Hendrick Motorsports team would have to adapt, and do so better than anyone else, if they hoped to win a title.

For the first time in thirty years, since Yarborough's title runs, NASCAR was changing the points system, creating the Chase for the Championship, with only the top ten drivers after twenty-six races being allowed to compete for the Cup. And Winston departed as naming sponsor for the sport's premier series after thirty-three years, with Nextel signing on. The replacement of a tobacco company with a wireless communications company spoke for itself: It was now easier to promote—the sport to its growing fan base; especially to kids. NASCAR was in the midst of its $2.4 billion TV contract with Fox Sports/FX and NBC/TBS. There was more exposure than ever. The sport boasted 75 million fans, nearly half of whom were women.

As in Yarborough's day, only a handful of major organizations had the resources to compete for titles and the majority of wins. However, these were now multi-car teams, with the wealth spread to as many as four or five drivers each. Add the few additional talents who rose to the occasion and you had a sport where, on any given Sunday, as many as twenty drivers had a bona fide shot of making it to victory lane.

On paper, all these shifts worked in Jimmie Johnson's favor. Team owner Rick Hendrick might not have been a ready jack man, but he was the ideal owner for his era, a businessman willing to put his resources toward winning, and a man capable to getting the best out of his employees. His teams won five championships in the seven seasons from 1995 to 2001, including four with Gordon, Johnson's closest teammate.

"If you tried to do a comparison between Junior Johnson and Rick Hendrick, Junior Johnson would probably tell [a driver], 'If you don't like the conditions, boy, go on. There's somebody else out there wants to work on this racecar,'" says Fox racing analyst Larry McReynolds. "Rick probably would say, 'What do you think we can do to make it better for you?' For the era that they were owners, they had the perfect concept of how to own and run a race team."

Throughout the 2004 season, talk of an inevitable Jimmie Johnson championship grew louder; it was practically foretold, given his skill, team, and results. The driver set a blistering pace in the standings through much of the season, taking a commanding lead in the points and patiently answering the media's questions about his hope for a title. But from midsummer through early fall, the No. 48 team had a sudden spate of mechanical issues, with engine trouble leading to three DNFs in a row. When points for the top-ten drivers were reset after Richmond for the first-ever Chase, Johnson had dropped to second, and while he was now only five points behind his teammate Gordon, the team had lost momentum.

Bad finishes in the first four races of the Chase found Johnson incongruously mired in ninth place, 247 points out of first, with virtually no chance of winning.

Years later, it remains an amazing feat that they managed to come as close as they ultimately did. For everyone at Hendrick Motorsports, the last six races of the 2004 season offered incredible swings of triumph in the face of the worst tragedy any racing organization had ever dealt with.

The numbers for Johnson in those last six races still astound: Four victories, one second-place finish, and one sixth. It was after the second of these victories, at Martinsville, that Johnson learned about a Hendrick company private plane carrying ten people on a flight from Concord, North Carolina, that had crashed in the foggy mountains seven miles from Martinsville's Blue Ridge Airport. All ten on board were killed. They included Rick Hendrick's son Ricky, his brother John, Rick's two nieces, the company's chief engine builder Randy Dorton, and Hendrick general manager Jeff Turner.

It was impossible to calculate the enormity of the heartbreak. Johnson, who considered Ricky Hendrick a close friend, felt ripped apart. Chad Knaus, who'd learned so much from Dorton, was devasted. The entire organization huddled around Rick Hendrick, attempting to regroup and somehow, between Johnson and Gordon, win a title to honor those they loved and respected.

But after the finale at Homestead, Roush Racing driver Kurt Busch hoisted the first-ever Nextel Cup. Jimmie Johnson was an aching eight points behind him in second, with Gordon another eight points back in third.

There was no chance for Johnson to wallow or even catch his breath; twenty days after the Homestead race, he married Chandra Janway, the Wilhelmina model from Oklahoma whom he'd met in 2002. It would take a long while before Johnson could gain perspective on the season.

"To lose my close friend Ricky Hendrick, Randy Dorton, that whole crew: nothing has ever rocked me and stopped me in my tracks like that," he said months later. "I look back and it was almost like a daze we went through. Then almost winning a championship and then getting married, it was a year of extremes from the lowest of lows to the highest of highs. I can look back and say, I've really learned a lot as a man and a racecar driver. It may be one of my biggest years of growth, period. And being big doesn't mean it was easy."

The 2005 season offered something of a repeat performance for Johnson. Through midsummer, he led the standings, but a terrible, concussion-producing crash at Indianapolis for Johnson put race-winner Tony Stewart into the points lead. After Richmond, Johnson was in fourth place going into the Chase. His Chase numbers were not as good as the previous year's, but going into Homestead, he stood fifty-two points behind Stewart in the title run. Homestead, however, ended less than halfway through the race for Johnson, because of a punctured tire; he finished fortieth, and a disappointing fifth in the points.

"We went to Homestead and it goes away again and I thought, I just had two shots at a championship. I didn't expect to have *a* shot. And in fact, did I miss my window?" Johnson said of the pressure of those days.

In fact, pressure had already been building to a destructive level within the No. 48 team. For the workaholic Knaus, a sense of responsibility had turned into obsession; he alone was bearing the burden of these title runs, and another loss exponentially increased everyone's frustration. Perhaps he'd gone as far as he could go with Johnson; perhaps his driver felt exactly that way. Johnson and Knaus's constant arguing said as much.

Rick Hendrick knew better, and as rumors swirled that Knaus was considering a departure from the team, Hendrick brought both crew chief and driver in for a sit-down. As the Associated Press's Jenna Fryer reported, he served both men milk and cookies on Mickey Mouse plates at the meeting. It is testament to Hendrick's particular skill as an owner that he chose the gesture to tell the men to stop acting like children, or they'd have to stop working together. Knaus and Johnson aired their grievances, and Knaus, in particular, agreed to step back a bit, trust in his crew a lot more, think about the big picture, and not sweat the small stuff.

At the start of the 2006 season, he was immediately forced to put this into practice. NASCAR discovered an infraction in the No. 48 car during qualifying for the Daytona 500 and suspended Knaus from competition for four weeks, leaving lead engineer Darian Grubb to sit on top of the box and make race-day decisions. The defiant but chastened Knaus was forced to watch the races on television and hope the crew would deliver. It was enlightening, perhaps even humbling, for Knaus, when the year started off with two victories—including the Daytona 500—and a second-place finish in those first four races.

After its successful early start, and with Knaus back in tow, the No. 48 took off in 2006, gaining wins at Talladega and, after many stumbles in previous seasons at the storied track, the Brickyard 400 at Indianapolis. Johnson qualified second for the Chase but four subpar races in, he'd moved down to eighth, 156 points back. And yet, for the first time in a long time during the Chase, the team felt no sense of panic. Knaus went around lifting everyone's spirits, reminding them that there was little to lose, and that in 2004 they'd marched through the late-Chase races.

Incredibly, the 48 team nearly had a repeat of that success, with Johnson scoring one victory and five second-place finishes in the next six races. After Homestead, he'd topped Kenseth by fifty-six points and captured his first Cup title.

In 2007, NASCAR was transitioning between the standard-design car and the safety-centered Car of Tomorrow (COT). The Chase was tweaked to include twelve drivers instead of ten, with the playoff field set based on number of victories earned during the twenty-six-race regular season. And Dale Earnhardt Jr. signed on toward season's end to race the following year for Hendrick Motorsports, replacing Kyle Busch.

These were the most discussed topics and issues throughout the 2007 season. Meanwhile, Hendrick drivers went about annihilating the field, winning ten of the first fourteen races of the year. Gordon in particular put up eye-popping numbers, highlighted by twenty top-ten finishes in the first twenty-two races.

But with the new Chase format favoring victories, Jimmie Johnson went into the final ten races with a slight edge over Gordon, thanks to his six wins. And as good as Gordon was, Johnson was, once again, that much better during the Chase. He rode into the finale at Homestead with an eighty-six-point lead, and a four-race winning streak. He ended the season with ten wins and a second-straight championship.

In 2008, it was now Joe Gibbs Racing's Kyle Busch, riding a head of angry steam after being unceremoniously dropped by Hendrick, who quickly began to dominate, along with Roush Racing's Carl Edwards. Both drivers quickly set strong marks for consistency.

The best indication that Johnson would have trouble keeping up with them came in the season's third race, at Las Vegas, one of the 1.5-mile intermediate tracks that continue to dominate the sport's schedule. With Hendrick Motorsports hosting a roster of Lowe's execs at the track, the No. 48 team performed horribly, qualifying thirty-third and finishing twenty-ninth, racing at lap speeds a good two seconds off race-winner Edwards's pace.

"We just happened to have every Lowe's store manager and supervisor worldwide in a tent in turn two, and we had to walk up in front of all those people and apologize for the worst race the 48 car had ever had in its history, and I think it really sparked a lot of fire," said Rick Hendrick.

"Vegas was like the first part of a three-step recovery program for an addict," Johnson added months later. "First we had to recognize we had a problem, then we had to address the problem, and then we had to change."

The work began to settle down in the July race in Chicago, where Johnson passed Kyle Busch for the lead with sixteen laps to go. Busch regained the lead with two to go and took the win—his third victory in four races—but Johnson now knew he was competitive again.

Johnson entered the Chase in third place, forty points behind Busch, after consecutive wins at Fontana and Richmond. But as successful as Busch had been during the regular season, his complete reversal of fortune seemed to kick in the moment the Chase began. And once again, Knaus and Johnson, so skilled at peaking during the right time, turned in an incredibly solid run with three wins in the final nine races.

Edwards won at Homestead, but it wasn't enough: Johnson captured his third consecutive Cup championship, tying Yarborough's mark. And as with Yarborough, Johnson's crew well understood that winning titles meant being the master of a points system.

"Cale Yarborough had to do it for thirty some races straight and beat everybody through the season," says Dale Jarrett. "Jimmie figured out, okay, our job is to get into the Chase and do the best job we can for ten races. And they do a better job than anyone. It really encompasses where the sport was and where it is now."

Johnson's most astounding statistic came in his performances in races thirty-one through thirty-five each season. These races—at Charlotte, Martinsville, Atlanta, Texas, and Phoenix—are the year's most pressure-filled, the ones leading into the Homestead-Miami finale that strike like a dagger into the heart of the Chase. In the fifteen such races that Johnson ran during these three title-winning seasons, he finished either first or second twelve times.

"I really don't think I'm going to understand how special these three years have been until I retire and step back," Johnson said after the 2008 season was over, sitting at Foley's bar in New York City, after buying a celebratory drink for the house. The banquet, and his on-stage moment with Yarborough, was days away, and yet he was already looking ahead. "Right now we're really focused on next year and what we have to do to keep going," he said. "It's not because we're focused on some great plan and have all this confidence about being a four-time champion. It's because we're racers; that's what we do. We can't sit still."

* * *

Johnson hadn't promised Yarborough anything; not really. As Yarborough pointed out, he'd only *tied* the record. "And that's motivation," said Waltrip after the 2008 season.

But a changing of the guard seemed likely as 2009 got underway. Edwards had secured more wins, top fives, and top tens than Johnson in 2008, and carried momentum into the new season. And there was a sense that Kyle Busch had gotten that one bad Chase out of his system, and would be a good bet.

The playing field shifted as well: The recession had taken its toll on the sport and its players. Trying to keep costs down, NASCAR prohibited all testing at tracks where series races were run in 2009. Bankruptcy among the auto manufacturers meant a great reduction in financial support for teams. With much less money, once-unthinkable merger combinations among storied franchises gave birth to amalgams such as Earnhardt Ganassi Racing with Felix Sabates. The famed No. 8 car that Dale Earnhardt Jr. had driven through 2007 ceased to exist two months into the 2009 season, itself a victim of a balance sheet without sponsors.

It was no surprise, however, that Johnson, Knaus, and the No. 48 Hendrick Motorsports team remained a constant, still planning strategy incomparably well and calling an audible whenever necessary.

"They never sit still or rest on their laurels," said McReynolds. "They know that if they win in Michigan in June, when they go back in August, they probably oughta take a different racecar, and go in with a different approach because the worst thing in the world—and I was guilty of it many times as a crew chief—is you win some races, you get successful, and then you kind of roll back a little bit."

Twenty-five races into the 2009 season, with only Richmond left to decide the Chase field, Johnson had notched three victories—at Martinsville, Dover, and Indianapolis—and stood third in points behind Stewart—now enjoying his first spirited season as owner—and Gordon. Only Kyle Busch and Johnson's teammate Mark Martin notched more victories, and stood to inherit the series lead once the Chase field was reset based on wins.

But along with triumphs, marked inconsistency plagued Busch all season. And after Brian Vickers's storybook climb continued at Richmond, it was the driver of the Red Bull Toyota who improbably gained the final Chase spot, with Busch ending up a mere eight points shy of qualifying for the championship field. One of Johnson's main rivals was out of the Chase.

And then, in a performance as towering as it was typical, Johnson plowed through the standings yet again. The first seven races of the Chase produced three victories, five top fives, and seven top tens. His finish at the November Talladega race proved to be his most Houdini-like performance. Sitting in twenty-seventh place with five laps remaining, Johnson snaked through and survived two vicious cautions—the first of which left Ryan Newman on his roof, needing to be cut from the car—and ended the race in sixth. Going into Texas, with three races left, he led second-place Mark Martin by a whopping 184 points.

However, three laps into the Dickies 500 in Fort Worth, a wiggling nudge and slap from Sam Hornish's 77 AAA Dodge pushed Johnson's 48 car up the racetrack. Johnson held tight and rode the brakes hard, but after whipping up and back like a teacup in an arcade ride, he spun and slammed full and hard into the track's inside wall. The jolt rode through him. He let go of the wheel of his stopped Chevrolet, flexed the fingers on his tingling left hand, and made for the garage.

Up on the pit box, Chad Knaus slammed his left hand on the video screen and then went to supervise a slew of repairs. By race's end, Johnson would be scored in thirty-eighth place, his lead now cut to seventy-three points.

Such a finish might have steered some teams to play the prevent defense and protect their lead, but Johnson and Knaus had too much good history in the Chase not to be confident and aggressive. Kurt Busch had the car to beat early on the next week in Phoenix, but Johnson, who'd won three of the previous four races, remained on his tail. On two occasions, Johnson used slower cars ahead to block Busch and make passes from second to first. By playing traffic perfectly, Johnson bolted to the lead pretty much for good by lap ninety, and went on to top second-place Jeff Burton by a second. The finish padded his series lead to 108 points, rendering the Homestead finale a formality, barring any Texas-like collapse. And when the checkers flew the next week, Johnson had captured consecutive Cup title number four, with his Hendrick teammates Martin and Gordon finishing second and third in the standings.

After the race, Johnson and his team celebrated long into the night. Hanging at a local lounge at 2 a.m., someone put on "We Are the Champions." As Johnson later told a group of reporters, "That song doesn't really mean much until you're a champion. When you hear it, you swear it's your anthem."

Driver and teammates stood on couches, singing at the tops of their lungs.

Days later, Johnson was standing high above Manhattan, on the observation deck at the Empire State Building, having flipped the switch to ensure the building would light up blue, white, and yellow to match team colors on the city's Jimmie Johnson Day.

"I don't think myself or Chad had this mindset of, all we want to do is win a championship and we're done," he said, as fans gawked and New York Yankees World Series MVP Johnny Damon stood by. "We hoped that we could win one and were fortunate enough to have that happen early in our careers and still had a lot of racing and desire ahead of us, so we just show up, re-rack, and do it again."

The champion's banquet was held a week later, for the first time in Las Vegas instead of New York. Ryan Newman, accepting prize money for a ninth-place finish, seemed to sum up the drivers' thoughts on Johnson by saying, "Jimmie, congrats, awesome job; hope you enjoy your retirement."

The accolades poured in. Chief among them: Johnson was voted the 2009 AP Athlete of the Year, the first motorsports player to be honored on a list that, historically, has included the likes of Michael Jordan, Lance Armstrong, Tiger Woods and, in 2008, Olympian Michael Phelps.

If only the jokes about retirement could slow the man down.

In 2010, challenges to Johnson, as many racers and writers detailed, came at him both inside and outside the racecar. The birth in July of his and Chandra's first child, their daughter Genevieve, came on the Wednesday between Daytona and Chicago; both Johnson and his team struggled for the couple of months that followed, while chief rivals Denny Hamlin and Kevin Harvick kept up their share of enough consistent finishes.

And yet, once the Chase began again, Johnson and Knaus dusted off those same magic tricks everybody has seen and nobody has figured out. After a subpar showing at the opening Loudon race, they reeled off, in that last nine-race stretch, a victory, two seconds, two thirds and no finish outside the top 10. Texas—the third to last race of the season—made the going dicey, however: Johnson's normally rock-solid crew suddenly began to falter. After a series of poor pit stops, Knaus made the incredibly radical decision to switch crews with those of Johnson's teammate Jeff Gordon, whose car was already sidelined by an accident. Johnson finished the day in ninth, but Rick Hendrick decided Knaus could keep Gordon's crew for the remainder of the year—a move that seemed to foretell the Hendrick team shifts after the season's end.

Suddenly thrust out of first place, Johnson watched and waited as new title favorite Denny Hamlin tried to remain calm in the gravity of the moment, even as his crew chief Mike Ford began a little premature trash talking. In fact, it was Hamlin and Ford who blew calls at Phoenix, and went into the season's final race with a slim 15-point lead. Johnson, clearly annoyed by all the chatter, struck back, hoping aloud that Hamlin would lose sleep all week.

He need not have worried. A wreck early at Homestead-Miami put enough hurt on Hamlin's car that Johnson quickly erased his deficit. When race winner Carl Edwards was doing his post-victory cartwheel, he did so inside the cloudy haze coming off Johnson's celebratory tire smoking. Johnson had captured consecutive Sprint Cup title number five, by 39 points over Hamlin and 41 over Harvick.

As part of the post-season celebrations before the championship banquet in Las Vegas, top racers played an exhibition game of celebrity *Family Feud*. The question arose: Who's the driver you'd least enjoy seeing in your rear view. Names were called out; when Johnson's came up, the survey produced the loud "Honk!" signifying a choice that didn't make the cut. Johnson smiled incredulously; how was it possible for the five-time champ to be thusly treated? The shrug that followed seemed to be Johnson's best answer: He couldn't really have cared less. He was, as his teammate Mark Martin had tabbed him, the sport's Superman, and game show answers aside, nobody on the circuit had yet discovered the kryptonite.

*   *   *

Time will judge Jimmie Johnson in relation to his peers and the sport's greats; it has already given Yarborough his due. He was as tough as one could be on the track. "They give the distinction to Dale Earnhardt but I think Cale was the first Intimidator," says Hammond. "He was just as tough as anything or anyone I've ever had the privilege of being around."

And yet, Yarborough didn't capture the public imagination the way his top competitors did. Fred Lorenzen was the Golden Boy; David Pearson, the Silver Fox; Richard Petty, the King; and Bobby Allison headed the Alabama Gang. For Yarborough, "the Timmonsville Flash" didn't exactly sing. Race reports would sometimes describe the five-foot-seven Yarborough as "pudgy" or "stubby." And in terms of visuals, when thinking about Yarborough it's tough not to first recall the driver's place in that most inglorious of images: the ending of the 1979 Daytona 500, with Yarborough on the ground and Bobby Allison holding his foot, as Yarborough's eyes burn with the angry look of a bested man.

Jimmie Johnson will also one day leave the imprint of a tough, seasoned competitor who, despite Martin's assertion, doesn't have the fancy nickname or the flash that often sends fans into paroxysms. He's not

Smoke or Junior or Shrub—something he shares with Yarborough. But there's that other thing they share: They were nearly perfect for an incredible stretch of time and nobody has been able to touch them.

"Jimmie Johnson is one of the most talented drivers to ever buckle on a helmet," says Hammond. "He's smart, he's personable, he's fearless, and he's not afraid to do a lot of different things to make things happen behind the wheel. But he is just not overly charming, he's not overly reckless, he's not overly anything. He's just good in every area that everybody else wishes they were."

Bobby and Judy Allison, happily reunited, in April 2003.

Epilogue: Bobby Allison Reclaimed

October 2010

"I'm faced with whatever today brings. And I am fortunate there are some things I do enjoy doing. So I try to focus on the positive."

—BOBBY ALLISON, Pocono Raceway, July 1999

M Y INTERVIEW WITH BOBBY ALLISON WAS SET UP FOR A MID-afternoon hour on a steamy July day at Pocono Raceway, in 1999. While searching for Bobby as our appointment drew near, I paced along the wide gulf between the Winston Cup drivers' haulers and the line of garage slots, where the press and anyone with a "Cold Pass" can patrol during practice sessions. You could hear the maddening groan of the cars on the tracks, while the wondrous smells of gas, oil, and burned rubber filled your nose, and I walked and studied the faces of fans, racers, and legends.

I was at the track to do interviews for my first book, *NASCAR Generations*, about the incredible draw of families to the sport. It was very clear to me that I never would have been working on such a book—and I never would have been a fan of the sport—had I not met Bobby Allison six years earlier. But the irony of speaking with Allison at Pocono was not lost on me: It was there, on June 19, 1988, that this man who'd changed my life by passing on the honest lessons he'd learned about doing something constructive, almost lost his own life in a terrifying first-lap crash in the tunnel turn.

It was because of my conversation with Allison in 1993 that I understood the need to keep writing about stock car racing, because the athletes who played this sport were special. You cared about them because they met your eyes when you asked a question, considered what you said, and answered with a refreshing honesty that most other athletes did not. I had just come from twenty minutes of standing face to face with Dale Earnhardt in his hauler, watching his gruff mien change to vulnerability and warmth when talking about the time that he wished he'd spent with his children, and the hope of getting the chance to do more of that with his namesake son, who'd be running his first full-time Cup season the following year. He joked about races he'd won with a generous bump, and recalled every use of the word *sumbitch* in a memorable back-and-forth with a one time crew chief. When he sensed that exactly twenty minutes were up—the allotted time for the interview—his eyes suddenly grew tight and he said, "We done?" in such a way that I knew the answer had to be "Yes." Not once did he use a tired phrase such as "We'll take it one day at a time," or "I'd like to cut up that trophy and share it equally with all my guys."

As I walked past haulers, I soon caught sight of Bobby; he was just done talking to Jimmy Kitchens, an ARCA driver from Bobby's hometown of Hueytown, Alabama, whom he's been advising. Bobby still had the hitch in his gate that he'd had six years before. He was now sixty-one, and fans parted around him and stared back in his direction and whispered respectfully among themselves.

I approached and offered a hand and we moved toward the pressroom, where reporters stopped what they were doing to greet him. As we settled into a small private room, I tried to muster up the kind of necessary dispassion of a doctor who's job it is to inflict uncomfortable therapy.

I needed to ask Bobby, here at the track where some of his memory was robbed from him, to cast his mind back again to the deaths of his sons Clifford and Davey, and more recently, to his bitter separation from his wife, Judy.

As he spoke, his eyes betrayed no pain; instead, there was pride in his boys, and resignation about the things they'd never have the chance to do. With Judy, there were lists of details and the cold stare of bitterness at the way things turned out. I'd been told correctly that due to Bobby's anger and resentment over their parting, he refused to refer to her by name.

Judy had decided at one point to try to auction off the couple's one-time house in Hueytown, after being told that selling the house—and whatever memories they'd accrued inside—would bring her much-needed money.

"And I said, 'I can't stop it,'" Bobby told me he'd said to Judy about the auction. "I wasn't around. And they sold an awful lot of it: the furniture, the pictures off the wall, the special things I had down there. Some of the things sold because of what they were, and some of the things sold because they had been mine. And so the bidding started on the house, and the person with the high bid was a friend of mine that she did not like. She had the option that anything she didn't like the price of, or anything that she decided not to sell, she would not sell. And so she said, 'No sale.' So then there sat the empty house that the stuff had been sold out of."

It was, it seemed, a terrible coda to an already fractured family's life. Anyone looking at the situation could see with clarity that the tragedies the pair had endured became too much for them to handle as a couple.

After the auction, Bobby and Judy continued to argue over property. Finally, Judy took an apartment in Birmingham. "I went over there and visited her a couple of times," Bobby said, "and I thought, This just doesn't make sense. And so she said, 'Okay, we're gonna go on with the divorce.' So we did that." And it wasn't very long before Judy showed up at a racetrack with a new boyfriend. "And I don't know where in the picture the boyfriend came in," Bobby said, his stare clear. "I accepted that as one of the things in life that I didn't like that I didn't have a good remedy for, so I had to just accept it."

We parted perhaps ten minutes later, after I'd reminded Bobby of the words he'd told me years earlier—that, at times, he wished he'd died in his Pocono crash, but having lived, he'd embraced the idea of doing something constructive with his life. Given these latest setbacks, it was hard for Bobby to see the value of those words; and yet, courageously, he ultimately refused to look at his glass as half-empty.

"Some days I think it's really a piece of some kind of good fortune that helped me make it through those things, and some days I think it's a piece of really rotten luck that I didn't die," he admitted. "And so I'm faced with whatever today brings. And I am fortunate that there are some things I enjoy doing. I really enjoy owning and flying my airplane; that gives me an accomplishment that's special. And so I try to focus on the positive."

I remember, as I watched him get into his car and drive slowly toward the twisting roads leading out of the track, that I wished only for some kind of reclamation for Bobby Allison. I had come to love this sport in part because it had always been, and continues to be, rife with stirring comeback tales. Why couldn't something occur to bring a bit of solace to the life of someone who'd given fans such joys?

*   *   *

Sadly, it would take another tragedy to induce a change in Bobby Allison's life.

May 12, 2000, ranks high among the worst days for any fan of stock car racing. That afternoon, Adam Petty was killed during a Busch Series race practice session at Loudon's New Hampshire Motor Speedway.

Bobby heard about the tragedy while attending the marriage of Liz Allison—Davey's widow—to Ryan Hackett. The wedding was the first time in months that Bobby had seen Judy, and when they both learned of the news about the Pettys, they agreed to set aside whatever differences they had, and offer Kyle and Pattie the kind of solace that can only come from shared experience.

Afterward, they came to realize that it wasn't differences that had set them apart, but the great gulf in their lives created by grief. Talking it all through suddenly brought them closer once again. They'd needed this time apart, and now they needed to be together again.

On July 3, less than two months after Liz's wedding, Bobby and Judy remarried at Jefferson County Courthouse in Bessemer, Alabama. It signaled the healthy continuation of a healing process, and a chance for Bobby Allison to better accept his legendary place in the sport. In the ensuing years, he cowrote an autobiography with Tim Packman, and lent support to a book about him and his family by Peter Golenbock. Appropriately, the book is called *Miracle*.

I've spoken to Bobby Allison a few times since he and Judy have remarried. On one of those occasions, I saw them in April 2003, in Talladega, Alabama, where we were attending the festivities leading up to that year's induction ceremony for the International Motorsports Hall of Fame. I had begun researching what would become my second book, a biography of Curtis Turner, with whom Bobby had once infamously tangled at Bowman Gray Stadium, before later becoming friends. During two days of meals and events in Talladega, I sat at a table that included Bobby and Judy; Liz Allison; Curtis Turner's widow, Bunny Hall, and her husband, Tommy; and famed racer Tiny Lund's widow, Wanda. At one point, funny hats were passed out to many in attendance to celebrate someone's birthday. Judy playfully placed a hat on Bobby's head, and I snapped a picture of the moment. Looking at the image later on, it was, thankfully, that much harder to recall the desperate coldness on Bobby's face at Pocono years earlier. It was as if the bad times had been wiped away.

They hadn't been, of course; they'd continue to serve as a lesson. I thanked Bobby once again during those days in Talladega; he accepted my sentiments kindly and cordially, yet he appeared a bit uncomfortable with such appreciation. He'd earned these lessons I spoke of through perseverance, through survival more than triumph.

Thinking about it years later, as I began to work on this book, I realized it has always been Bobby Allison's resolve that has meant the most to me. The true legendary tales of this sport always involve the ability to put all bad memories in perspective—from one kind of loss to another—and move forward, down the road where, one hopes, better tidings await. Has anyone ever done that better than Bobby Allison?

I remember asking Bobby, after that Talladega Hall of Fame event, about the Bowman Gray race where he and Curtis Turner put on a demolition derby exhibition, angrily banging each other until their cars sat in the infield, immobilized and beaten. One week later, they were on friendly terms, with both preparing for a race at Darlington.

"My attitude from day one through my career was whatever happened yesterday was yesterday," Bobby said. "It cannot have any effect on today, as far as a direct effect. Now, it certainly can teach you to be careful of a certain thing or whatever, but you never took yesterday's problems to today's race. So I went to Darlington with that attitude. This is a new place, and this is a new day."

* * *

I wouldn't see Bobby Allison for another seven years. But it was clearly a much different Bobby I saw back at Talladega Superspeedway in October 2010.

He'd been riding a huge high: two weeks earlier, he'd been on hand in Charlotte for the NASCAR Hall of Fame announcements, and had been inducted in the second-ever class.

There were endless discussions afterward about the vote; many people had predicted he'd go into the Hall with contemporary rivals Darrell Waltrip and Cale Yarborough. But among those three, only Bobby made it in this time. Some spoke of all that he'd lost through his career, and his willingness to remain a great supporter of the sport. It was clear, however, that he basked in the wonder of such an honor.

At Talladega, the gleam in his eyes from two weeks earlier remained. After decades of inspiring incredible sympathy, he was now surrounded, applauded, and lauded. Something had truly lifted.

I shook his hand, had a photo taken with him and watched him walk through the Media Center at the superspeedway that would always remain the hometown stop for the Alabama Gang.

The track at Talladega adjoins the International Motorsports Hall of Fame Museum and Library. With all its materials and exhibits, cars and collections, the place clearly favors Bobby and his family. Later that afternoon, as I stood in the library, researching photos for this book, Bobby came in with a group of friends. He was talking about a missing trophy from an old race he'd won; he recalled details of the race with clarity. It struck me that having been robbed of some of his greatest memories, he remains determined to hold fast to others. And I thought with gratitude of my own memories of Bobby Allison, going back seventeen years to our first meeting, in the days when I'd just gotten married, years before the births of our three kids.

Bobby spoke cordially to the volunteers at the library and then, with a smile and a wave, turned to go, and walked past the glass memory cases containing victory photos and checkered flags from some of his thrilling victories.

"You know, there's no one like Bobby Allison," one of the volunteers said. "A lot of drivers, they're in the sport, and then when they're gone, you never hear from them again. But not Bobby," she said with an admiring shake of her head. "Bobby Allison never forgets."

Acknowledgments

There are plenty of people I must thank as I consider the enormous help and generosity of family, friends, colleagues, and participants in the glorious history of this sport I love. But I have to start with my dad.

I am one of the very lucky ones. My father was a great source of support, who boasted of his children and took endless pride in their accomplishments. During the last nine months of his life—a period smack in the middle of the writing of this book—he and I had the privilege of saying the simple things you hope to say to someone you love and are losing. And as bad as things got—and they got bad—the upside was the time it pressed my mom, my dad, my brother Dave, and I to share.

I'm not sure that I found distraction or solace while writing this book. But I looked for, and found, my dad in every step of this process. I stumbled on a piece of information I'd never known: that Bill France lost his father not long before NASCAR's first-ever "strictly stock" race, a race that could have broken the sport but which ultimately propelled it forward, thanks mainly to Big Bill's insistence. And I found my dad again and again in answers that came to me from the loving, respectful sons of this sport—and the fathers as well. And as open and forthcoming a man as Dale Earnhardt Jr. continues to be, he has always been incredibly eloquent about dealing so publicly with the loss of his father. His words have helped a bunch.

So, it was good to spot my dad in a sense guiding me from stop to stop, when I was missing him most. It's not a surprise: guidance was always one of his greatest strengths. Thanks, Dad.

Among the folks I spoke to for this book, I'd be remiss if I didn't call out Larry McReynolds, Andy Petree, and Humpy Wheeler. Each man went out of his way to offer vivid details and terrific stories.

Beyond that, I have to thank the following for their continued aid. Bunny Hall, my terrific friend, who cares so deeply for the legacy of Curtis Turner, and her wondrously warm husband Tommy; my superb agent John Silbersack, whose friendship has been a true beacon for me; Peter Mayer, the publisher who has come to see all that's exciting about NASCAR, and is happy to have my books on the shelves at The Overlook Press; and Bruce Ramey and his staff at the International Motorsports Hall of Fame library at Talladega Superspeedway who, carrying on in the absence of the indomitable Betty Carlin, bent over backward to help.

Stephanie Gorton inherited this book at Overlook, then embraced it and shepherded it with great patience. I relied once again on notes provided by Wendell Scott biographer Brian Donovan, as I did years ago while working on my Curtis Turner book.

I'm grateful to three transcribers. Abby Royle did a bulk of this work with speed and care. David Tanklefsky did a bunch as well, with dedication, interest, and humor. And my daughter Rachel proved to be a mighty adept help when I needed her most.

Of the bosses who gave me the gift of time, I must thank Ben Grossman, editor in chief at *Broadcasting & Cable*, along with his predecessors, Max Robins and Mark Robichaux. Their support proved enormous.

I keep telling my toweringly talented friend Mike Hembree all the reasons why his confidence, counsel, and encouragement mean the world to me and I don't plan on stopping anytime soon. The first NASCAR writer I told about this project was the late David Poole, a generous mentor and friend whom I miss greatly. I treasure my friendship with, and the advice I get from, Jeff Gluck; the same goes for the warm support of Allen Gregory. More help came from Monte Dutton (for correcting the longtime misspelling of "Glenn Dunaway") and Andrew (*The Weekend Starts on Wednesday*) Giangola. And the public relations staffs at Bristol Motor Speedway (specifically Wayne Estes and Lori Worley), Infineon Raceway

(Jennifer Imbimbo), and Texas Motor Speedway (Louis Mora) were immensely kind enough to provide many photos for the chapter breaks.

I continue to trust the editing counsel of Bret Watson above all others. I received only enthusiasm and top-notch guidance after manuscript reads from Phil Thron and David Singer. No small support has always come from Jeff Iorio, Michael Davis, Miriam Wolf, Rob Copeland, Barry Krostich, Russ Rieger, Mark Lasswell, Marc Lichter, Erik Arneson, Richie Narvaez, Jay Fader, (Uncle) Larry Helner, and Ray "first time" Wilson. I'm quite grateful to Vincent Giannangelo, whose letter remains near my desk. And though my friend Dave Glatter laughs when I tell him this, the truth is, I never would have started writing about this sport had it not been for him.

My in-laws were, as always, immensely supportive. It had been my hope for Suzanne Rose Ginsberg to take this book's author photo, with an assist from Butch Ginsberg, and they came through much better than anyone could have expected, given the subject. I can't thank them enough. And I'm also mighty grateful to Ellen and Mike Scammon for their help.

I must thank Jill Mosley, curator of the works of her father Zack, who sent me great *Smilin' Jack* comics from 1949. And I've said it before and will again: If you love this sport, you *must* own the sea-blue-cover *Forty Years of Stock Car Racing* books by the incomparable Greg Fielden.

I am left, finally, to consider the impact of my family. I cannot give a shout out to my dad without offering the same thanks to my mom; they did everything together, and that included raising my brother Dave and I to be supportive of whatever we've each tried to do. If I can continue to live my life by my mom's example, I'll be pretty fortunate. That said, I've learned more about life from Rach, Nellie, and Jake than from anyone else. Their loving acceptance of their dad's schedule is what has encouraged me to follow these writing dreams of mine.

Then there's Loren, who makes everything possible, doable, and enjoyable. I am happy to admit that if you enjoyed this book at all, it's because my wife literally chopped 20 percent of the fat out of it. The fact is that being married and writing a book is not possible without love and teamwork. In this respect, I am also one of the very lucky ones.

Please give generously to the Victory Junction Gang Camp.

Photo Credits

Sources

Interviews

Many quotes for this book were taken from interviews conducted over a several-year period. New and updated interviews were also done over the last year. Major interviews were conducted with the following:

Racers, Crew Members, Race Managers, Family Members, Promoters:

Bobby Allison, Donnie Allison, Buck Baker, Buddy Baker, Paul Cawley, Dale Earnhardt, Dale Earnhardt Jr., Bill Elliott, Wayne Estes, Ray Fox, Bunny Turner Hall, Jeff Hammond, Kevin Harvick, Dale Jarrett, Ned Jarrett, Jimmie Johnson, Junior Johnson, Fred Lorenzen, Mark Martin, Larry McReynolds, Bud Moore, Don Naiman, Marvin Panch, Benny Parsons, Jacques Passino, Andy Petree, Adam Petty, Kyle Petty, Maurice Petty, Pattie Petty, Richard Petty, Tim Pistone, Paul Sawyer, Tony Stewart, Darrell Waltrip, H.A "Humpy" Wheeler, Glen Wood, Leonard Wood, Smokey Yunick

Members of the Racing Press:

Chris Economaki, Greg Fielden, Barney Hall, Hal Hambrick, Tom Higgins, Bob Moore, Max Muhleman, Hank Schoolfield

Books

Chapin, Kim. Fast as White Lightning: The Story of Stock Car Racing (Updated Edition). New York: Three Rivers Press, 1998.

Cotter, Tom and Al Pearce. Holman Moody: The Legendary Race Team. Minnesota: MBI Publishing Co., 2002.

Edelstein, Robert. NASCAR Generations. New York: Harper Entertainment, 2000.

Edelstein, Robert. Full Throttle: The Life and Fast Times of NASCAR Legend Curtis Turner. New York: The Overlook Press, 2004.

Fielden, Greg. Forty Years of Stock Car Racing, Volume One: The Beginning 1949-1958. South Carolina: The Galfield Press, 1992.

Fielden, Greg. Forty Years of Stock Car Racing, Volume Two: The Superspeedway Boom 1959-1964. South Carolina: The Galfield Press, 1988.

Fielden, Greg. Forty Years of Stock Car Racing, Volume Three: Big Bucks and Boycotts 1965-1971. South Carolina: The Galfield Press, 1989.

Fielden, Greg. Forty Years of Stock Car Racing, Volume Four: The Modern Era 1972-1989. South Carolina: The Galfield Press, 1990.

Fielden, Greg. Forty Years of Stock Car Racing, Forty Years Plus Four, 1990-1993. South Carolina: The Galfield Press, 1994.

Fielden, Greg. Rumblin' Ragtops: The History of NASCAR's Fabulous Convertible Division and Speedway Division. North Carolina: The Galfield Press, 1990.

Golenbock, Peter. The Last Lap. New York: Macmillan, 1998.

Golenbock, Peter and Greg Fielden, Editors. The Stock Car Racing Encyclopedia. New York: Macmillan, 1997.

Higgins, Tom and Steve Waid. Junior Johnson, Brave in Life. Arizona: David Bull Publishing, 1999.

Hunter, Don and Al Pearce. The Illustrated History of Stock Car Racing. Winsconsin: MBI Publishing Co., 1998.

Levine, Leo. Ford: The Dust and the Glory, A Racing History, Volume I (1901-1967). Pennsylvania: Society of Automotive Engineers, Inc., 2000.

Morris, Dr. D.L. Timber on the Moon: The Curtis Turner Story. North Carolina: Colonial Press, 1966.

Sowers, Richard. The Complete Statistical History of Stock-Car Racing. Arizona: David Bull Publishing, 2000.

Wilkinson, Sylvia. Dirty Tracks to Glory: The Early Days of Stock Car Racing as Told by the Participants. North Carolina: Algonquin Books, 1983.

Magazines

American Racing Classics. January, 1992. "Darlington Raceway" by Godwin Kelly, p. 111.

— April, 1992. "Curtis Turner" by Herman Gary McCredie, p. 118.

— January, 1994. "Joe Weatherly" by Gene Granger, p. 18.

Car & Driver. March, 1966. "The Editorial Side" by Brock Yates, p. 6.

— June, 1966. "The Daytona 500: Almost a Runaway for Richard" by Brock Yates, p. 75.

— November, 1966. "Who the Hell Do You Think You Are? Curtis Turner?" by Brock Yates, p. 60.

Circle Track. August, 1985. "Pops" by Bob Myers, p. 42.

Illustrated Speedway News, 1956. Various: May, June.

Motorsport. March, 1951. "Sportraits: Bill France," p. 3.

NASCAR: The Early Years, 2002. "The Cost of Race-Watching," p. 139.

Speed Age. March, 1956. "Bill France Predicts: The Year Ahead for Stock Cars" by Bill France, p. 26

— July, 1956. "Let's Save the Dirt Tracks" by Bob Russo, p. 24.

— January, 1957. "Toughest Driver in the World" by Hank Schoolfield, p. 39.

Sports Illustrated. August 21, 1961. "Scorecard: Race to Organize," p.4

— November 28, 1966. "A Wild, Wicked Race to the Big Time" by Kim Chapin, p. 84.

— March 6, 1967. "Demolition Run at Daytona" by Kim Chapin, p. 20.

— February 26, 1968. "Curtis Lives!" by Kim Chapin, p. 48.

Stock Car Racing. May, 1966. "C'mon Back Curtis" by Bob Myers, p. 6.

— May, 1966. "Stock Car Racing: 1965," p. 14.

— July, 1966. "ARCA 250: Curtis Turner Turned 'em All Back in the World's Richest Modified Stock Car Race," p. 16.

— November, 1966. "Ford Defectors Speak Out!" by Hal Hayes, p. 8.

— January, 1971. "Southern Strategy" (column), by Bob Myers, p. 7

True. February, 1971. "Death of a Race-Car Driver" by Bill Kilpatrick, p. 78.

Newspapers and Websites
In addition to reports credited in the text:

CBS SportsLine.com. "Tony Stewart: Lighter, Kinder. Can That Be?" by Jeff Owens, June 29, 2005.

Charlotte Observer. Various dates through the following years: 1958, 1960, 1961, 1962, 1963, 1965, 1966, 1967, 1970

NASCAR Scene. Various dates through the following years: 1995-2010

National Speed Sport News. Various dates through the following years: 1947, 1948, 1949, 1950, 1951, 1952, 1953, 1954, 1956, 1957, 1959, 1960, 1961, 1962, 1970.

St. Petersburg Times. "Stewart's Big Comfort of Home: Being Home" by Brant James, Aug. 7, 2005.

Government and Legal Papers

Florida

Volusia County, Seventh Judicial Court, in Chancery

Curtis Turner and Tim Flock (Plaintiffs) vs. National Association for Stock Car Auto Racing, Inc., a corporation, and Bill France (Defendants), Complaint for Injunction and Other Relief (Complete file).

Race Films

1979 Daytona 500

1999 Goody's Headache Powder 500 (at Bristol Motor Speedway)

Various races from the following years: 1988, 1989, 1992, 1993, 1998, 2001-2010

Miscellaneous

Mosley, Zack: *Smilin' Jack* comic strips, June 6-11, 1949

Index

K

Kahne, Kasey 59-60, 214, 229-230, 237-239
Kennedy, John F. 59
Kennedy, Robert 12
Kenseth, Matt 142, 164, 167, 229, 245, 275-276, 283
King, Clarence 59
Kitchens, Jimmy 294
Knaus, Chad 238, 267, 275, 281-283, 285-289
Korn, 178
Kulwicki, Alan 11, 123-124, 126, 188
Kvapil, Travis 133-134
Kyle Petty Charity Ride 243-245, 256, 257

L

Labonte, Bobby 134, 151, 161, 182, 237
Labonte, Terry 94, 96, 115, *136*, 138-140, 148-156
Ladyga, Tim 238
Lakewood Speedway 30
Lamar, Berney 245
Larson, Mel 47, 72
Las Vegas Motor Speedway 284
Letarte, Steve 218
Liguori, Ralph 65
Logano, Joey 217
Long, Dustin 142
Lorenzen, Fred 53, 55, 81-85, *106*, 110-114, 133, 248, 290
Lund, Tiny 45, 56, 70, 107, 297
Lund, Wanda 297

M

Maggiacomo, Jocko 116
Mantz, Johnny 270
Marcis, Dave 149
Martin, Mark 59-61, 145, 151-152, 159, 164, 200, 216, 227, 229, 252, 270, 286-288, 290

Martinsville Speedway 30, 71, 285-286
Massey, Jimmy 42, 72
Matthew Good Band 178
Matthews, Banjo 270
Mattioli, Joseph 48
Mayer, Peter 15
Mayfield, Jeremy 147, 151, 181
McGrew, Lance 215
McMurray, Jamie 131, 142
McQuagg, Sam 270
McReynolds, Brandon 135
McReynolds, Larry 108-109, 116-118, 120, 122, 124, 126-130, 132, 134-135, 143-144, 156-157, 211, 267, 280, 286
Melling Racing 275
Menard, Paul 133
Michigan International Speedway 286
Miracle 297
Moody, Ralph 73, 82-84
Mook, Gary 226
Moonshine Running 27, 29, 39
Moore, Bob 34, 52
Moore, Bud 68, 112
Moore, Greg 161
Mosley, Zack 29
Muhleman, Max 112
Mundy, Frank 65, 69
Murchison, Clint 74-75
Myers, Billy 72-74
Myers, Bobby 72
Myers, Danny "Chocolate" 126

N

Nab, Herb 277
Nadeau, Jerry 148
Naman, Don 56-58
Nardelli, Bob 228
NASCAR:

About the Author

Robert Edelstein is the author of *Full Throttle: The Life and Fast Times of NASCAR Legend Curtis Turner* (named Best Motorsports Book by the American Auto Racing Writers & Broadcasters Association) and *NASCAR Generations: The Legacy of Family in NASCAR Racing*. He is the exclusive motorsports writer for *TV Guide Magazine* and a contributing editor at *Broadcasting & Cable*, and he writes frequently about sports, travel, and health for several other publications. He lives with his family in New Jersey.

Sample pages from *Full Throttle* by Robert Edelstein

PROLOGUE
July 23, 1967
"I don't really think I'd be happy if I wasn't in some sort of trouble."

Easley, South Carolina, about ten miles west of Greenville as the crow flies, is a town where everyone knows everybody else. On this hot July Sunday in 1967, with the mercury having hit ninety for the second day in a row, folks are greeting neighbors while giving thanks for each bit of breeze as they head into church for the evening service. There are 5,000 people living in Easley's eleven square miles, and about a hundred area churches serve the faithful. Nearly half of these are Baptist churches. G. B. Nalley has just built Town and Country Plaza, the first mall in the area. It's doing a good bit of business.

There is an old saying in town: "You can easily do better in Easley."

One thing Easley doesn't have is an airport, but it doesn't need one. Greenville-Spartanburg Airport is only twenty-five miles to the east.

This fact of geography is relatively inconsequential on most days. On July 23, however, it matters a lot.

At first, the few folks walking at dusk near the Southern Railroad tracks—which run right behind where Main Street turns into Highway 123—hear only an odd, insistent buzz. But the volume reaches that of a swarm very quickly as a large, loud twin-engine Aero Commander grows in view in the near distance. There is nothing strained about its approach; the pilot seems to be holding the craft's line steadily without wavering in the orange-gray sky, and his path continues with confidence. The only problem is, if the plane keeps this course, it will touch down in the heart of Easley.

Inside the Glenwood Baptist Church and the Faith Missionary Baptist

Sample pages from *Full Throttle* by Robert Edelstein

Church, which both sit along the same stretch of Saco Lowell Road—a stone's throw from the railroad tracks—it is getting harder to hear the organ. Parishioners have given up trying to sing over the din of the plane. Many are wide-eyed with fear that they may be under attack.

None of this concerns the pilot of the Aero Commander, who's busily searching for the right place to put his plane down. He is Curtis Turner, a handsome, self-assured, baritone-voiced forty-three-year-old business-man; he is also an entrepreneur, legendary party animal and arguably the most popular and daring stock car racer of his day. If NASCAR is the only other religion followed as rabidly in the region, Turner may be its most worshipped, beloved and bedeviling practitioner. He quietly smokes a Camel and adjusts his aviator shades and trusty Stetson. The open seat-belt dangles off his lap.

For Turner, this will be an emergency landing: he and his three pas-sengers are dangerously low on whiskey, and the Easley resident on board—Mr. Nalley of the Town and Country Plaza—has suggested they land in town and maneuver through the streets to his house so he can jump out and "refuel."

For most people, such a suggestion will inspire little more than an appreciative chuckle. But the time it usually takes Curtis Turner to con-sider all the drawbacks of such a startlingly odd idea is equal only to the few seconds that a sly little grin forms on his face. Yes, he thinks, we're goin' in.

Turner has landed in rougher spots than this—small grassy fields, backstretches of raceways, parking lots, tiny single-engine landing strips on chicken farms, icy banks near the edges of cliffs, places no one would even consider touching down for reasons he can't quite understand. He'd once gotten into trouble trying to land his plane at an airport socked in by terrible weather. The tower commander told him to turn around and land elsewhere. Turner made one last pass and radioed the tower, saying, "Pop, I think I can make it." Then he switched off the radio and came on in any-way. Man's gotta land his plane, after all. Much like he is behind the wheel of a race car, Turner, when up in the sky, is a master of control who always understands his limitations. There aren't many.

But a man can go only so long without a "shooter" of Canadian Club and Coke, especially with a close friend and two women in your plane on a lazy, dusky Sunday evening.